About the author

Marjory McGinn was born in Scotland and moved to Australia as a child. She later became a journalist, working in Australia and then in Britain. Her stories have appeared in *The Sydney Morning Herald*, *The Sun-Herald*, and British newspapers, including *The Daily Mail*, *The Times* and Scotland's *The Herald*.

A youthful work/travel year in Athens inspired a lifelong fascination for Greece. In 2010, together with her partner Jim and their Jack Russell dog, Wallace, she set off from Britain on an adventure to the southern Peloponnese that lasted nearly four years, the first year of which is recounted in this book. The sequels are *Homer's Where The Heart Is* and *A Scorpion In The Lemon Tree*.

In 2018, Marjory published her first novel, *A Saint For The Summer*, also set in Greece.

Marjory also writes a blog with a Greek theme on the website www.bigfatgreekodyssey.com and she can be followed on Twitter @fatgreekodyssey and Facebook at www.facebook.com/ThingsCanOnlyGetFeta

Things Can Only Get Feta

Get Feta

Two journalists and their crazy dog
living through the Greek crisis

(Book 1 of the Peloponnese series)

By Marjory McGinn

Things Can Only Get Feta

Published by Createspace Independent Publishing Platform, 2015. First published by Bene Factum Publishing, 2013.

ISBN-13: 978-1508496069.
ISBN-10: 1508496064.

Cover illustration and design, and chapter illustrations, by Tony Hannaford, www.anthonyhannaford.co.uk

Formatting, editing and back cover design by Jim Bruce, www.ebooklover.co.uk

Dedication

For my parents, John and Mary, and Euphamia.

Acknowledgements

Sincere thanks to the villagers of Megali Mantineia for allowing me to rattle about inside their hitherto quiet lives, and for sharing their stories. Thanks to the families: Kosteas, Avramis, Kozombolis, Mihaleas, Papadeas, Manikis, and not forgetting Papa Miltiades.

With fond memories of a gentle village matriarch, the late Nikoletta Kostea.

Thanks to author Peter Kerr for his wisdom and guidance. I would like to acknowledge the informative guide book *Inside the Mani* by Matthew Dean, which was a constant companion on trips through the Peloponnese.

Most importantly, thanks to my partner Jim Bruce for his enthusiasm and good humour on our Greek odyssey. Also for his editing and formatting of this edition through www.ebooklover.co.uk and to Anthony Hannaford, www.anthonyhannaford.co.uk, for his cover illustration.

And finally, Wallace the dog, for his big, willing heart and for keeping us entertained for years.

Author's note

This book is based on real events and characters. While I have kept the name of the hillside village in which we stayed, I have changed the names of most characters to protect their privacy. Lastly, no goat, one-eyed cat, or donkey was man-handled in researching this book. I wish I could say the same for the scorpions.

Note – Modern Greek

Modern Greek is a complex language and some word forms may confuse readers. Basically, articles, nouns, adjectives and most pronouns change according to gender, number and their position in a sentence (whether subject or object).

The noun *xenos*, for example, meaning foreigner or stranger, in the masculine form, sometimes appears in the text in plural form *xenoi*, or feminine singular, *xeni*.

Masculine names that end in 'os', 'as' or 'is' will drop the final 's' in the vocative case (when addressing someone directly). The name Dimitris, for example, will change when you say: "Dimitri, are you listening?"

Contents

1

Wild woman of the Mani

O N a remote Greek hillside in early summer, a woman in a broad-brimmed hat loped into view on an overloaded donkey. She was riding side-saddle, drumming her welly-booted legs on the animal's belly to urge it along the ragged, pot-holed road.

From a distance she looked like she was transporting half a house, or at least the sun terrace. Tied across the donkey's back was a white patio chair, turned on its side, and a rolled-up sun umbrella, its ends poking out a foot either side of the overburdened beast.

A jumble of plastic bags dangled from the pommel of the wooden saddle, along with two long-handled cooking pots. Finally, a fat sheath of olive wood branches was bundled along the far side of the saddle. What she was doing with this jarring mix of objects was hard to determine, but no less so than the woman herself.

She was mannish looking – stocky legs in trousers and a bright plaid shirt. The minute she noticed us, she quickened her pace, waving a long stick and bellowing in loud, incomprehensible Greek. She looked frightening.

"Hell," said Jim. "Do you think she's waving at us?"

I gazed at the image for a moment. The woman charging towards us looked as if she had some long-standing score to settle, her donkey-laden cargo juddering about, making a racket, like feral cats fighting in a garden shed. And I was filled with excitement.

"I damn well hope so," I said, turning around just to make sure there was no-one behind us on the road. There wasn't.

When we moved from our Scottish village for a year to escape Britain in recession and one of the coldest winters for decades, we were desperate for an adventure. We picked the rural region of the Mani peninsula in the southern Peloponnese because it promised soaring temperatures and deserted coves, but most of all it was described as untamed and remote, all the better to find colourful characters, raw edges, and even the odd calamity. This was particularly the case because as journalists, now freelancing, we were keen to turn our experiences into feature articles so we wouldn't slide into the abyss along with the failing Greek economy.

Meeting this wild woman right at the beginning was good fortune indeed and by the time our encounter with her was over, we had decided the nearby hill village of Megali Mantineia was where we were going to spend the next year of our lives.

Or more to the point, the woman on the donkey decided it for us.

An hour earlier, it was quite a different story. We had come to Megali Mantineia to meet up with a real estate agent who had been showing us rental properties in the Mani region that were suitable for a couple and a manic, but lovable, Jack Russell dog called Wallace. The place we had come to see here was a traditional village house sensitively renovated by its British owner. While it had a pleasing exterior with beautiful stone work and the interior was in better condition than most of the houses we'd so far seen, we weren't keen on its tiny size and its location. One end of the house was built about a foot on to the main road through the village and promised to be noisy.

Then there was the problem of the resident one-eyed cat called Cyclops, a big bruiser of a beast. The good eye was mean and spoiling for a dust-up, the other clamped shut in a ragged line like a badly repaired stuffed toy. The agent told us the cat lived permanently on the property and my stomach was cartwheeling at the thought of how Wallace would survive a few rounds with this monster. Lastly, the rent was expensive.

What the house mostly had going for it was the fact that it was the very last suitable house for a couple and a dog that we'd seen in the Mani, and if we couldn't find long-term accommodation soon, we were facing a quick return to Scotland. Slightly disappointed with this final offering, we told the agent we'd give her a decision in a day or two. After she'd driven away, we walked through the village with the dog to mull things over.

The village ended abruptly with a church and a small cemetery, its stout walls overhung with wild jasmine. We kept walking and reached the high point on the road where the land either side was thickly terraced with olive groves and fig, orange and mulberry trees, and sloped gently down to the wide Messinian Gulf, with Kalamata city spread along its head. At the edge of the road were poppies, purple daisies and wiry clumps of wild thyme and sage. As our legs brushed against the herbs, the air filled with their succulent, strong aromas.

Hidden among the orchards were small goat farms, the animals grazing around rocky outcrops ringed with wild flowers. As a sea breeze picked its way up through the olive trees you could hear the sweet melodic tinkling of goat bells. And brooding over this expanse of orchard and sea were the unforgiving peaks of the Taygetos mountains that define this rugged north Mani region.

The location at least had won us over, but it was the woman on the donkey, bursting on to the scene – with her promise of rural authenticity, tinged with craziness, and the hope there were more characters like her, toiling away on the hillsides – that really stirred our interest.

When she stopped in front of us she was still bellowing in Greek and I was lost. My Greek language skills, acquired years earlier during a youthful working holiday in Athens, were rusty and I struggled with her thick rural accent. After several attempts at engaging with us she finally stopped shouting and offered a simple twist of her big meaty hand that seemed to say, "So, what's happening here?"

From under the straw hat, with its comically oversized brim, we could see an unexpectedly handsome face – piercing blue eyes, high cheekbones and a generous mouth. There was a hint of Ingrid Bergman in her features, though not necessarily from her sexy *Casablanca* era. She levered herself off the donkey saddle, landing heavily in front of us, in a puff of dust.

She pulled the animal to the edge of the road, never taking her eyes off our dog. She pointed her stick at him, talking more of her loud patois. Wallace started to growl. I asked her to go slower with the language, *"siga, siga"* and finally I understood. She was asking what Wallace WAS. I laughed heartily. It was a question I had often asked myself over the nine years we'd had this crazy, beguiling beast.

"It's a dog."

"That's a *dog*?" she said, wrinkling her nose. "Funny kind of dog. It looks like a sheep."

It is true that Wallace is sheep-like, because he is a white, thick-coated Parson Russell terrier, to give him his proper title, with long, stick-like legs. He has a V-shaped blaze of white on the centre of his forehead and big black patches over his eyes and ears. Perhaps this was what her haste had been all about, to check out these funny foreigners taking a sheep for a walk.

She moved closer for a better look and Wallace started growling again. It had a familiar, gurgling edge to it.

"Don't come too close," I said, but it was too late and Wallace let fly with the screamy, hysterical barking that is his trademark and that is so loud and shrill at times it stops conversation cold. He has perfected this skill over the years and uses it when he sees anyone who doesn't square up to his canine expectations, or is 'odd' to his skewed sensibilities. Wallace is a clever and lovable beast but he has the crazy gene and a hang-up about personal space. Being a terrier, he thinks it's all his. His territorial obsession was one of the things we worried about when we decided several months earlier to move from a Scottish village, where dog-tolerance is high, to Greece, where it hovers around zero.

One Scottish friend was horrified when we told him our plans. "You're not taking Wallace to Greece? Haven't they got enough problems there already?"

Wallace carried on barking and the woman watched, slightly amused. It wasn't until he turned on the donkey, snapping at its muzzle, that her tone changed. She pushed the end of her stick right up to the tip of his nose, offering a few verbal threats. Wallace finally gave up.

She stood by the roadside, hands on her hips, steaming inside the thick plaid shirt. There was a beading of sweat on her smooth forehead.

"What are you doing here on the road?" she asked.

"We've just looked at a house in the village. We're thinking of renting it."

"What house?"

I told her.

"Ah, that one," she said, wiping the side of her big hand across her forehead. "It's noisy there. But it's a good house.

And the roof doesn't leak," she said, putting as good a recommendation on the house as we were likely to get. "What's your *patrida* (homeland)?" she asked.

"*Scotia*." Scotland.

The big blue eyes looked blank. I didn't think she knew where Scotland was exactly, like many other rural Greeks we had already met, but the name at least sparked some cultural recognition. She started pointing excitedly at her knees, shouting "*foustaneles*" (kilts), and performed a manic jig by the roadside, her wellies kicking up dirt.

"We have *foustaneles*, too," she said, slightly out of breath.

It wouldn't be the last time that Greeks would claim brotherhood with Scots because of men wearing skirts, since the white 'kilt' is part of the traditional costume of many rural Greek men and the ceremonial uniform of the Presidential Guards (*Evzones*) in Athens. It claims its origin in the ancient Greek male tunic. *Foustaneles* are short, pleated and frothy, accompanied by white tights and black shoes with woolly pom-poms on top that no Scotsman, however, would want to be seen dead in, and probably would be, if he ventured out in this get-up on a Glasgow street at midnight.

"How long will you stay?" she said.

"If we take the house, a year or so."

"A whole year?" she said, loudly.

She moved closer to me now, as I was doing all the talking, and became serious, putting her big hand on my shoulder and staring into my eyes for a peculiar length of time. It was unnerving, the same feeling you get when a horse comes close and looks at your soul through your eyeballs. I have no idea what she was searching for there.

"You'll call by at my *ktima* (farming compound) one day, where I keep my goats, and drink a coffee? I make good coffee."

"Where is your *ktima*?"

She waved her stick back along the road. "The place with the metal gate. Come soon." The hand pressured my shoulder blade.

We'd seen her *ktima* briefly from the car that morning – a sprawling compound with a high wire fence that looked like the backblocks of Soweto. It had a goat enclosure and a rambling wooden building with sheets of corrugated iron on top, held in place with a vast collection of old car tyres. Her *ktima* had the usual rustic assemblage of wood piles, bits of scrap metal and thin scatty cats. In no sense did it seem like a place where you could sit a while and sip a coffee – or even want to.

"I can't promise to come. We haven't decided if we'll take the village house or not."

"Why wouldn't you take it?" she said, with the forthright manner of the rural Greek, looking me up and down, sternly, as if searching for a clue to my dithering behaviour.

"I don't know," I said.

My mind was fried by her laser logic. I looked at Jim, needing some direction here, and realised he hadn't understood a thing. Jim was still struggling with Greek, and hadn't got much further than the alphabet. He barely knew his arse from his *epsilon*.

I translated her last bit of conversation. Jim nodded. "She's right I suppose. Why wouldn't we take the house? And we're running out of time anyway."

We had talked about the house all the way along the road and I was slowly coming around to this idea myself now, especially with the addition of this larger-than-life character.

"Okay, maybe we'll come by one day," I told her.

"I have a kitchen, water and *petrogazi* (small gas cooker). I make good coffee. Ask anyone in the village what kind of coffee Foteini makes," she said, winking.

"So your name is Foteini. That's nice," I said, slightly mispronouncing it.

She put her face close to mine again. "It's Fotein-ee," she said loudly, with the emphasis on the final letter, instead of the way I'd pronounced it. The name means luminous or bright, as in candlelight. Except in her case, a flashing neon was more appropriate.

She asked my name and I told her. She fumbled with it a few times, but I didn't insist she get it right because Greeks can't pronounce the 'j' in Marjory without great difficulty.

"Ach! I'll call you Margarita. I like that name better, okay?"

That's how Foteini rechristened me Margarita, a name that stuck for the rest of my time in Greece. And somehow, that's how Foteini decided our fate with a short, amusing encounter in this rural outpost. Yet I had no inkling then that this meeting with Foteini would be the start of the most unusual friendship of my life, with a woman who in many ways might have been from another planet, let alone another culture, for all that we had in common.

When she left, she shouted loudly over her shoulder: "*Sto kalo.*" The words mean "go to the good", a common and heart-warming farewell in Greece.

As Jim (or Dimitris, as Foteini had rechristened him because there was another troubling 'j' to deal with) and I walked back towards the village, we talked about the stone house and agreed we could do much worse than live in Megali Mantineia. We would contact the agent the next day and give her our decision. I also gave Jim a quick translation of my exchange with Foteini.

"I'm not sure about the coffee invitation though, in the goat compound," he said, squeezing his chin between his fingers. "I'm not sure I can handle café latte with unpasteurised goat's milk."

16

I knew exactly how he felt, but further down the road the decision was made for us on that score as well. We came across a woman collecting herbs in the fields. She seemed keen to chat, and spoke some English. She asked us where we'd been and I told her about Foteini.

"Did she grab your cheek?" she asked.

"No," I said, slightly mystified.

"Good. The women in the village have told her not to grab cheeks. People have complained. She has hands like steel. It hurts."

"Foteini grabbed my shoulder though."

The woman considered that for a moment. "That's okay. I think shoulder is okay."

"She invited us for coffee at her *ktima*," I added, keen for her opinion.

"Did she now?" said the woman, her wily brown eyes full of mirth. "And so you must go. You will find it ... interesting, as foreigners. There is no-one like Foteini in the Mani. She is what we would call a *paradosiaki yinaika*, a traditional woman. But a little ... I forget the word ..."

Pleasantly bonkers came to mind, but I said, "Eccentric?"

"Yes, that is it ... *ekkentriki*," she said, reminding me that Greeks invented eccentricity as well.

"We'll have to take Foteini up on the offer now and find out more about this 'traditional woman'," I said to Jim as we walked towards the village. "It's why we came on this adventure, isn't it, to embrace the unfamiliar?"

Jim sighed. "I don't remember smelly goat sheds and salmonella being high on the wish list though."

We moved to Greece in the late spring of 2010 for a year's sun-kissed adventure and to escape from one of the biggest upheavals we had ever experienced during three decades of working in the newspaper industry. During 2009, with Britain deep in recession, there had been a harsh restructuring of journalism in Scotland which, for me, had wiped out much of my regular freelance work. But for Jim, who worked full-time on a Glasgow daily newspaper, the draconian changes made by the proprietors meant his paper, and its sister publications, were locked into waves of industrial strife, redundancies, and untenable working conditions which forced us both to rethink our future in this contracting industry.

By the end of 2009, we faced even more challenges. Scotland was suddenly gripped by one of the coldest winters for years, which turned our otherwise picturesque village into a vast ice rink with hill views. It ended with Jim breaking his wrist after performing a spectacular triple toe loop across the ungritted driveway of our apartment block. This was just a year after he had broken his other wrist, very badly, falling off a ladder during a DIY session, showing a clear tendency to be accident prone. The first broken wrist had required a lengthy operation and the insertion of a titanium plate with 14 screws, which inspired one of his specialist doctors to joke that he now had more metal on board than the Forth Road Bridge.

After the wrist healed, the second unlucky fracture on ice seemed to be telling us something we already knew. It was time to change our lives. Time for a move away, at least in the short-term, and Greece came to mind. We were confirmed Grecophiles with many Greek holidays to our name, and I had worked for a year in Athens in my twenties, teaching English, and at least had some Greek language skills.

As the exit strategy barrelled along there was no time for doubts, or to consider what we'd do when we came back – if we came back. Or whether we were walking away from financial security forever. All we could think of as the days tramped on through a long, bitter winter was blistering sun, pebbled beaches, the sea flat and hot, like oil, as they say in Greece. The plan seemed perfect, except for one major drawback: Greece was on the brink of economic collapse, with debts spiralling to 300 billion euros.

Since joining the euro in 2001, Greece had mismanaged its economy and had gone on a debt-funded spending spree, especially with expensive public projects like the 2004 Athens Olympics, which went seriously over budget. As well as soaring public sector spending, the country's GDP had been hammered by widespread tax evasion, and the crisis was further deepened by the global financial downturn of 2008. With increasing anger amongst Greeks over debt and government corruption, the socialist party Pasok, led by George Papandreou, won a landslide victory in the 2009 elections, promising to tackle these deep-rooted problems and to fix the near-bankrupt economy. However, with Greek debts mounting, within weeks of coming to power, he was forced to seek an international bailout.

In May 2010, with Greece edging towards a default on its debts, the International Monetary Fund and the eurozone countries approved a bailout package of 110 billion euros to be paid over three years. In return for this, the Greek government was forced to implement stringent austerity measures which sparked a general strike and violent protests. Three people died after a petrol bomb was lobbed by rioters into a bank in Athens, prompting Greece's revered President

Karolos Papoulias to say the nation was on the "brink of the abyss".

So, with Greece teetering on the edge, there was no telling how this catastrophe would affect a couple of new arrivals like us, and our ability to live and work there and produce the feature articles we planned for mainly British publications. Though negative stories on Greece would never be in short supply, we planned to be based near the southern city of Kalamata, which was seriously affected by the crisis but not in the vortex of angry protest.

Even before the crisis started to escalate, friends and family warned us it wasn't the right time for an adventure in troubled Greece, but with Britain in recession and journalism in crisis what was there to fear from Greece on the edge? And as the Greeks have since taught us: live only in the minute and don't worry about the rest of the clock face, which is what we did. The fact that this is the philosophy that got the Greeks into economic strife in the first place, with no forward planning and no regard for consequences, didn't really occur to us then.

We left Scotland in a howling gale. Our friend Mark came to see us off and laughed when we showed him all the luggage we had yet to cram into our tiny Ford Fiesta, all of it stacked in the driveway in the pouring rain, on the spot where once Jim had performed his ice folly.

"So you're really going. It must have been a difficult decision, eh? Scotland or Greece?" he said, looking up at the leaden sky, with a sardonic smile.

After we had packed the car he asked: "Where's Wallace going to fit?"

It was a good question as, after cramming in the luggage from floor to roof, there was no room left for the dog. It was Mark's idea to squeeze Wallace's soft dog bed into the passenger footwell and put Wallace in it. I think our minds were too fatigued to have figured that out. And so we travelled for five days across Europe, Jim driving and me sitting with my feet (without the boots) in Wallace's bed, as there was nowhere else to put them, and Wallace lying on top of them.

Wallace slept through the journey, mostly, but woke without fail every time we stopped at motorway toll booths in France and Italy, where he jumped on to my lap for a screamy confrontation with toll collectors. He was either in accord with the anti-toll lobby, or just being a typical Jack Russell. We had to drive off at speed from every toll both, with curses in different languages ringing in our ears.

Jack Russells aren't model house guests and there were problems even in the dog-friendly hotels we'd booked. He barked and snarled in the foyer of a large Italian hotel as we were checking in, along with 50 local police officers, mostly men, who were staying for a two-day convention. Under their steely gaze, we made a great show of putting on Wallace's cage-shaped muzzle, turning him into a diminutive Hannibal Lecter. The cops probably thought this was part of the convention entertainment and offered nods of approval, with some of them laughing all the way to their meeting hall. It was probably the last laugh of their stay, judging by the peaky faces over the breakfast buffet the following morning.

The Mani region was perfect for our year's adventure as it was much less familiar than the mainly island destinations we'd been to in Greece. Part of the Messinian region of the southern Peloponnese, the Mani is diverse and beautiful with the Taygetos mountains forming a ragged spine the whole length of the 70-mile peninsula – the middle of the three prongs that hang down from the southern mainland like pulled roots.

Once riven by clan warfare, vendettas and invaded by the Ottoman Turks, the Maniots created splendid retreats out of mountain villages and built hilltop castles and tall fortified towers to protect themselves, though many are now only walls with views. The Byzantine churches, with original frescos, have survived in better shape, well guarded in hillside villages, or hidden away in olive groves. Down the Mani coastline from Kalamata – the region's capital and famous worldwide for its juicy black olives – to Cape Tainaron, is an abundance of small fishing villages and pebbled coves. At the tip of the cape is the ancient entrance to Hades, the doorway to the underworld. Heaven and hell, all in one place. Some would say that summed up crisis-torn Greece at the time of our arrival.

We only had two real conditions with the house we rented. It should be in a traditional village in the hills, so we could savour authentic Greek life and work on our language skills. The other condition was that the property should have some kind of fenced yard to stop Wallace from following his inherited tendency to sprint off in pursuit of rabbits, real or imagined, without watching for speeding cars, or from terrorising passers-by.

Wallace had been with us through good times in our decade in Scotland and cheered us through some turbulence as well. But we knew he would narrow our chances of getting a decent house, as Greeks have harsh ideas about keeping dogs as pets, and if they have dogs at all they are mostly for guard duties and hunting, and tied to trees on long chains. They are not kept inside the house and treated to human comforts. And we were told to be careful taking Wallace to the beach as well, because if we did, Greeks would have a massive strop. Anxiety over economic meltdown would be nothing compared to it.

In our first few weeks in the Mani, we rented a holiday house from an English owner who was happy to accept a dog. From there we contacted estate agents and went to see every suitable long-term rental on their books. We knew it wouldn't be easy but the choice of houses was abysmal. 'Furnished' often meant spartan, with old battered pieces that wouldn't have looked out of place in a London squat. Apart from furniture, the main issue was always the lack of a fenced yard.

One agent at least, an English woman called Rochelle, who had lived in Kalamata for 27 years, had a better idea of what we wanted, and was sympathetic to the dog. When she showed us the stone house in Megali Mantineia, at least the village itself seemed perfect. Although only a 30-minute drive from Kalamata, it seemed a world away from the city's popular marina area and café society. Megali Mantineia was old Greece, a working rural village where most locals survived on goat farming, olive harvesting and running the four tavernas and one *kafeneio*. The fact that most of the village Greeks only had a few words of English was a bonus in our search for authenticity. But the modern addition of internet connections meant that at least we could work at the village house.

Megali Mantineia (Great Mantineia) is built along the saddle of a hill, one side of it sheared off by the deep Rindomo Gorge. It has views of the sea, mountains, the Messinian peninsula to the west, and Kalamata is clearly visible from the northern side of the village, its apartment windows sparkling in the summer sun like a scattering of diamonds.

After we finally told Rochelle we'd take the house, we went back a couple of days later for another viewing and to decide what furniture we would need. Although the house had no furniture in it at the time, Rochelle assured us the English owner Desmond, who was due back in Greece in a week or so, would provide everything.

Desmond had his own renovated stone house in the heart of the village and a spare set of furniture stored in its basement. The decision to take a 'furnished' house without seeing the furniture first probably ranks as one of the crazier things you can do in Greece but we had no choice.

The house had two floors, with an open-plan lounge/dining room/kitchen upstairs where the front door was located. It had a large front balcony with steps down to the front gate, and a view towards the village. But its tiny side balcony that could fit only two small chairs, side by side, had the best view of Kalamata and nearby Mount Kalathio, one of the highest peaks of the north Taygetos. This was the good end of the house.

The other end was nudging on to the narrow but busy main road through the village, with some of the lower level of the house, mainly the bathroom, below ground level. The bathroom was closest to the road and traffic was sometimes so loud you felt like you were showering in the pits at Brands Hatch.

But at least the house satisfied one of our main conditions – an enclosed yard for Wallace. There was a large front courtyard and although it was below the level of the road, it had a low fence on top of the boundary walls so that while everyone could look into it as they passed, Wallace couldn't escape. Standing in the sunny courtyard that day with Rochelle, after our second viewing, as giant hornets buzzed overhead in the old mulberry trees and young men on motorbikes droned along the road, we were relieved to have found a house at last and philosophical about its negative points so far. Until Rochelle mentioned expats.

"I should tell you there are a lot of them in the village," she said, casually, waving to a middle-aged British couple she knew as they walked past the house. "About a quarter of the villagers are British," she added.

That seemed steep, out of a population of 250. While we didn't object to expats in theory, the numbers here seemed to make a nonsense of living in a traditional Greek village. Yet, as most villages in the Peloponnese and many other parts of Greece now support British expats as well as many other Europeans, particularly Germans and Austrians, we had to face the fact that Greek villages without a few incomers were hard to find, unless you chose a mountain eyrie, of which there were many in the Mani, miles up dirt tracks and freezing in the winter, with no broadband.

"Don't worry. Everything will be fine," said Rochelle, with a slightly dismissive wave of her hand. "The village is still very Greek and most of the expats only have holiday houses here. You'll hardly see them."

When she said that I had a sudden flashback to a TV movie I'd once seen where a handful of people were camping in north America and obsessing over brown bears. "They're not that common really," said the camp leader the first evening. "You'll hardly ever see them." But by morning the camp leader had disappeared, eaten by a brown bear with the midnight munchies.

In the coming weeks, however, we discovered there was more to worry about in the undergrowth than expats, or brown bears.

2

Goats, polecats and Paul Newman

"HERE'S where the farmers sometimes skin goats before feast days," said Desmond, our landlord, pointing to an overgrown lane as he took us on a tour of our new village, a few days after moving in. He must have seen my look of disgust.

"Well it's rural Greece, not Kew Gardens," he said, with a shrug.

I didn't think we needed to know about goat-skinning so soon, especially since the lane was a few minutes' walk from the house we'd just signed a year's lease for, and too late for a change of heart.

While there was no shortage of beauty spots in the village, Desmond seemed to be on a mission to show us the more ramshackle parts of it, to reinforce the issue of it being 'a proper working village' which he said was becoming something of a rarity, even in the Mani. And in a sense we approved of some of its rough edges because it smacked of authenticity. But we made a mental note to always avoid what we later dubbed Goat Lane.

The villagers, it seemed, had been very inventive in recycling crumbling houses and turning them into chicken runs, or goat pens. Even vehicles were given new lives, like an ancient campervan, its bodywork spray-painted in a psychedelic design, which Desmond told us had been abandoned years ago by hippies on the overland trail from Mumbai to Europe. It was left where it expired, nudging an old stone wall and finally turned into a 'barn' where one wily farmer called Eleftheria kept her animal fodder. It was the kind of thing that might have won first prize for rural ingenuity at a village fete in England.

Garrulous and friendly, Desmond, a retired public servant, liked to tell a story, very much embellished. He also took us to a point in the village where we could see - if we had a mind to - the giant, menacing polecat which sloped about the rooftops in the evening, "as big as a German shepherd". No-one else in the village had seen this polecat, however, and we later came to the conclusion that Desmond had a knack for exaggerating invisible threats while playing down the ones that were right under your nose and a lot more threatening.

Whenever we seemed slightly repulsed by the garish 'highlights' of his tour, he would shrug in an exaggerated Greek fashion, with arms straight down and rigid, palms facing outwards. After 10 years of coming and going between England and Greece, Desmond hadn't mastered much of the language but he had a gamut of interesting Greek shrugs and facial expressions that he used constantly, mostly to avoid awkward questions.

The Greek he did speak, however, was a kind of Gringlish, with more English than Greek. And he also produced strange sentences with no verbs. He told everyone he met, while pointing to us emphatically: "*Ena chrono, spiti mou.*" One year, my house. We heard it so many times that day that we jokingly christened the house Spiti Mou, My House, since Desmond had curiously never bothered to give the old place a name.

"Journalists," he also said to everyone, pointing and making a scribbling sign with his hand to indicate stories. "About *horio* (village), maybe."

It was hard to tell from their expressions if the Greeks were delighted with that or mortified, or perhaps they hadn't understood a word he said. Finally, on the main road near our house, we saw a man in blue overalls, leaping off an orange-coloured tractor.

"There's your neighbour Leonidas," said Desmond, ushering us forward. "He lives in one of the old stone houses across the road, but keeps goats up in the hills."

Desmond did a similar Gringlish routine and I think Leonidas got Desmond's drift, even though he appeared to have not one word of English, which was promising, in my bid to improve my language skills. More promising still was the fact that he was incredibly handsome, with a sunburnt complexion and pale, dazzling blue eyes. Goat farmer be damned. This man, with those eyes, was Paul Newman, reincarnated on a Greek hillside. The neighbourhood had gone up a notch in my estimation.

Desmond told us that Leonidas would come to the house in the autumn to prune the mulberry trees and take away the leaves to feed his goats. These trees had always been coveted by the villagers, not only for the leaves but also the quality of the fruit. They were old trees, too, which are much prized in the Mani. This region was called Morea in medieval times after the word for mulberry tree, *mouria*, which were once plentiful here.

"He collects the leaves every year. It only takes a morning. He's fearless and he works fast," said Desmond.

How could you doubt it? Especially with the heroic name Leonidas, the Spartan king who led the Greeks at the great Battle of Thermopylae in 480BC.

While we didn't see a single expat as we toiled about the laneways that day, Desmond knew them all and offered a lengthy commentary on the more flamboyant ones in a strange David Attenborough whisper, as if he were indicating exotic, endangered species. Most of them seemed to be living out hippy fantasies on the hillsides. One elderly couple had set up home in a large Mongolian-style yurt that was self-sufficient with a generator and an eco-sewage system; another couple had built their own Khubla Khan folly palace, dedicated to the female form, with giant roof domes shaped like breasts and a sculpture by the front door of the Virgin Mary (topless). Desmond assured us the expats mostly kept to themselves but, if we wanted, he could introduce us around. But we weren't in a hurry to take up the offer. I was reminded of George Bernard Shaw's famous quote: "I dislike feeling at home when I am abroad."

Desmond wasn't strong on history, however, and we were left to glean the origins of the village ourselves. Megali Mantineia had been in existence on the hillside since the late Byzantine age and probably in ancient times as well as Homer was said to have referred to the area as Iri, in the *Iliad*, including its sibling Mikra (Small) Mantineia, on the coast below. From the early 1800s, after the Greek War of Independence, in which the Greeks finally ousted the Ottoman Turks after 400 years of occupation, many families came down to Megali Mantineia from mountain villages to settle, and their descendants were still living there. It once had a school, police station, a bank, bakery and several shops. Now it had only one general store.

Spiti Mou was one of the most historic houses in the village, and Desmond was fond of telling us that after he renovated it some of the older people came to thank him for bringing this old stone relic back to life. We found out on our first day, however, there was more to this old house than memories.

A round of screamy barking drew us out of the house and into the courtyard. Wallace was at the front gate, fizzing over the sight of an old man, standing on the road, dressed in a black suit and black cap. He was leaning on a stick and staring at the house with lively interest.

When we went to the gate to get hold of the dog, he said: "This house will probably explode one day, you know." Which must rate as one of the more curious introductions to a new home.

We thought he was joking, but then he explained that during the Second World War, when the southern Peloponnese had been occupied by Germans, like the rest of Greece, Megali Mantineia had been raided many times by German army units based in Kalamata. During this time, the house had become the headquarters of local resistance fighters, *andartes*. The old man, whom we later discovered was called Pericles, believed that a cache of hand grenades, and other explosives, had been stored in the thick stone walls in the 1940s for safekeeping ... and had never been found.

"Be careful," he said, rolling his eyes skywards. "It will all go up one day."

When we asked Desmond about this dramatic claim he just shrugged in his typical fashion.

"Look, it's a village myth, that's all. Most of this house has been dismantled and rebuilt, and nothing was found. Mind you, if you want to start hammering nails into walls, you'd better come and ask me first," he said, grinning.

After our tour, Desmond took us to the village *kafeneio*, called the *Kali Kardia* (Good Heart) for a drink, to seal our business relationship. The *kafeneio* was endearingly messy. It was built high above the road with a large terrace overlooking the village. Over the years it had become the unofficial heart of the community, as the village, unusually for Greece, lacked a central *plateia*, a square, where people could gather in the evening.

The terrace was decorated with bits of ancient memorabilia, an old saddle belonging to an ancestor, the long wooden slats of a dismantled loom, *argaleios*. At one side of the terrace was the 'cabin', a small roofed structure with roll-down, scuffed plastic sides which housed the massive wood burning *soba*, stove, where everyone would congregate in the winter.

In the corner of the cabin sat the owner Ilias at his '*grafeio*', office, as he called it, the table nearest the TV, which was resting on an up-ended wine barrel. Around him was more ancient junk: boots hanging by their laces from ceiling joists, bits of outmoded farming equipment, all of which made him look like the slightly scatty curator of a village folk museum. Ilias would grizzle over TV news reports and occasionally have volcanic arguments with some of the village men over politics that would boom down the road on a Sunday morning. He had a wily personality and twinkly eyes and very little of what went on the village escaped his attention, which made him a useful person to know.

The owner's son, Lefteris, had the day-to-day running of the *kafeneio*. When he wasn't serving he was to be found in the inside 'dining room', sitting under wall-mounted ancestral pictures, adding slapstick video clips to his Facebook page. He was the only Greek in the village with fluent English, and Desmond told us he would be invaluable, particularly for deciphering telephone and electricity bills when they were wrong.

We sat on the terrace, drank beers and ate lunch – a rustic mix of potatoes, peas and artichokes, cooked by the owner's wife. Angeliki was a cheery, round-faced woman with a soft, high-pitched voice and a cheeky sense of humour, but who could also be uncomfortably honest in her observations. But primarily she liked *parea*, company, and would often join you at your table, before or after your meal, and occasionally during it, as Greeks tend to put *parea* above all else and don't consider it bad manners to interrupt you for a chat. One thing she didn't like, however, was dogs.

On that first meeting, Desmond told her we had a small white dog and we might bring it with us sometimes.

"Yes, I've heard the dog...yesterday was the worst."

I remembered that day. Wallace had discovered Cyclops the cat for the first time and had gone off in hot pursuit, chasing it around the courtyard, the two of them finally leaping off an eight-foot wall to a lower terrace as if they were competing in the Grand National. The chase ended on the last terrace where Desmond had olive trees and a thin attempt at growing grape vines. The two had a stand-off, Wallace barking loudly and Cyclops shrieking like the protagonist in a Chinese opera.

"Don't worry. Wallace is usually a good boy," I told Angeliki in Greek, slightly tinkering with the truth.

She doubled up with laughter and we all exchanged puzzled looks. I asked her what was funny.

"We can put him in a *horiatiki salata* (village salad) then?" she said, wiping tears from the corners of her eyes.

It was clear she didn't like dogs, but this was going a bit far.

"You've just told me your dog's a good cucumber," she said, her eyes still brimming with amusement.

"Did I?"

She explained that I had said *angouri* (cucumber) instead of *agori* (boy).

That's the thing about Greek, too many similar words, too many vowels. It wouldn't be the last time I made Angeliki weep with laughter at my language skills.

"All right. Bring the dog along sometime. But don't let him get too close to me. I don't like that," she said, suddenly looking anxious, making me wonder if we should let Wallace out of the house at all.

"That went down well – I think," said Desmond, his lower lip in a pout, as we walked back down the road after lunch.

"I'm sure she'll get used to Wallace in time. I don't know about the barking though. And I've got nowhere else to keep Cyclops," he said, looking panicky.

"How long has he lived at the house?"

"He turned up when we were renovating the place, probably looking for critters disturbed by the builders...you know, mice and scorpions."

"SCORPIONS?" I said. "In the house?"

He shrugged. "Well, not in the house exactly...in the perimeter walls...er maybe."

I'd never even considered the notion of scorpions around houses – until now.

"This is rural Greece, remember?" he said for the ump-teenth time. "But don't worry, you'll probably never see one." Just like we'd never see expats or brown bears, I thought.

When Desmond left for the day we went home and reflected on our village tour. Although we were happy with the choice of village, more Greek than we could have dreamt of, and excited about the year ahead, we wondered how difficult it might be to really become a part of this traditional farming community. The people we had met so far were delightful, but there was a well-documented toughness about the Maniots, because of their violent past – and even the punishing landscape must have shaped their character, particularly in the *Mesa Mani*, Deep Mani. Among the various explanations for the name 'Mani', some academics have suggested it comes from the female adjective of the word *manos*, meaning dry, treeless, waterless.

One expat we met early on was a man in his late 70s, who had a holiday house in Megali Mantineia and had been coming to Greece for 40 years. He warned us: "No matter how long you live in a village like this, even if you speak some Greek, you can only ever scratch the surface."

It seemed like a sad comment after four decades, and even if it had a kernel of truth in it, I was quite determined to prove him wrong - and have a damned good time in the process.

@@@@@@@

After a few weeks in Spiti Mou, we quickly discovered that its location was both a curse and a huge blessing. It was noisy, right on the main road, and there was a row of industrial-sized garbage bins opposite that we knew would be a problem sooner or later. But the fact it was close to the heart of the village meant we were steeped in the richness of its life. The *kafeneio* was diagonally opposite and next to that was the 17th century church, the *Koimisis tis Theotokou*, which literally translates as the 'falling asleep (death) of the God bearer (Mother of Jesus)'. From here, the hypnotic sound of the Orthodox chant in the Sunday service would float down to our open windows on summer mornings.

Everyone in the village, and beyond, passed the house sooner or later: goat farmers with their herds, boys on motorbikes, weekly hawkers in pick-up trucks announcing a strange mix of commodities ("We have tomatoes, watermelons and chairs"), over a crackling loudspeaker. We saw men riding horses bareback and priests in black robes roaring by on tractors. Once we saw Leonidas on his tractor, pulling a small open trailer in which Foteini sat propped up on heavy sacks, eating from a glistening bunch of grapes like some B-grade Cleopatra for the rural masses. And carloads of Kalamatans would drive past on the weekends for lunch in the village, or to see how the hayseeds lived, and occasionally stopped to scrump the mulberries from Desmond's trees.

In the first few weeks, many people in the village seemed to be taking their evening *volta*, stroll, up and down the road past the house, mainly, I felt, to check out Wallace and his reign of terrier in the front courtyard, especially when Cyclops was skulking about. From their comments, we realised they had never seen a Jack Russell before, or even a pure white dog with a black-patched face, like a Zorro mask, that to the rural mind resembled a miniature sheep or goat.

The adults were more wary, but the children at least appreciated Wallace's daft behaviour, though none of them ventured through the courtyard gate. They liked his armoury of tricks, the way Jack Russells leap up and down like Masai warriors, as if their legs are made of industrial-sized springs.

Then there was his 'bathroom trick' that made kids howl with laughter and has kept us amused since he was a puppy when he first performed it for our slightly more conservative Scottish villagers. At just a few months old, Wallace had the peculiar habit, when he was in the mood, of peeing while standing up on his front paws, the back ones up in the air like a gymnast, with a stream of liquid flying out the back. In time, he could even walk a few yards in this position, urinating as he went. It was hilarious.

Once, while writing a light-hearted feature called 'Do Dogs Need Psychiatrists?', for a Scottish newspaper, I mentioned Wallace's 'trick' to several dog trainers I interviewed. They were amused and mystified. Since there was no physiological reason for a dog doing a handstand piddle, in the end it was decided that, basically, Wallace was eccentric, and also a bit of a joker. If he'd been human I think he might have become a stand-up comedian.

One of the children in the village, delighted by Wallace's routines, was a gentle girl called Irini, whom we were told had learning difficulties. Many times she would sit on the courtyard wall and watch Wallace, and despite an initial volley of barking, he usually gave up quickly with Irini, sensing, as animals do, that she was unlike the other children, and also less threatening. If only Wallace had been this compliant in every situation. But being a Jack Russell, unpredictability had been stitched into his genes.

In our first weeks in Spiti Mou, I thought over what a Scottish friend had said about taking Wallace to Greece. "Haven't the Greeks got enough problems already?" And didn't we also have enough challenges of our own? But at least if we could get Wallace to fit into this year of change, and the rural and cultural unknown beyond the perimeter fence, and accept boisterous Greeks and expat colonisers, surely we could as well?

3

Dancing on tin sheds

FOTEINI was standing just beyond the front metal gate of her *ktima* with her goat herd quietly assembled in front of her. She turned around but didn't seem surprised to see us there, or to hear we'd just moved into the stone house after all. It was as if she had expected it all along.

In the small space of time her back was turned on the goats, they must have agreed on a crazy turn because they all roared off at the same time, kicking over buckets and hay bales. Several managed to leap-frog on to the roof of the long wooden building, tap dancing up and down the length of corrugated iron. The noise was hellish – as if Jack Russells were let loose in the percussion section of the London Philharmonic Orchestra. Foteini ran after them, shouting and hurling bits of wood over the top of the building. The sky was now raining goats, as they leapt off the roof, dancing away in every direction.

We ran for cover under a sprawling olive tree, where Riko the donkey was tied up with its saddle on, and siphoning water greedily from an industrial-sized feta cheese tin that now served as a drinking trough. We waited there while Foteini rounded up the goats and our eardrums settled down. Up close, the donkey seemed very small and its traditional wooden saddle was fantastically solid, with a folded-up blanket underneath to protect the animal's back. I was trying to imagine what it might be like riding a donkey through the olive groves when Foteini came rushing back, the goats having been chased into their pen.

"Go down to the *kaliva*, shed. I need to fill the goats' water troughs. It will take a few minutes, but don't follow me. The goats are shy." Or words to that effect, I thought. She pointed to a hut, down a set of overgrown steps.

"You know, when Foteini talks I could swear she's speaking Hungarian or something else I don't know a word of," said Jim mournfully.

Jim was still battling with the Greek alphabet, and verb conjugations, and the fact that the word 'the' for example has around 16 different forms, depending on gender and case. Greek was hard enough but Foteini's dialect defeated him, as it did me in those first weeks, and still does at times.

"What did she say?" he asked.

"I think she said the goats are shy."

"The hell they are! Goats dancing on tin sheds – that's not shy!"

The area outside the shed bore no relation to any kind of café haunt in the world, apart from the white plastic table and a pair of wobbly plastic chairs like the one strapped to Riko's back the first day we met Foteini. This was no sun terrace either, but a rough patch of dried earth under a low-hanging fig tree, around which fat hornets buzzed. There was an old metal sink nearby, propped up at one end on a block of wood and at the other on a rusty ironing board. There was a water tap and a makeshift soap holder (the sawn-off bottom of a plastic bleach bottle) nailed to a post.

The round plastic table was a piece of rural ingenuity. It had lost its pronged base and instead the centre post of the table had been jammed into an old plastic paint tub, with several jagged stones around it to keep it aloft. A rickety cupboard was propped up against the outside wall of the shed. It had a jumble of water bottles, bags of food, and tools of indeterminate usage.

"I hope the coffee's good at least," said Jim, trying to find a flat piece of ground to set down the wobbling legs of his plastic chair.

I was beginning to see why Greeks weren't habitual visitors to Foteini's compound. Yet when you looked beyond the perimeter fence of the *ktima* at the olive orchards and fruit trees, a nearby hill with a ruined castle perched on its rounded peak, the mountains beyond, you realised that clearly location, location, location was everything here.

Foteini finally joined us, took off her straw hat and hung it on a nail outside the shed.

She went to the sink to wash her hands, and we realised for the first time that the water from the tap sluiced into the metal sink and straight out the plug hole onto the grass below, which was thick and green. It was one of the eccentricities of this *ktima*.

Her shed was a curious place inside, dark with a patina of smoke and age. A handwoven rug was pinned over an old divan bed, and there was a solid wood dresser with deep drawers, where she kept her coffee and other foods, "because of the mice", she whispered. In one corner she had an ancient two-ring gas cooker, *petrogazi*, as she called it. When she lit the ring, the flames roared up around an old *briki*, (small Greek coffee pot), the course coffee and water mixture spitting and crusting around its rim. The *briki* was blackened with age and had a piece of twisted wire coathanger for a handle.

She poured the coffee at the table into tiny white cups. It was strong and sweet and surprisingly good, and Jim offered a nod of approval in my direction.

"Where's the dog?" she suddenly said, looking about her.

"He's back at the house."

She nodded, looking mildly relieved. I was, too. Putting Wallace into this crazy mix of runaway goats would have been disastrous.

"Foteini, why did you say the goats were shy?" I asked her.

"Ach, when they're out of their pen, and they see *xenoi*, they go mad. They're frightened."

We took *xenoi* to mean foreigners, expats like us, thinking of the word in its more obvious form, and I laughed. I shared the goats' anxieties about expats, especially some of the ones we'd already met in Megali Mantineia. But she meant *xenoi* in the broader sense of strangers, any strangers – even Greeks from outside the village.

"The goats only know me. They're frightened of other people. Sometimes I come here straight from church and when they see me in my black clothes they don't know me, and run away." She clasped her hands together and smiled, and it lit up her whole face, her pale eyes dancing with glee.

"They're rather silly creatures then?" I offered.

"Maybe, but that's the way they are and I've had goats since I was a little girl living up in my mountain village."

She talked a little about her life, and I was grateful we'd come on this visit, but I was struggling to keep up with the language. It was not only her dialect that was difficult but her habit of chopping the ends off words and slurring words together. But she was patient, repeating things many times, and she waited while I looked words up, as I nearly always carried a Greek/English dictionary in my bag.

I had started learning Greek in my twenties while working for a year in Athens, giving private English lessons. But my fascination with Greek and the country goes much further back, to my childhood, to a circumstance that must have fixed Greece in my mind before I was even conscious of it. Although I was born in Scotland and had returned there later in life to live, I had spent my childhood in Sydney, where on my first day at school as a nine-year-old, I was introduced to the 'buddy' system to help newly arrived migrants, including many from the UK, to settle into their new Aussie school. The buddy was someone who shadowed you all day, showed you where everything was, and held your hand if need be. My buddy was Anna, an Australian-born Greek girl, whose family had come from the mainland, perhaps even the Peloponnese, though I now couldn't remember.

Anna was chubby faced and good natured and not only did she facilitate my life at the school as a newly-arrived, shy Scot, but we also became great friends and she made me part of her extended Greek family. I spent weekends at her house, which included the long Sunday lunch. I could still recall her serious, black-clad *yiayia*, grandmother, sitting at the table, never speaking anything but Greek. It was a language that, to my young Scottish ear, sounded madly exotic and I must have absorbed something of its magic at least, without later remembering a single word.

Yet the time spent with Anna and her family stirred my interest in Greek subjects and I chose to study ancient history at high school with a particular interest in Greek history, though sadly it didn't include the language. When I left Australia in my twenties to travel around Europe, as most Australian kids do sooner or later, I went straight to Greece and worked in Athens.

That was how my love affair with the country really began and years later it still burned as intensely. But if I thought that spending a year here in middle age would have me speaking decent Greek in no time, even with the private lessons I'd had over the years, I now knew differently. Like so many other things in this adventure, I would be like King Sisyphus, battling with a rock and a steep ascent.

That day, Foteini wanted to know everything about us, which is common when you first meet Greeks. How old we were? How many children? Did I know her third cousin Theo, who lived in Sydney? She was pleasant company, liked a good laugh. It hadn't occurred to me that we would go on visiting Foteini regularly, yet I liked the idea that given time and better Greek I might get to know more about her. She intimated she had a few tantalising stories to tell, which was honey to my journalistic ears.

She did have one annoying habit though, despite the tendency to shout when she was excited, and that was the fact she couldn't take her eyes off the road outside. She knew every passing car and who was in it, as the road brought her many good things – the weekly greengrocer in his truck and farming comrades – but also itinerant thieves who stole things they could easily sell on, like the piles of olive wood she gathered after the harvest, for fuel. Or scrap metal, like the ancient metal *kazani*, cauldron, she still used to wash her clothes. It had legs long enough to set a wood fire under and it seemed like a domestic appliance from the Dark Ages.

When she told us about the thefts, it made me wonder if, as well as using this spartan compound for her farming work, she lived there as well, but I was too embarrassed to ask. Foteini also knew which cars belonged to which expats and knew many of these people by name, though she'd only spoken to a few of them. After one expat drove past in an ancient, beaten-up car, she explained that he lived in a large house on a hilltop overlooking the road. Despite the old car, she called him the "*arhontas*".

"But that means 'lord'," I told her, and imagined we were living in the shadow of a titled and distinguished aristocrat.

"The *arhontas* gives me things," she said, with girlish pride. "When he comes back from London, he stops at the gate. He never comes in, but he always hands me a box of chocolates."

And she scrambled about inside her shed, bringing out a square box of chocolates that were battered, soft, and probably mouse-nibbled, and tipped most of them into a plastic bag for us to take home.

As it happened, a few weeks later we met the *arhontas*, whose name was Bernard. He later invited us to his house for sunset drinks on the roof terrace. He wasn't a lord in any sense, though I could see how village people had misconstrued the fact that this flamboyant character with a rambling stone house full of antique furniture couldn't be anything short of a lord, particularly with his formal, very correct Greek. In reality he was part of an interesting partnership with a man involved in the London arts scene, and they were also the only gays in the village, a fact that Foteini was, sweetly, unaware of.

Bernard told us an amusing story of how he had stopped in his car one day in front of the *ktima* to have a quick chat with Foteini, and in the passenger seat was a woman friend from London.

"Come by one day for a coffee," Foteini had told Bernard, "and bring your *nifi* (bride) with you." Bernard laughed hysterically when relating this tale.

"Have you been to this *arhontas's* house?" I asked Foteini when she first mentioned Bernard. She looked at me as if I'd just asked her if she'd ever been abducted by aliens.

"No," she said. "I've got no reason to go all the way up there." Which was true.

"I'd rather go up to my own village, where I was born," she said, indicating the Taygetos mountains. She pointed to one sharp, denuded peak right at the back. "My village is further back than that. A long way. Maybe we'll go one day?"

It seemed like a curious idea, taking this farming woman, whom we knew so little about, all the way through the mountains to the lofty Altomira village. It was so high up that even olives couldn't grow there. But as it turned out, getting Foteini up a mountainside would prove to be harder than getting Greece's national debt under control.

4

Driven to distraction

"WHY do you want to mothball your Ford Fiesta and buy a Greek car?" said Desmond one day, when we were asking him if he knew of any decent cars to buy here. "Why not just drive the Ford around with no tax, MOT or insurance, with the number plates taken off, just like the Greeks do?"

In our first few months in Greece we had seen some old wrecks on the road, and a few of them slumped about the village, used for local trips mostly because the police presence in the Mani was said to be non-existent. Greeks were driving cars up to 40 years old – ancient Ford Cortinas and Datsuns – like a scene from the British TV cop show Life on Mars. Some cars were patched-up Frankenstein monsters with bodywork plundered from other wrecks. Many Greeks, we were told, refused to spend money on new cars, especially as the latest round of austerity measures began to take effect with VAT on the rise, and neither did they like paying for road tax and insurance.

Many non-conformist Greeks won't do this because they don't like rules, and even among Greeks themselves, Maniots had a reputation for being more anarchic than most, which is why on roads with hairpin bends all over this region 'cowboys', young farmers with hunting rifles, had shot out the safety mirrors just because they could. But also because they don't like government directives. Sometimes the cowboys just scrawled graffiti over the mirrors, so they were useless anyway.

Ironically, our eight-year-old Fiesta with nearly 100,000 miles on the clock, which we had driven from Scotland, was in better condition than the village cars, but the UK tax disc and MOT was about to run out. The car would have been illegal to drive unless it was re-registered here, a process that only a masochist with deep pockets would want to pursue. So we decided to buy a decent Greek car, as one of the aims of this trip was to see as much of the southern Peloponnese as possible.

However, buying a second-hand car in Greece had been one of the things we feared most, apart from being run over by an unregistered, uninsured heap, and Greek drivers themselves. Greeks seem to have a personality change the minute they hit the ignition, especially men, who seem otherwise warm and considerate. They love their families, adore their children and wouldn't want to leave them father-less, and yet we had seen the craziest driving in Greece. Cars on the wrong side of the road, overtaking on blind bends. Perhaps the most maverick – and comical in other circum-stances – display we'd ever seen was a guy in a clapped-out car on a busy winding road into Kalamata, slumped back in his seat, steering the car with his knees while rolling up a cigarette.

Expats were keen to offer advice on car-buying in Greece. Many had horror stories to tell and in the end advised us to buy a car from other expats because "expats are more honest". Desmond, who claimed to have Greek contacts for all vicissi-tudes, promised to take us to see a woman car dealer in Kalamata, called Dimitra, from whom he had bought his latest car, which we did on a day when the thermometer was nudging 40 degrees.

Her showroom was on a frenetic strip of road that is the old Athens highway, where car repair shops and tyre depots hunch up against greasy souvlaki joints. Dimitra was charming, especially to 'my dear friend, Mr Desmond' and took down all our requirements, promising to have three different second-hand cars delivered to the showroom within a week, from all over the southern Peloponnese, for us to test drive. Too good to be true? Of course it was.

Weeks later, the cars hadn't shown up and frantic calls to Dimitra produced many excuses as colourful as they were complex. We told her we only had a few days before our British car became illegal, but she didn't seem to grasp our sense of urgency in a country where everyone seems to be doing something illegal some of the time, at least. And since Mr Desmond was out of the picture now – back in Britain for a few weeks – we decided to forget about Dimitra.

"That leaves just one option," said Jim, adopting a crude shrug of hopelessness, so perfected by Desmond. "Let's hit the Kalamata car yards tomorrow."

"What if no-one speaks English?" I said, dreading the length of time I'd have to spend boning up on car vocabulary: engine size, number of previous owners, what's the mileage, what's this big puddle of oil on the ground under the engine, and so forth. As we drove the next day towards the phalanx of car dealers whose showrooms line the main road out to the city's airport, I realised how easy it was going to be for some Arthur Daley character to sell us a dazzling heap once he got wind of my patchy Greek.

It was crazy enough buying a car on our own, in Greek, but doubly worrying when, unlike the UK, none of the cars had prices on their windscreens, meaning we had no ball park figure to start with. But whether I got the Greek numbers right or not, every salesman used the same technique for a foreign sale of writing the price with a finger on a dusty side window, as if we were haggling in a market in Tangiers. The same technique was used for car mileage. After a couple of hours of this, standing in the blistering heat, we confused the mileage with the price, and were shocked that an eight-year-old Fiat Punto could cost 145,000 euros and had only travelled 3,000 kilometres.

As we moved from one car yard to the next, our fears were bubbling, and for the first time we experienced the frustrations of living in a country with its chaotic, old-fashioned systems and its Levantine bureaucracy. One car yard we passed looked like it was being run by gypsies, with a fleet of old bangers parked at odd angles between olive trees in a field bordering the main road. If they'd had a half-decent gypsy caravan, complete with a bow-legged gelding, we'd have bought it.

But just when we were about to give up and go home, we found the perfect Greek car salesman, the tall and charming Andreas, who spoke good English as well. He let us test-drive a small Fiat, allowing us an illegal U-turn at a major intersection. Once back at the showroom, we bought the car on the spot. Crazy? Yes. But this was Greece, after all. The car was a Fiat Panda, four years old, and two years on it still went like a charm.

Insuring the car was much less daunting. We had a recommendation to visit an efficient broker, who arranged fully comprehensive insurance, or what he called in English "the full packet". However, we had to wait about 10 days for the paperwork to arrive, during which time we only had third-party cover, and drove the car around as if it were a Ming vase on wheels.

When we returned to pick up the paperwork the broker told us there was a hitch. We had been knocked back by the preferred insurance company and another would have to be arranged. When we asked why we had been rejected he told us the first company was no longer insuring foreign drivers in Greece as they were a high risk.

"Do you mean they think we are poor drivers?"

"No. The company says foreigners don't know how Greeks drive," he told us, throwing out his arms in frustration. When we burst out laughing, he offered a wry smile. By then we knew exactly how Greeks drive – at high speed, on the wrong side of the road, while rolling up cigarettes, eating souvlaki, slurping coffee, talking loudly on the mobile. Doing anything, in fact, but driving.

@@@@@@@

Now that we had our new, legal car, we were keen to start exploring the vast Mani region in earnest. But instead of picking something easy and accessible, we set our sights on a mountain village with a terrifying drive to it, known locally as the 'travmatikos dromos', the traumatic road. When we mentioned to the villagers that we were attempting this ascent, they told us we were mad and that most Greeks wouldn't dream of taking it on.

From the side balcony of our village house we had a panoramic view of Mount Kalathio, one of the highest peaks in north Mani sector of the Taygetos mountain range, at 4,500ft. Three-quarters of the way up Mount Kalathio is the tiny village of Ano (upper) Verga, clinging to a craggy slope and one of the highest villages in the Mani. Sometimes wreathed in morning mist, or glittering gold when the setting sun lit up the windows of its large cliff-edge taverna, it had fascinated us from the first day. At night, an arc of lights from the street lamps along its narrow main road hovered in the darkness like the landing lights of a UFO. It seemed to indicate a fantasy village of shy beings who liked to keep themselves apart. And it wasn't far from the truth.

The drive up the side of the mountain to Ano Verga was far more treacherous than we thought, with scree-showered hairpin bends and deep ravines below and no guard rails anywhere. We found the village strangely quiet for a morning in late June and drove to the other end it of without seeing a soul. Here, the church of Agios Dimitrios is built near the cliff edge and from here you get your first vertiginous glimpse of the city of Kalamata, spread out below, a cubist vision of white apartment blocks from the sea to the hills at the back. Up here you might as well be floating on air, or hang-gliding without all the paraphernalia. It's about as close as you get to heaven, without dying first.

An old stone *kalderimi,* donkey track, at the back of the village ascends the mountain further, but you don't need to go very far to get the second best view from this village – the whole eastern flank of this peninsula looking south. From here, the last 50 miles of the Taygetos mountains forms a blue/grey big dipper of peaks running all the way down to the bottom and tapering out completely just before Cape Tainaron.

Driving through the village we passed its only inhabitant so far, an old guy dressed in baggy trousers and wearing a black captain's hat with straggly grey hair hanging down below it. We stopped the car and I wound down my window to ask him where everyone was. He stood for a moment in silence, looking to the back seat, where Wallace was screamy-barking because the poor man was encroaching on his territory.

He launched into a stream of excitable rural Greek, flashing one single blackened tooth that protruded from his upper gums. It drew your attention by its sheer eerie perseverance.

50

A tooth that would last until the end of time. He didn't seem to want to stop talking and in the end we had to just drive off, beeping the horn and waving goodbye.

"What did he say?" said Jim.

"Haven't a clue."

We parked the car and took a steep path to the old part of the village where once-elegant stone houses were now wrecked and leaning together, their roofs caved in, their balconies crumbling. In the courtyards was a chaos of wild fruit trees and weeds. There was no sound, except for a gentle wind toying with old shutters sagging on their hinges, and the droning of hornets and wasps around the mouth of an old spring water outlet.

Much of this desolation was caused by earthquakes, especially the most recent one in 1986 that destroyed much of Kalamata and many villages in the Messinian region, which comprises the left hand peninsula, the Kalamata area and most of the central peninsula. This earthquake has probably been the biggest factor in the social changes that have taken place in this region since the 1950s, with people leaving their scarred villages, their wrecked lives, for other places, other countries.

If Ano Verga seems now like a beautiful ghost village, its flashier sibling, just below at some 1,200ft, called Kato (lower) Verga, has the glamour gene, with expensive houses and a few trendy nightclubs. Two centuries ago the area attracted a different kind of hell-raiser. During the Greek War of Independence, started in 1821, the Maniots fought valiantly against the Ottoman Turks, but a decisive battle was fought and won in Verga. With Turks advancing on the Mani in 1826 under the leadership of Egyptian general Ibrahim Pasha, defence walls were hastily built up the side of Mount Kalathio. The Turks were eventually beaten in Verga, which meant they were unable to seize control of this strategic north Mani region, the gateway into the whole peninsula.

At Ano Verga, we trudged along overgrown paths, past more deserted houses, yet somewhere nearby, a door banged loudly, making us jump. A voice boomed over a high wall.

"Who's there?" said a male voice. "Are you looking for work?"

Jim and I stared at each other. What kind of work would these mountain dwellers have in mind in these crumbling backblocks? A metal door in the courtyard wall swung open to reveal a middle-aged man standing before a large courtyard. He was irritable.

"Well," he said. "Are you looking for work?"

"We're *xenoi* (foreigners)," I offered, nervously, which was to be the start of my predilection for using that phrase every time we encountered a strange, or unnerving experience as if, by being foreigners, we are forgiven for all lapses of good taste.

"We're exploring your village," I added.

"We don't get many tourists up here. There are *xenoi* in the village with holiday houses. They come in summer." His head jerked towards the road below. "Where are you from? Are you German?" he said, in the sharp, usual manner that Greeks use with this question, because of German occupation during the war.

"We're from Scotland."

He looked blank, just like Foteini and other Maniots we'd met. Clearly Scotland had an image problem in this part of the world. The man was suddenly more relaxed.

"Come in and have a coffee with us," he said, opening the metal door further.

In the middle of the courtyard, surrounded by messy piles of junk, sat an old man at a wooden table, toiling lustily over a heap of vegetables on a broad plate. He smiled and waved a fork, gleaming with olive oil, in our direction, as if our presence was expected. I would have recognised that solitary tooth anywhere.

"It's them," the old man said to the other, or at least that's how it sounded to me. I wondered how he had managed to scramble up here so fast.

We declined the offer of coffee, but I asked the first man: "How many Greeks are there left in the village?"

"Just a few of us left now. It's cold in winter. We get snow here. Most people go down to the plain then."

"But you stay?"

"Mostly," he said, with a frown. "We have some animals. We do some olive harvesting a bit further down."

Another man stepped into the courtyard, hovering around the periphery, with a long face, messy hair, old farm clothes. They now looked like a gathering of hillbillies from the Appalachian Mountains in America.

"Come in and have a drink," said one-tooth man, waving his fork again.

Now it was a drink. Rough mountain liquor, some 50 per cent proof sage brew, or similar.

"Yes please!" said Jim, loudly, after I'd translated the drink offer and my thoughts on mountain tipples.

"Don't even think about it," I said.

"You're always saying you want adventure, and plenty of it ..."

"Remember the drive back down. Hairpin bends ...sheer drops."

Jim frowned.

The first man was observing us closely now. "So you're from Scotia, eh? Is that part of England?"

Jim and I looked at each other and grinned. How do you summarise 1,000 years of Scottish history? I didn't bother.

"Scotland's nearby."

"We had an English soldier here during the war…after the Battle of Kalamata…do you know about that time?" he asked.

He was referring to the heroic rear-guard action by the allies against the Germans invading the city from the north in 1941. Heavily outnumbered, however, the British, Australian and New Zealand troops had massed on the beaches at Kalamata, awaiting evacuation to Crete by Royal Navy ships, in a dangerous manoeuvre known as Operation Demon.

Although most were evacuated, several thousand troops were left behind. Most of these were captured by the Nazis and taken as prisoners of war. A small number managed to escape down the Mani coast. Eight British soldiers mounted a daring escape by stealing a rowing boat and taking it 160 miles to northern Crete. Others hid out in the mountains, in lofty villages like Ano Verga, or further back in the Taygetos.

"Someone in this village hid the soldier for months in his house," said the first man, "until he was able to make his way to the coast and escape by boat."

"Where was he hidden?"

"Further down the village. The house is gone now in any case, and the family who lived there."

I couldn't imagine anyone making it up this mountain from the beaches below in wartime or how this place must have seemed to a British soldier then. In peacetime, however, in the summer, this village must have been glorious – families in every house, children, laughter, wedding processions to the village church with the shady plane trees, midnight services on Easter Saturday, *paniyiria* (fetes) with spit roasts in the church forecourt, long tables groaning with food and people. All gone.

We said farewell and he shouted after us: "*Sto kalo* (go to the good)."

We scurried back down to the car, moving quickly from the crumbling laneways of the past to the tiers of neat new holiday homes near the main road. It was like a geological core sample you could find in mountain villages all over the Mani. What was left of Greek life in Ano Verga, like the family in the courtyard, seemed shockingly raw, scratching out a living with animals and olives, in dire surroundings while the rest of their villagers slowly gave up and moved away.

We would see families like this all over the southern Peloponnese during our stay, even before the worst of the austerity measures were introduced. Yet it was hardly the image most holidaymakers still have of Greece – smart clubs and tavernas along a whitewashed Mykonos seafront, or even poolside at the luxurious Costa Navarino golfing resort in the western Peloponnese, with its clipped fairways. Over the next year or so, these two sides of Greece would start to seem more and more incompatible.

5

Icons of our times

ON Sunday morning, Jim woke me up, moaning loudly. "I think I've suddenly developed tinnitus," he said in a groggy voice.

"Don't be silly. It's the church bell."

"That's not a church bell. That's right inside my head."

That's what it sounded like, as Spiti Mou was not far from the church, and the bell when it was rung, was end-of-the-world loud and insistent. I looked at the clock. Seven. Time to get up.

The Sunday service in Megali Mantineia was something of a mystery. It wasn't held every week because of a lack of parish priests, which was a problem here as it was elsewhere in Greece, as young men no longer wanted to take on this demanding role for a modest salary. In Megali Mantineia the *papas*, priest, had to cover for three or four churches in different locations. The service at our local church took place, well, when it took place, without any logic obvious to a foreigner. I was keen to take part in everything that went on in the village, including the Sunday service, and what better place to observe our fellow villagers than in church?

Greek women usually always know when a service is imminent. They have a gift for it, like wild elephants sensing the coming of a tsunami. Yet here, even that wasn't always the case. One day at the Good Heart *kafeneio*, I asked Angeliki when the next Sunday service would be held. She stared at me blankly, then shrugged.

"I don't know, but just do what we do, listen for the bell. You won't miss the bell," she said, with a knowing smile.

Of course she was right. This is Greece. There are no schedules, timetables, plans. Listen for the bell is a metaphor for life here. I had no problem with that. And so the bell started at seven.

"Get up," I said to the bleary Jim. "Your hour has come."

Or two to be more precise. I hadn't bothered to tell him that the Sunday service here is long but, unlike British church services, there is no pressure to stay for the duration, or even for more than five minutes. Greeks come and go, like guests at a smorgasbord table, piling up their plates, then leaving. They troop into church, light a candle, kiss an icon and depart. But while this devotion-lite approach was cool for Greeks, I thought it would be frowned upon in foreigners.

It was nearly eight by the time we arrived at the village church. The chanting had also begun, a great apocalyptic wave of sound rippling out from the loudspeaker at the front of the building and all over the village. At the church door I could see candlelight, a cloud of incense, a dark priestly figure flitting about like a moth in a jar. It was a long time since I'd been to a Greek church service. I panicked. Would we seem like party gatecrashers? No time to find out as old Pericles, the man who predicted bombs in our house walls, shuffled up the stairs behind us and nudged us inside, muttering: "What are you waiting for?" Indeed.

Men to the right, women to the left, a residual nod to rituals of the Greek Orthodox Church that haven't changed for at least 500 years, and every surface of the church was painted with frescos of august-looking Byzantine saints and apostles.

"Sit on my side," I said to Jim, tugging his arm towards an empty row of wooden chairs on the left, near the back of the church. I sensed many eyes upon us – and not the sad, soporific eyes of the saints. Along our side wall, sitting on high-backed wooden chairs with arm rests, were the old women in black, sitting motionless but watchful, some of them with a dismissive stare. While no-one openly condemned foreigners for joining services, clearly not everyone welcomed it either.

Two *psaltes* (chanters) stood at a lectern on the right of the church, singing, one with the voice of a saint, sweet and clear, the other with a deep throaty refrain, but the face slightly distracted and pained, as if he were constructing a mental shopping list he couldn't quite get to the end of.

The priest was standing at the altar in the *bema* (sanctuary), which lies beyond the *iconostasis*, the richly carved wooden partition covered in icons. His back was turned to the congregation, engaged in intricate rituals we could only guess at. When he turned around, however, it was Robert Downey Jr, dressed in a long black robe. Had he given up acting, was he researching a new role as a priest?

"Robert Downey," I whispered in Jim's ear.

"What?" said Jim, too tired on a Sunday morning for Spot the Celebrity.

"Don't worry about it," I said, tapping him on the arm.

Okay, so it wasn't Robert Downey Jr, but his doppelganger anyway, with black soulful eyes. He looked modern for a priest, with short cropped hair instead of the long hair tied back, and a bit of a beard and moustache. At the bottom of his robe, peeking out, I could see very fashionable shoes, highly polished. And to complete this wealth of Sunday morning riches, to our right I could see Paul Newman tidying up the candle stand, his blue eyes twinkling in the soft glow of light. Our friendly farming neighbour, whom we had met with

Desmond, was also an elder of this church. Suddenly the Greek service seemed a lot more interesting, even if brevity was never going to be its strong point.

Apart from its use of Ancient and Byzantine Greek, most of its rituals are incomprehensible to the foreigner. There was a great deal of standing and sitting. Up and down we went, like players in a sombre game of musical chairs. During one long standing segment, my eyes wandered to the woman directly in front. Dressed smartly in black, a shiny handbag over one arm, her dark hair was flecked with grey, and slicked back with a tortoiseshell headband. As if she'd felt my stare, she turned slightly.

I gasped. "Foteini, is that you?" I said loudly, as if I were in the arrivals hall at Gatwick Airport waiting for a long-lost Greek relative.

Jim, well over his tinnitus now, nudged my side with a manly elbow. The women in the high chairs twitched like a line of crows on a power cable, ready for flight. The priest frowned and swung his censer, on its long silver chains with tinkling bells, in a vigorous arc up the aisle, plunging the female corner into thick clouds of fragrant, choking smoke. This lusty toying with the censer, we were to discover later, was the whim of many parish priests, especially this one. Foteini smiled, the unmistakable pale eyes giving nothing much away. I caught a glimpse of a well-pressed cotton blouse, a gold chain at her neck, a smart black jacket. Jim shot me a quizzical look.

The rest of the service floated by and whether it was the early start or the incense, I felt drowsy and stared at the vision in front of me, wondering how the woman we'd last seen, skimming blocks of wood across a tin roof at tearaway goats, dressed in her layered *ktima* couture, could be this sedate, rather elegant woman here. It was as mysterious to me as the mellifluous Byzantine chanting, now drawing to an end.

A basket of blessed bread was produced from the sanctuary and the congregation jostled each other along the aisle to the front to receive a piece from a seated Robert Downey Jr. I thought it best just to slip away and attract no more attention. Jim nodded towards the door and scurried outside. The women in the high-backed chairs clambered down and gave me a disapproving look, apart from one very old, tiny woman bound tightly in black, including a headscarf, the favoured outfit of the very old and devout. She struggled towards me, bunching her fingers together, pointing towards her open mouth, with only a few teeth left, very spaced out.

"*Faye*," she said, her eyes darting towards the bread basket. She told me to eat.

I shuffled up the aisle with the woman behind me, her cold twiglet fingers goading the back of my arm. The priest handed me two bread squares without making eye contact, not well pleased, I thought, with my earlier noisy outburst. I was quickly elbowed out of the way by several hungry matrons and propelled back along the aisle to the door.

I found Jim outside with Foteini. I decided not to comment on her outfit but came to the conclusion that there were obviously two Foteinis – the one on a donkey carting half a house, shouting at goats, and this normal village woman.

"How are you getting back to your *ktima*?" I asked her, wondering if her donkey was tethered nearby.

"I'm going to my house first," she said, giving me the strange look that Greeks reserve for foreigners because we never seem to grasp the 'obvious'.

"You have a house?"

"Up the path there," she said, pointing a nugget of bread towards a group of dilapidated houses. "The one with the blue door."

It was a house we could plainly see from our front balcony, though we'd never seen its occupant so far. I felt relieved she didn't live in the ramshackle *ktima* after all.

"Come by again for a coffee."

"To the house?"

She grimaced. "No, not there. It's an old place ... I meant the *ktima*." And she turned and left, muttering something about goats...and *xenoi*.

Ah, the *ktima*, I said to myself with a heavy heart. The place of dancing farm animals, sinks leaning on ironing boards, and a 'café terrace' patrolled by hornets. But at least Foteini had a village house, with neighbours and an assortment of rough comforts, I imagined.

"Foteini doesn't invite many people to her house," said a voice behind me. I turned to find Angeliki. She had obviously overheard the conversation.

"Why? Because it's old?"

"No, not that."

"Why then?" I asked with a journalist's natural curiosity.

Angeliki raised her eyebrows, shutting her eyes at the same time, which is the unique, often maddening, gesture of Greeks, often paired with a tutting noise, all of which is the equivalent of "no comment". It is a gesture that invites no more dialogue and only the foolhardy would push a Greek further than this point.

But her gesture implied some mystery I hoped I might whittle out of her in time.

"You heard the bells this morning then," said Angeliki, smiling and showing a row of tiny white teeth.

"The priest's very handsome. He looks like Robert Downey Junior, don't you think?"

"Who's that?" she said, looking blank.

My eyes pleaded with Jim for help. "Don't look at me. I don't buy into all your crazy ideas," he said.

"Did you see his Italian shoes?" asked Angeliki, with more enthusiasm.

"How do you know they're Italian?"

"In a village, everyone knows the shoes of a priest."

I smiled. It sounded like a kind of village *parimia,* folk saying, to which there was no rejoinder.

Later, while taking Wallace out for his morning walk, we called into the *kafeneio* to prove to assembled villagers that despite his barking and fights with Cyclops the cat, Wallace had a dignified side. But Wallace is a typical Jack Russell, a dog with the Freudian inclination to only do the one thing you don't want him to do.

The minute we walked on to the terrace and Wallace set eyes on the table of young Albanian stone masons, who were talking loudly and smoking like the funnel on the QEII, he started up a round of screamy barking. The Albanians laughed at the sight of this white ball of angry fluff – and that just made him worse. Angeliki, still in her Sunday black, was sitting in the cabin in front of the TV that was blaring out the morning news with its gloomy reports on Greek affairs. She half-turned and shouted: "He's very loud for a cucumber, isn't he?"

Ilias, who was sitting nearby in a cloud of cigarette smoke, reading a Sunday paper, looked up and laughed heartily and the sunburnt skin around his eyes crinkled like Biblical parchment. Ilias was a man who never said very much but his face conveyed a great deal, whether it was just in the merest twitch of a smile or the arching of an eyebrow. When he watched customers walking into the courtyard you could tell from his trace expressions exactly what he thought of them. Generally, he also liked a good wind-up, just like Angeliki. After watching screamy Wallace for a few moments, he did that peculiarly Greek thing of making a claw of his hand and twisting it back and forth at the side of his head, while going "*Po, po, po!* (bloody hell!)", which meant "the dog's bonkers".

I nodded in agreement and we took Wallace to a table at the other end of the terrace. Moments later, Angeliki brought Greek coffee on a tray and a plate of *melomakarona* sticky honey biscuits. She sat at the table, pulling her chair back a little distance to create a buffer zone between herself and the dog.

"Why don't you like dogs?" I asked her.

"We've got dogs," she said, pointing to a plot of land across from the *kafeneio*, where three slavering dogs were tied to trees on long chains. As if they had heard and understood, they started yapping loudly in unison.

"My other son Stavros keeps them for hunting. He looks after them. I don't go anywhere near them. I just don't like them. I'm sorry," she added.

Fearing she'd caused offence, she leaned forward and twitched the corner of the tablecloth back and peered down at Wallace, who was sitting hot and bug-eyed underneath, but quiet at least.

"This one's okay I suppose, as long as he doesn't get too close. He's got a cute face. What's his name?"

We told her it was Wallace, but said she'd find it difficult to say. Greek doesn't have the letter 'w'. She tried to say it several times and failed.

"Why don't we give him a Greek name. Call him Vasilis," she said with a chuckle. "That's close. Or Vassie, for short. I like that name."

"Okay. Vassie it is then," I said, feeling very pleased that Angeliki had come round so quickly to liking Wallace. But the satisfaction was short-lived.

"Don't think I'll like him more for having a Greek name."

As we walked down the road back to the house we talked about Wallace and his new name.

"Do you think Angeliki watches too much television and Vassie is her take on Lassie?" said Jim.

"It's his first step to becoming Greek," I said. "The next time we take him out in the car he'll want to wind down the window and hang one paw out in the breeze the way Greeks do."

We chuckled as we walked along the road, but not for long. As we reached the opening of Goat Lane we heard a noise and stopped. At the top of the lane, in a clearing where there was an old shed, we saw two men we didn't recognise standing beside the body of a skinned goat. It was dangling from a hook on a wooden beam, projecting from the side of the building.

The large pale body twirled slowly on the end of the rope and sunlight flashed off the long smooth surface of a knife. The man holding it was motionless, with wary eyes, a cigarette hanging from the corner of his mouth. He seemed annoyed that we'd somehow caught him out. Yet there was no attempt to hide the deed and it was clearly visible from the road. I got the feeling the pair were working fast, trying to get the business finished and the goat ready for Sunday lunch perhaps. We stood for a few moments silently watching, even Wallace seemed transfixed and never made a sound. Jim pulled me away by the arm.

"I wish we hadn't seen that today," I said, mournfully.

"Don't think about it. Farmers probably slaughter their own animals all over Greece. They don't do village abattoirs," said Jim.

I shivered. Goat Lane with its shed and butcher's hook was close enough to being an abattoir.

"Desmond said it was only now and then," said Jim, pulling Wallace along the road now because he kept stopping, turning his head back towards Goat Lane and sniffing the air. "It's not our concern what the locals do with their animals."

Not long afterwards, we saw Desmond on one of his regular visits to the house. This time it was to drop off letters, as all the mail, for the expats at least, went to one of the village tavernas, where it was piled up against one wall. Everyone would flick through it with great relish, looking to see who had final demands for electricity bills, who had subscriptions to dubious magazines. Community-minded Desmond took it upon himself to deliver mail to some of his fellow expats. As we took our letters, we asked him why the goat was being skinned on that particular Sunday.

"Probably one of the farmers was having a birthday and wanted to roast the goat on a spit, something like that. I never ask about these things, best not to," he said, looking uncomfortable.

Greeks celebrate their birthdays as name days. As most people are named after a saint, they celebrate on the feast day of the relevant saint. On Christmas Day those called Christos or Christina, for example, will celebrate.

"Do they slaughter a goat in the village every time there's a name day?" I asked.

Desmond chortled. "Hope not, that's a lot of goats, isn't it?"

"It's a lot of goat skinning as well," said Jim.

Desmond looked away, stumped for a reply.

We were quickly beginning to learn that nothing in Greece is ever the way it seems.

6

Hounds of Hades

"DO you realise that when we go back to Britain we can say: 'When we were in Greece we went to hell and back – literally'," I said to Jim as we drove down the coast road on a sweltering summer's day towards the tip of the Mani peninsula.

"Yeah, and it has nothing to do with the Greek crisis – or buying cars," he said, chortling.

This was a trip we had been keen to make from the very beginning of our adventure because it is impossible to live in a region that boasts the "the gateway to hell", or rather the ancient entrance to Hades, as one of its main attractions, and not want to cross its threshold. As journalists, it drew us like a ghoulish magnet.

The drive took us from the top of the peninsula, where the Taygetos range has some of its highest peaks, right the way down to Cape Tainaron at the bottom, the southernmost outpost of mainland Europe. Here, on a rocky headland, the ancient entrance to Hades is said to exist.

In Greek mythology, Hades was the god of the Underworld, from which this macabre realm of souls also takes its name. The entrance to Hades was also the portal to some pretty outlandish quests in the mythological world, for both gods and mortals, the tales of which have become the crucial filaments of western literature. It was here that charming Orpheus, the poet and musician, descended to retrieve his beloved wife Eurydice. It was here that the demi-god Iraklis

(Hercules) carried out his 12th labour, dragging out the snarling three-headed dog Cerberus (Kerbaros), referred to in ancient times as the Hound of Hades, the guard dog who stopped dead souls from escaping.

If we couldn't find the entrance to Hades with our own hound in tow then we would be abject failures, I thought.

I turned and looked at Wallace, snug on the back seat, wearing his special car harness that plugged into the seatbelt jack and stopped him from pinballing about while the car was moving. I made the mistake once, when Wallace was young, of letting him sit on the passenger seat while I was driving. It ended with him in my lap, standing on his back legs with his paws on the steering wheel, barking at oncoming traffic, while I tried to see over the top of his head. It drew a few wild stares from other drivers, yet in Greece, that kind of dangerous caper wouldn't have seemed at all out of place.

The entrance to Hades, or *Adis* in Greek, is not just a figment of mythical imagination. A real entrance was referred to in ancient times by Pausanias and Homer, but our research for this journey showed there was some mystery over where the actual portal was. To make things more difficult, there are three possible entrances described near Cape Tainaron.

The main contender was a cave overlooking the atmospheric Bay of Asomati, close to an ancient temple dedicated to Poseidon, god of the sea. Pausanias, the famed geographer and traveller of the 2nd century AD, in his book *Description of Greece*, wrote: "On the promontory is a temple like a cave, with a statue of Poseidon in front of it." This gave us a few clues at least.

Yet that other great travel writer of more recent fame, the late Patrick Leigh Fermor, who penned the book *Mani*, claimed the entrance to Hades was in a sea cave on the western side of this middle peninsula. Intrepid traveller and war hero, best remembered for his daring exploits in Crete during the Second World War, when he abducted a German general, Leigh Fermor first came to the Mani in the early 1950s, where he said the way of life had "survived in a fierce and enchanting time warp". He was convinced the entrance to Hades lay in a cave beneath towering sea cliffs, close to Cape Tainaron (also known as Cape Matapan).

To reach the cave, Leigh Fermor hired a local boatman from the village of Marmari and got him to wait while he swam into the mouth of the 30-foot high opening. But, as he wrote in his book, he was disappointed to find that the floor of the cave had probably sunk and there was no submerged entrance to the cave system he expected to find.

Other Greek scholars have confirmed several entrances to Hades. Robert Graves, in the *Golden Ass of Apuleius*, talks of "ventilation holes of the underworld" in and around the ancient site of Tainaron. A Greek friend of ours in Kalamata, Evangelos, who is a keen historian and environmentalist, agreed with this theory, telling us that some ancient ruins beside the water at Asomati Bay, which has the remains of Roman mosaics, had probably once contained a ventilation hole in the form of a staircase leading down to Hades, which sounded like something Stephen King might play around with.

As for the sea cave entrance to Hades, Evangelos believed, like Fermor, that there probably was an opening here in ancient times but that a rising sea level and local earthquake activity had probably wiped it out. The famous Dirou caves, not far away on the west coast, are thought to be part of vast subterranean lake system dating back to Neolithic times. Perhaps this inspired the notion of an underworld, since in Greek mythology Hades had five rivers including the Acheron (River of Woe) across which Charon the boatman was said to ferry the souls of the dead for the fee of one coin (*obolus*), placed in the mouth of the deceased. Our journey to Hades then was potholed with mystery.

The road from north Mani to Cape Tainaron covers some of the most rugged terrain in Greece, but also passes some of the prettiest coastal settlements, like the ancient town of Kardamili. Mentioned in Homer's *Iliad*, the town is said to contain the tomb of the mythological twins Castor and Pollux. Most of the present town was built in the 1700s, when it became the stronghold of a clan chieftain, Panayiotis Troupakis. In the 1960s it became better known as the home of Patrick Leigh Fermor, who had a monastic house built on a secluded promontory.

A few miles further south is the tourist town of Stoupa, most famous for its sheltered beach of Kalogria, where the Greek writer Nikos Kazantzakis lived in 1917/18 and drew inspiration for his novel *Zorba the Greek*. Kazantzakis had come here to run a lignite mine, still in evidence in the foothills of Stoupa, and hired the real-life George Zorbas as foreman. Kalogria beach was the inspiration for the famous scene in the novel where Zorba teaches the protagonist (the writer) how to dance the sirtaki.

Halfway down the peninsula, at the village of Otylo, overlooking the wide bay of the same name, is the point where the Outer Mani ends and the Deep Mani (*Mesa Mani*) begins. From here the landscape becomes hot, parched and inhospitable. If you wanted to conjure up the perfect landscape to draw you on down to Hades, you could find none better than this area.

The main town of this region, Areopolis, defines this region. Despite narrow laneways with boutique hotels in listed buildings with immaculately restored stonework, trendy cafes and museums, you can feel the weight of history here and a sense of wariness in its residents because of its clannish, warring past.

The Mani has a long and turbulent history from the early days of 1200 BC, when its first residents had to take refuge from invading Spartans. Over the centuries there were waves of other invaders: Slavic tribes from eastern Europe, and Franks, which has added to the melting pot of Maniots. In the 17th and 18th centuries the violence was stepped up with blood-curdling clan warfare, mostly about land. It was enough to keep even the Turks away, despite four centuries of domination in the rest of Greece.

While the Turks launched punitive raids into this peninsula, they were continually outwitted by the wily Maniots and their powerful *Kapetanioi*, the clan leaders like the great Theodoros Kolokotronis, who led the revolutionary army that trounced the Turks in Kalamata in 1821, thus starting the Greek War of Independence. Even the women here, who were trained to shoot, were famous for their cat fights with the Turks.

I had no doubt about this when I met one of Areopolis's oldest, toughest matrons in the old-fashioned *artopoleion*, the bakery in the centre of the town. The bakery has a traditional wood-fired oven for making the village loaves so loved by older people in Greece, with crusts that are volcanic and probably explains why few people over 60 have any teeth left. She was formidable, dressed in black, with dark eyes as tight as wingnuts. She was not amused when I asked for the softest loaf, as I feared for my own dental work. She riffled through the loaves, her claw-like hands squeezing them in turn.

"This one's soft," she said, smacking a round loaf down in front of me with a great thud. I tried to feel it for myself but it was rock hard. I don't think even a power saw would have made a dent. I took it anyway and left with a polite "*Yiasas, kai kalo mesimeri*" (goodbye and have a good afternoon), which won me nothing but a deep stare of suspicion.

The car park at Cape Tainaron is the end of the road, with an azure sea shimmering into the distance towards Africa. A dry track snakes off towards a lighthouse at the cape's tip. It felt peaceful here under an impossibly blue sky, with waves lapping gently at the nearby three coves that make up Asomati Bay. Yet it was hard to believe that the stony land here had once supported an important and thriving ancient city.

The signpost here didn't muck about. "Sacred and Death Oracle of Poseidon" it said, pointing to the Church of Asomati, where we thought we'd begin our quest to discover Pausanias's "temple like a cave" with the entrance to Hades. We set off towards the church, Wallace pulling us along, desperate for movement after being confined to a hot car for three hours. Or had he got some mystical whiff of the Hound of Hades?

The church is mostly in ruins, apart from thick outer walls with massive stone blocks that seemed to indicate an ancient temple, possibly to Poseidon, though a newer Byzantine church had been built inside. The stone altar had become a repository for modern-day votive 'junk': rusting keys, coins, a hammer and, curiously, a Red Nose Day plastic cap on its piece of elastic, as if visitors here had emptied their pockets of things they no longer needed in this life. But there was nothing inside resembling an entrance to Hades.

We wandered about in circles on this windswept point, covered in long grass and myriad tall wild thistles, a nod perhaps to the swaying Meadows of Asphodels, one of the zones of Hades where 'neutral' souls (neither good nor bad) were said to gather.

As we scrambled about, Wallace pulled hard towards a cove below with a few colourful fishing boats at anchor. Wallace's favourite thing, apart from roast chicken, is a swim in the sea, and on this hot, dry day, the sight of cool water tickling the pebbled cove was too much for him. He had his swim, shook himself and then made straight for a line of shrubs obscuring a section of cliff-face that was topped by the Asomati church.

He relieved himself with great ceremony on each shrub and then bolted through the curtain of greenery, leading us straight to Hades, which seemed fitting, of course. Beyond the shrubs was an enclosed, dank area ringed by ochre-coloured rocks but open to the sky. On one side was a long, low cave with a mouth like a gummy giant's smile and an entranceway with a classical carved stone either side, and low dry-stone walls.

The cave seemed like a dead-ringer for the gateway to Hades from all the descriptions we'd read, even though there was no sign of a Poseidon statue. The cave was certainly neglected though, its walls blackened and damp from centuries of dripping water, and the scrubby forecourt smelt strongly of goats. Yet inside the cave, we found the most curious indicator of subterranean capers. In one damp corner was the outline of a stone-lined shaft, now filled in with compacted earth and rubble.

I had trouble, however, seeing Iraklis dragging the slavering Cerberus into the light through this shaft. And was this the place where the touching story of Orpheus unfolded as he descended in search of his wife Eurydice, who died after a snake bite? Orpheus was said to have softened the hard heart of the god Hades with a sweet tune on his lyre and was allowed to bring his wife out of the underworld.

But Hades set one condition: that Orpheus must walk in front of Eurydice and never look round until they were safely back in the upper world. Poor Orpheus, almost at the end of his quest, and just to reassure himself his wife was still there, turned, and she was snatched back again into the depths of hell.

"Is this it then?" Jim and I said to each other as we pondered this desolate portal that the fates had not treated kindly over the centuries.

In a whimsical nod to this strange, eerie place, we propped Wallace on to one of the entrance stones of the cave and took his photo, a one-headed hound of hell with a lolling tongue and a glassy stare. We thought Cerberus would have been no match at all for the mad and indefatigable Jack Russell dog.

We walked from the cave along the shore to a walled, ruined site with lovely circular floor mosaics, featuring a spectacular wave design alluding to the sea god Poseidon. We looked for signs of another ventilation shaft of Hades but couldn't find one, so we trudged on, despite the heat, to the lighthouse at Cape Tainaron's tip. It was a long, hard trek on a rocky path with stones that were as punishing as giant cheese graters, where one false step would send you pinging off a cliff into the sea below.

The lighthouse was predictably on a lonely, rocky outcrop looking towards Africa. Swallows capered along the cliff edge and below, in an inky blue sea, several divers were exploring the coastline. Were they looking for more gateways to the underworld? Perhaps...

On our long drive back towards north Mani and Megali Mantineia, the mountains and the towered hillsides had a slightly gloomy feel after sunset. We were exhausted from the day's trek. Wallace was on the back seat, engaged in compulsive dog therapy, licking a scraped paw over and over again, the result of the lighthouse walk.

"Okay, we can say it now. We've just been to hell and back," I chirped as we drove through a winding mountain pass with an impossibly bright moon to light our way. I pondered the irony of Greece possessing the fabled gateway to hell. Were we mad to even go looking for hell when it was already creeping over the whole country in the form of economic ruin and punishing austerity measures, with a road block at the exit, just like the compacted shaft in the Hades cave?

But hell comes in many different forms, we were soon to discover.

7

There's a scorpion in my slipper

ONE afternoon, Jim came in from a walk with Wallace and found me crouched beside the open storage area under the stairs – motionless.

"What are you doing there?"

"Scorpion!" I said, my voice as tight as a circus high-wire.

"What's it doing?" he asked, taking Wallace's lead off and shutting him in the bedroom.

"What do you think it's doing?" I said, soaked in sweat and my knees aching from crouching on floor tiles for 20 minutes. "Skulking in the corner, sending Tweets from its mobile phone?"

"Very cute. Let me see." He crouched down beside me and I pointed under the stairs to the black critter in the corner.

"Holy Mother! It's got an erection, if you see what I mean."

Only a man can see a scorpion and think of sex. The poisonous black tail was certainly very up though, and jabbing in our direction.

"I've been trying to keep an eye on him all this time. We can't let him escape or we don't know where he'll end up," I said, starting to become hysterical.

"Okay, calm down. I'll look for the insecticide," said Jim and he ran upstairs and rattled about in the kitchen cupboards. He took so long that I thought I'd faint.

When we first came to live in our hillside village, a few of the expats took great delight in winding us up about noxious critters – especially scorpions, the one creature we had feared the most. And Desmond hadn't helped matters at the beginning when he mentioned scorpions in the stonework here before renovation. I knew then that we were destined to meet this hideous creature that looks almost prehistoric – the outsized claws, the pitch-fork tail at the back; half-crab, half-devil. We had heard stories about massive black scorpions falling out of olive trees, or hiding in wood piles.

Then there was one story from an English expat called Derek, who seemed to be something of a scorpion magnet, having been bitten twice in a matter of months. The second scorpion, beige-coloured and more deadly, bit him painfully on the stomach while he was lying in bed. Derek claimed the critter must have hidden in his pyjamas while they were hanging on the washing line earlier. His wife managed to get the scorpion into a jar for identification and it required a midnight scramble to Kalamata Hospital, where he was not in good shape – and neither was Derek.

Placed on an antibiotic drip, he survived the attack, but the scorpion expired and was returned to Derek, by his doctor, sealed up in the same jar with the addition of formaldehyde. It was now a kind of *memento mori* that Derek liked to bring out on a tray with cold beers and nibbles when had had people round for drinks in the summer.

We were warned by Desmond not to lift rocks in the courtyard without wearing gloves, or to poke about in the perimeter stone walls. Given that grenades might appear before scorpions, we had no intention of doing this. He also warned us not to leave objects lying on the floor for more than a few days because if scorpions did come into the house they would hide under them. This was the first time Desmond confessed to possible scorpion interlopers.

I had been clearing out the space under the stairs and moved a gym bag that had been there for weeks when the scorpion skittered out. Jim came running back down the stairs, a spray can in his hand.

"Okay, let's hit it with this," he said, and instantly sprayed enough insecticide under the stairs to poleaxe a brown bear. Then we pulled everything else clear of it and got it on the end of a sweeping brush.

"I think that stunned it, anyway," Jim said, taking the brush outside, the scorpion dangling on the end of the bristles, and gave it a mortal bashing on the paving stones.

"Thank God we got rid of that," he said.

"They travel in pairs, you know," I told him, recalling something I'd read.

"Nonsense, of course they don't."

But if there's one rule in life it's this: whenever you say a thing won't happen, it generally does. A few days later I walked into the bedroom and screamed like a woman confronting a hooded intruder with a machete. Jim came running in.

"What is it?"

"There's a scorpion in my slipper!" I shouted.

Crawling around the inside rim of my sheepskin slipper was another black scorpion, bigger than the first one, its tail up and quivering in my direction.

"They don't seem to like me," I croaked as Jim mobilised the spray and the sweeping brush and took the scorpion outside while I pushed shoes around the floor, trying to rumble any more scorpions. Jim came back and viewed the bedroom floor grimly.

"I suppose you're going to say now they travel in threes."

As it happens, I found a third black scorpion some weeks later, trying to crawl into a crack in the stonework around the front door. Only its long tail was hanging out. This was the biggest one yet. We lived in fear of more of them.

"I thought Cyclops was supposed to stalk scorpions," said Jim, revving up his insecticide tin.

Poor Cyclops, with his dirty white fur, like the froth on a café latte, and his bleary one eye. I doubted he could even see them properly or that cats hunted scorpions anyway, even though their sting was not supposed to affect them, or dogs, the way it did humans.

We told Desmond about our scorpion 'infestation'. He looked surprised at first but then admitted that previous tenants had found some in the house, around six in one year.

"Six?" We calculated therefore that three in a matter of weeks augured a few dozen of the nasty little blighters in one year.

"You've been leaving objects on the floor for too long and not moving them around the house like I told you to," he muttered, like some grand master of the telekinetic arts.

"Look, a scorpion bite is no worse than being stung by a wasp," he added.

"Have you ever been bitten by a scorpion, Desmond?"

"Em, no," he replied. "They're shy creatures. They don't like noise and movement. I think they've come inside because of the road works, to get away."

I had instant sympathy for the poor shy scorpions. If only the rest of us in the village could have escaped the disruption of council workers digging up parallel trenches in the road for half the summer, with a huge digger that looked like a giant Triffid, booming along the road with its long neck and menacing metal teeth. The village was to have new water pipes laid, which was long overdue, apparently.

The digging was supposed to be over in a few weeks, but months later the roads and lanes were still being gouged out and mounds of discarded dry earth appeared around the village. Across from the house, beside the rubbish bins, was a patch of bare land where once a green metal bus shelter had stood. The shelter was now mangled and lying on its side, probably hit by a truck and left to rot. In front of it, a mound of rubble was added to every day by the road gang, a miniature pyramid that released sticky clouds of dust whenever a car sped by.

Every day on the road below the Good Heart *kafeneio* we would see Lefteris in a different sleeveless T-shirt, showing a forest of hairy arms and chest, hosing down his own rubble mounds on the road to stop the dirt from billowing up to the terrace above and settling on the tables. Lefteris was a genial soul, with a long nose and black, soulful eyes.

"How long do you think the road works will continue?" we asked.

"Who can say? This is Greece."

Apart from scorpions, the other creatures that plagued us in the summer because of the large mulberry trees in the front garden were hornets. The fruit was much prized by the giant hornets, *sfikes*, the ones with long dangling red legs that look oddly like jellyfish with wings.

"There are hornets building a nest at the front door," we told Desmond on another of his visits to the house.

"Nonsense. I checked the house completely for hornets before you moved in, and there were no nests," he said.

"Come and look then."

We showed him the cloud of hornets working on a small, perfectly formed nest in the space between the outer studded metal door and the inner glass door. With typical understated logic, Desmond told us to wave a tea towel at the hornets, as they hated air movement, and they'd be gone. Many of Desmond's suggestions had this much efficacy.

"Waving tea towels at hornets? I don't think that's going to do it," said Jim, shaking his head and reaching under the sink for the insecticide spray.

Greeks fear hornets for good reason. Their sting can be agonising. Whenever I saw a hornet I was reminded of a story told to us early on by an English woman called Celia. She had gone to a music recital at Ancient Messene, the wonderful archaeological site north-west of Kalamata, which in the summer hosts arts events in some of its amphitheatres. This was to be a rather refined gathering of music lovers. She wore an elegant floaty dress, perfect for a hot evening of inspiration and ancient ambience while seated on the carved stone (bum-numbing, notwithstanding) benches of the amphitheatre.

It was a perfect night, until a giant hornet hoved into view as people queued for seating. It spied her floaty dress, droned up within its cool, quiet folds and stung Celia on the bottom. After this attack she was transformed into a kind of whirling dervish, due to the searing pain, all of which the waiting guests might have thought was a subsidiary performance before the main act, and looked on bemused.

To make matters worse, there were no toilets free, or other place of refuge, where she could attend to her distressing situation alone, and after wandering about helplessly, looking for assistance, she threw herself on a female cellist who supplied her with some anodising medical cream. And while the stone slabs of the amphitheatre nagged more than ever, this night of pain and indignity was at least partly salvaged.

While we were just managing to cope with insect invasions, Wallace, however, was becoming frantic. First came the aversion to bees. The faintest buzz sent him straight to the 'dog bunker', under the bed. Next came flies, which had him displaying the oddest behaviour of all. He would sit resolutely in the middle of the room, snapping at them as they flew past, his teeth clanging together loudly like the ill-fitting dentures of an old man.

In our first few weeks in Greece we believed that Wallace was chilling a bit and losing his crazy behavioural routines, but here he was augmenting them. One thing that concerned us about bringing him to Greece was that the heat of summer (with temperatures in the high 30s and low 40s for two months straight), the critters and the cultural strangeness of it all would make him more crazy than he already was. Could he be more crazy?

8

A pinball with fur

WALLACE was born crazy, I'm convinced of that. We bought him from a lovable but eccentric breeder of pedigree Jack Russells in Edinburgh, called Brigit, who was a cross between Mrs Doubtfire and St Francis of Assisi. I suspect all her dogs had absorbed some of her unorthodox behaviour by osmosis. She lived on the edge of the city in a farmhouse that was a rambling theme park for Jack Russells.

Apart from the dogs she was breeding at the time were older members of her canine families. Many of these dogs were relatives of Wallace, like his grandmother Dumpy, his uncle Archie, and an assortment of scatty aunts that, if they were human, would probably be locked away in an attic somewhere. She also operated a kennel for regular clients who wanted their Jack Russells boarded while they were away. As Brigit often said: "Jackies need to be with their own folk, dear." I now know what she means.

Brigit's dogs were, to give them their correct title, Parson Russell Terriers, with longer legs than the generic Jack Russell, which is a cross-bred dog. They were originally bred in the early 19th century in England from fox terriers by the Reverend John "Jack" Russell. With their incredible stamina, they were designed to run foxes to ground, and run humans ragged.

On the day we went to collect Wallace, we sat in Brigit's living room, where the walls were thickly decorated with photos of some of her Jack Russell 'progeny'. On the floor, six two-month-old puppies were bouncing around. We ate hot bacon rolls and drank steaming mugs of tea and talked about the breed, but as we watched Wallace and his brothers playing, I began to feel slightly uneasy. The other puppies played with their 'toys' for a while and then dropped into a heavy sleep, one by one. But not Wallace. He was playing with his toy long after the others were asleep – and he played and played. Like the Duracell bunny.

"He's got a lot of energy," I said to Brigit.

"Och aye. He's a right wee rascal. He outlasts even my grandchildren. He never stops. You'll need to keep your wits about you, dear."

She must have seen my panicked look and she patted my knee.

"Och, you'll be fine and Wallace is a rare wee laddie. You'll never be bored – I promise you that!" Right, right, right on every point.

In the first few weeks after we brought him home, Wallace was beyond hyperactive. He was a bullet with paws, a pinball with fur. He wanted to play all day long and only slept when he flopped down eventually, knackered. A friend with a Jack Russell once said: "They don't start to calm down until they're five or six."

I felt faint. "It takes that long?"

As Wallace got a bit older, he added other behavioural issues to the hyperactivity, like his signature screamy barking when anyone came to visit. When people came through the front door, whether he knew them or not, Wallace rushed at them, often hurling himself at their knees. And then there was the trademark 'jump' – the repetition of high bouncy jumps, eyeballing the visitor at the same time. While it was a good way of keeping surly tradesmen in line, some visitors were terrified and it took years to get him to tone this down, although age and gravity has taken some of the height out of the jump.

Many dog-loving friends chastised us for years, saying that Wallace's behaviour was a result of us not training him properly – if at all – and we should have taken him to obedience classes. Every time we came close to enrolling him in a class, we would change our minds. Why inflict Jack Russell madness on 10 strangers – and that was just the other dogs?

Neither of us had had dogs since we were kids, so we were out of practice, and this was 2001, long before Cesar Millan, the American Dog Whisperer, appeared on TV, showing us all how to turn slavering psychopaths into docile lap dogs. But there were other reasons why dog training had been over-looked as we started building a new life in Scotland, and also dealing with a heartbreaking setback.

@@@@@@@

Going to Greece had not been our only serious adventure in life. Moving from Australia to Scotland had been our first, and had it not been for that, we probably wouldn't have gone to Greece for the year.

At the beginning of 2000, Jim and I left Australia to return to Britain, along with my mother, Mary, then in her seventies. We had liked Australia and its casual outdoor lifestyle, and after four years of living together, it seemed high time we bought a house and really settled down. But we just couldn't commit to Australia. Neither of us could put down roots there. Jim had migrated to Australia from England in his twenties to take up a job on a Sydney daily newspaper, but was now keen to return to Britain.

I had left Australia in my twenties to travel, and after a year of living in Greece, teaching English, and a move to England, I returned to Australia, securing my first real job in journalism. But after nearly 20 years there, I felt stifled and wanted a chance to work in the industry in Britain before it was too late. Family and friends said we'd lost our minds by going against the flow, leaving Australia when this was the Shangri-la that disgruntled Brits were desperate to emigrate to. And at the time, we both had satisfying jobs working on a mass-circulation Sunday newspaper, where we met. I was a feature writer and had spent several years travelling the country interviewing prominent Australians.

But I had also diverged into interviewing sports stars, including cricketers and rugby union and league players, even though I knew little about sport. Cricket was the worst. Even after the sports editor, who was in favour of my 'left-field' profile pieces, gave me a crash course in cricket, every time I heard the acronym LBW (leg before wicket), I thought it was the name of a radio station. But my sports ignorance made for interesting copy. During a lunch interview with larrikin Aussie cricketer Shane Warne in a smart Sydney restaurant, he went through the whole bread basket, bowling rolls across the table to illustrate to me his famous spin deliveries, like the 'googly' and the 'flipper'. It brought the place to a standstill.

I had had a ball, as it were, as a feature writer and along the way had met some wonderful people. Giving that up must have seemed foolhardy to others. It did to me as well, yet the desire for change was overwhelming. We decided to move to Scotland rather than enter the cut-throat environment of the London-based national newspapers when we were in our mid-40s because it would have been too tough. Glasgow had the second biggest newspaper industry in Britain, outside of

London, with Scottish editions of most of the English nationals. Scotland had now voted for devolution and we thought it would be exciting to be there at the beginning of this era of optimism and change for Scotland. For me, it was also a chance to reconnect with the country I'd left as a child.

The only sensitive point in this huge endeavour was bringing my widowed mother back to Scotland after having spent half her life in Australia. She was stoical about the move but I don't think the idea of returning to Scotland excited her much. Her abiding memories were its war years and the hardships of her twenties. We bought an old Victorian house in a picturesque Scottish village, with a backdrop of hills. Jim landed a job on a Glasgow daily and while I waited for a full-time writing job to come along I took up casual writing shifts on Glasgow papers. They weren't the kind of stories I had once written, but I couldn't complain about the range: sex-scandal priests, prison suicides, and one celebrity interview at least with a charming Donald Sutherland.

I was writing a piece about his first acting gig as a young man at Perth Theatre in Scotland, where my family came from. I had arranged to do the phone interview from the house, in the middle of which, however, he wanted to speak to my mother to reminisce about old times in Perth. I had pre-warned Mary about the interview and told her not to wander into the study with her morning coffee, but to stay very quiet in the next room until the interview was done. But then half way through the interview, there I was, taking the phone to her, saying: "Em...Mr Sutherland would like to speak to you."

It was one of the most bizarre moments of my life, and my mother's. As she took the phone from me, her hands trembling, she said in the sweetest Scottish accent, "Well, hello Donald", as if she'd known him all her life. I hovered around while they talked at length about Perth, until I managed to wrest the phone back. She dined out on that story for a long time – the day she spoke to a Hollywood legend.

In the beginning, our lives seemed to lack nothing, except that the house, meant for large bustling Victorian families, felt empty. What it needed was a dog, yet we never quite got around to it, until the first upheaval of the move hit us – my mother was diagnosed with cancer and faced an operation and gruelling treatment afterwards. We thought again about a dog, a puppy, something to divert our thoughts from the uncertainty that lay ahead. My mother had always loved dogs and her last one had been a fizzy, high-maintenance Shih Tzu called Benji.

"Get something small and cute like Benji that will lie beside me on the sofa while I watch my soaps," she said. And so we got Wallace, the dog that couldn't sit still anywhere for five seconds.

At least he made her laugh, and laughter was in short supply in the weeks after her diagnosis. One of Wallace's favourite exploits was jumping on to the back of her sofa while she watched TV and then leaping over the top of her head, landing on the floor. Then doing it all again.

"Och, he'll have my head off one of these days," she'd say, chortling nevertheless. "Is he never going to sit still?"

It was fairly obvious we were going to have to put in a lot of work to modify Wallace's daft behaviour, but while concentrating on our jobs, and my mother's treatment, his training programme was constantly put on hold. We turned a blind eye to his crazy behaviour because he was otherwise a brilliant dog who helped us cope with our anxieties.

While writing a feature on dogs some years later, I mentioned Wallace's more worrying behaviour to an animal expert. He believed that as a puppy, Wallace had picked up immediately on my mother's illness and the anxious vibes in the house and had cast himself in the role of family protector, trying to control our environment and keeping what he perceived as unwanted strangers away.

My mother died in 2002, and while we had family and friends with us, it was Wallace who constantly lightened our mood with his forceful personality. And a strong bond developed. Over the years I have thought about my Scottish friend saying that Jack Russells chill at five. Eleven years on, I'm still waiting, though he doesn't leap over anyone's head any more. And my mother, had she been alive now, would have approved of the way the wee guy turned out.

"Haven't you taught him to sit still on a sofa yet?" she might say these days. Yes we have, but only for half an hour – tops.

9

What would Hippocrates
have done?

WE were in the kitchen in Megali Mantineia one hot summer evening, cooking pasta, with a freshly-opened bottle of red wine on the benchtop. We were deep in a daft discussion over whether Greek red wine should be left to breathe a bit after opening, or was a Greek red just an impetuous little number, like the people them-selves, to be savoured straight away.

"Ach, it can breathe in my mouth, can't it?" said Jim, taking his first gulp.

We always had a drink early evening while we were cooking. Jim called it the "six o'clock muse". We were bantering away when there was a sudden hellish meowing outside, a scuffle and then a volley of petulant Greek, and Wallace started running about, barking madly. A face suddenly appeared at the front door, and squashed itself against the glass, the nose flattened, the eyes roving about the room. I opened the door and Foteini almost fell inside, dusty and flustered.

"Curses on that one-eyed monster cat," she said, "I tripped over him and nearly fell off the stairs."

"You mean Cyclops?" I said, smiling. Cyclops had taken to sitting on the front top balcony at night when we were cooking, flitting past the main glass door of the house, staring in with his one good eye, with the sole intention of winding Wallace up, which he did, without fail. We grew to like his raffish personality, however, and realised that his serious fighting days were over, notwithstanding the odd steeplechase with Wallace and a threatening swipe of his paws. We had started to leave a bowl of food out for him every morning in the woodshed.

"Yes, him," said Foteini, brushing imaginary cat hair off the mismatched layers of clothing and adjusting a dark patterned headscarf, the type she always wore, except to church.

She looked about the room, her hands on her hips, admiring the traditional wooden ceiling, the prints on the wall, the small wood-burning stove in the corner, the bubbling pot on the cooker.

"Did you come to see me about something?" I probed, gently.

She started gabbling, words popping out like gun fire, something about goats being sick. I couldn't make it out because several key words I suspected were local. The only thing I could definitely grasp was: "Do you have *kitrini skoni*, yellow powder?"

"What kind of yellow powder?" I replied.

"Yellow – you know," she said, staring at me impatiently.

"Do you mean like flour?"

I took her to the kitchen cupboards and started pulling out different kinds of powdery things: flour, baking powder, even caster sugar. None of it yellow, of course, but I couldn't think what else she meant. For a moment she seemed more interested in what we had in the cupboards and pulled a few other things out herself, turning them over in her big hands and staring with child-like wonder, going "Hmmmm!"

I had the sudden, dislocated image of Foteini as I'd seen her in church, looking smooth and dignified, and again wondered how that image and this lovably scatty woman beside me in welly boots and several layers of clothing could combine in one being. It was like schizophrenia without the mood swings and the messages from God.

"Is any of this useful?" I said.

"No. I need the *kitrini skoni* to make the goats better. If I can find what I want in the village I'll ride back to the *ktima* later with it."

"What is this yellow power then? A medicine?" I asked.

But the next wave of rapid Greek did nothing to enlighten me.

"Have you tried Leonidas?" I asked.

"He's not there."

"What about the shop?"

"Pah – they don't have the powder!"

I had no idea why she had thought of calling on us. Goat medicine had never been high on our wish-list of medical supplies.

"Look, don't worry. We have to go to the vet in Kalamata tomorrow morning with Wallace...Vassie..." I corrected myself, remembering that most people in the village now called Wallace by his Greek name. "I'll ask him about this powder, maybe he can help," I said.

Foteini seemed calmer now.

"What are you cooking?" she asked, sniffing the air.

"Pasta with artichokes."

"Hmmm," she said, looking at the pot bubbling on the stove.

"Would you like to stay and have some?" I asked.

She stared at me as if I had offered something unimaginable, and perhaps I had. Dinner with *xenoi* folk. Funny idea that. Or maybe dinner invitations weren't normal in her life, it was hard to say.

"No, I've had my meal, thank you."

91

I asked her what she'd eaten.

"Cheese and bread."

"Is that all?"

"That's enough, isn't it?"

Her eyes ranged over the fruit bowl.

"I'll have an apple, if you don't mind."

And so we all sat at the dining table while she peeled and cored an apple carefully and ate silently while her eyes again roamed every inch of the room. Her gaze finally fell on Wallace.

"What's wrong with Vassie?"

"Nothing. Just a check-up."

"*Kalo* (good)," she said.

Wallace was sitting nearby, keeping a suspicious eye on her and watching the apple in case it was something that might fall his way.

"What's that over there?" she asked, pointing to Wallace's soft bed with its cushion and blanket inside. I explained that it was the dog's bed.

"The dog has its own BED?" she said, spitting out the word and staring hard at the object on the floor with no less disbelief than if I'd just dressed up one of her goats in a pink party frock and kitten heels.

"The dog is spoilt, I know."

"Leave him with me for a couple of weeks. I'll toughen him up," she said, with a fiendish laugh.

I had no doubt that was probably what Wallace had needed his whole life – two weeks of boot camp with Foteini.

@@@@@@@

The next morning we took Wallace to see Angelos the vet. He had studied in Britain as well as Greece and had very good

English, with a mischievous sense of humour and a tendency to say the word "Rrrright" all the time, with great emphasis. It was also our first visit to a medical professional in Kalamata and to the Greek method of consultancy, which is so different from our own. Greek professionals, including doctors, favour a more relaxed style. Angelos had an old-fashioned wooden desk, bookshelves groaning with medical books, a rather lovely oil painting of a dog on the wall behind, and framed diplomas. There was none of the impersonal timekeeping of British professions, or supercilious receptionists with sing-songy voices. Just one man and his desk.

Angelos seemed to be having a slow morning. He told us the new austerity measures in Greece were starting to have an effect, with people cutting their expenses in every way they could. We sat and talked about Greece and the economy and a dozen other interesting subjects while people walked in off the street, whom he appeared to know well, some to buy medicines, or pet food, some to just shoot the breeze. Wallace was due to have his yearly shots and when Angelos set him on the table in the surgery I warned him that Wallace was grumpy with vets and he'd probably try to bite him.

Angelos looked sceptical and suddenly, in one practised movement, put his hands either side of the dog's chest and scooped him up, holding him about a foot off the examination table. Wallace's back legs thrashed madly but his teeth were well out of range of the vet's hands. He gave Wallace a cursory glance all over and announced to the dog: "Rrrright. You're a Jack Russell, nothing more, nothing less. Rrrright?" Then he put him back down on the table. It had to rate as the strangest canine diagnosis ever.

Before we left I asked Angelos to check out a small sore Wallace had on his face from scratching an insect bite.

However, when the vet tried to examine the sore, all hell broke loose, with a squirming/snapping display that I haven't seen since Aussie naturalist Steve Irwin wrestled on TV with crocodiles, before his untimely death. Angelos stood well back and looked at Wallace, half-bemused.

"Negative, negative!" he said, wagging his finger at Wallace.

"He's never actually bitten anyone," I said lamely, which was true.

"And I don't want to be the first. Rrrright?"

"Yes, right."

He gave us an antibiotic gel to rub into Wallace's face and before we left I asked Angelos about Foteini's mysterious 'yellow powder'.

"I don't do the farm animals here," he said.

"But the yellow powder – any idea what it is, what it's for?"

He sighed. "Ah, the rural people…they have many mysterious potions for their animals. I haven't any idea what they are."

But he gave us the name of an agricultural shop in the old part of Kalamata near the Frankish castle that sits atop a hill.

"You'll find something there. Rrrright? Goodbye Wallace, killer machine," he said, with a speedy pat on his head.

We later drove round and round the old part of the city but couldn't find the agricultural shop, so in desperation I went to one of the supermarkets we regularly used and bought things that seemed plausible, in a lateral-lite kind of way – a packet of flour because it was a well-known brand in Greece with yellow packaging, and some yellow, powered pudding mix, like custard.

When I returned to the car with the purchases, Jim shook his head.

"The goats want medicine, not a TV dinner."

We drove back to the village and found Foteini at the front of her *ktima*, stacking firewood. I showed her my purchases. She picked up the packet of flour and made a strange face.

"That won't do," she said. Then she picked up the custard power, reading the ingredients.

"Ah...this will do," she said, putting the packet on the woodpile. Then she left us a moment, running along the path that led to the *mandri*, goat enclosure.

"See," I said smugly to Jim. "That will help the goats after all."

Foteini returned with a young cute goat tucked under her arm. She turned herself around a moment so we had a better view of the goat's bottom. It was not a pretty sight. Jim made a noise, like a horse puffing air out between its lips.

"That's the problem," she said.

"Why didn't you say the goats had diarrhoea to start with?"

"I did."

"You used another word, a village word, that I don't know."

"Same thing though," she said.

I shook my head with exasperation. "I'm glad the pudding powder is going to help anyway," I told her.

"Pah! That won't help the goats. I'm having that for my dinner."

She said goodbye at the gate. "*Sto kalo.*"

Jim chortled all the way back to the car. "Have you had enough for today, Dr Doolittle?" he said.

"Shut up."

Several days later, I passed Foteini on the road. She told me the goats were fine now. Leonidas had tracked down the yellow powder for her.

"So what is this *kitrini skoni* you use? Does it have a more *exact* name, just so I know for next time."

She stared up at the sky a moment, thinking, then turned her big blue eyes on me. "It's *kitrini skoni yia tis yides* (yellow powder for goats)," she said, with a nod of her head, pleased with this elaboration.

"Thank you. That is, of course, much more helpful," I said with certain irony that went flying over the top of her oversized straw hat.

10

Hedonism and a stairway to heaven

THE ancient Greek philosopher Epicurus was probably the father of stand-up comedy. In the 3ʳᵈ century BC he was supposed to have said, "One must be able to philosophise and laugh at the same time", which is a very modern idea. He is probably better known, however, as the founder of *idonismos*, hedonism, the pursuit of simple pleasures. This philosophy has survived the centuries and is alive in Greece today. It is now called August.

This is a crazy, bubbling, blistering, happy month of eating, drinking, lying on the beach, sleeping and partying, in whatever order you fancy. *Sika*, figs, ripen in August and these fat fruits, full of strawberry jam sweetness, sum up the pleasure principle of August. They are delicious, plentiful, and in rural areas you can scrump as many ripe figs as you like, day after scorching day, until you're bursting. Then one day, curiously, you wake up and all desire for the fig has gone, which coincides magically with the end of the fig season anyway. And you will start to hunt out the next fruit sensation.

August in Greece is a long celebration of life. And despite the continuing gloomy talk about the economy and Greece's future in the EU, Greeks were still embracing hedonism to the max, enjoying the beach, the heat, long nights at tavernas in big boisterous family groups, as they have always. Why should this year be different, they would ask? After all, Greeks have survived worse calamities than this – earthquakes, civil war, a military junta, and Demis Roussos in kaftans.

With the daytime temperatures hovering around the high 30s to low 40s, we spent most of our time in August at the beach, where even the sea was so hot that Greeks would remark, *"i thalassa vrazei"*, the sea is boiling. We would return home for lunch and a siesta and often head back down in the early evening, sometimes taking a chilled bottle of wine so we could sit and watch the sun set behind the long, low rippling mass of the Messinian peninsula opposite. Those hours were often the loveliest of summer and as we sat hunched together on the sand, staring out across the gulf, we felt we had never been happier, and all the aggravations of previous years melted away.

Greeks pour on to the beaches in August as this is the month when they take their holidays en masse. Greeks have no issue about crowds and space, unlike the British. We like our personal space and exclusivity, whereas they adore *parea*, company, and closeness, which is why there is no word in the Greek language for 'privacy' as we know it. The Oxford Learner's (Greek English) Dictionary translates privacy with the Greek words for 'loneliness' or 'secrecy'.

One expat told me a charming story of how one August she had gone with a friend to an open-air concert in a Kalamata park and spread a big tartan rug on the grass. After becoming engrossed in the performance, she didn't notice a Greek couple had camped on the back of her rug and were in the process of spreading out their picnic lunch when they were discovered. So what else could the couple do but invite the expats to join them?

The beach we went to in July and August was Santova, a beautiful long stretch of pebbly beach that lies at the bottom of the narrow road that snakes down from the village. It was on Santova in August we first saw how deliciously crazy life is here when you mix Greeks with salt water, and shake it up a bit. It was here one morning while swimming in the still blue waters I saw a man who had spent an hour treading water a few yards further out while singing well-known Greek songs at the top of his voice. Other Greeks swimming past him yelled words of encouragement: "*Fantastiko repertorio kirie,*" (fantastic performance, sir) said one. Only a foreigner would ask why he was singing, which I did. He replied that as a member of a choir group in Athens he needed to practise in the summer and this was the only place he could do it without disturbing anyone, which was odd because Greeks rarely get disturbed by eccentric behaviour.

It was also on this beach we once saw an elegant, deeply tanned couple, who we christened the Rotisserie Twins because of their obsessive sunbathing. It involved standing together like statues by the water's edge as they each read a book. They turned ever so slightly every few minutes until in a half-hour or so they had completed a full revolution and every bit of skin had had a blast of melanoma-inducing August sun, and then they'd start the routine again.

The village tavernas were the best places to observe the Greeks at play, but they were also the venues where you would find the most expats. Yet there was never much integration on either side. The tables stayed resolutely separate, like opposing football teams. Most of the Greeks in August were from Kalamata in any case, seeking respite from their scorching city apartments, but expats rarely dined out in the village with the Greeks, partly because few of them spoke the language. As one village expat told me early on: "Greek is a difficult language for Brits, and everyone speaks English here." Sadly, that wasn't the truth.

But not all the expats felt this way. The retired English couple who lived in the Mongolian yurt at the top of the village were open-minded about most things and we often came across them in the *kafeneio* and tavernas in the summer. Harry and Bettina had had a peripatetic life. Bettina was a garrulous woman, and one of the few Brits who did speak some Greek. Harry had enjoyed a career in the RAF earlier in his life. He had a maverick soul, liked a good drink, and was outspoken, sometimes brutally so.

Over the summer we heard him unveil an ambitious plan for the special 70th anniversary of the Battle of Kalamata the following May, the same date as it has always been remembered in the city since the war. But this time he wanted to lean on some of his old RAF contacts to provide a fly-past by the world-famous Red Arrows aerobatic display team.

While living in the Mani, Harry had developed a keen interest in the 1941 Battle of Kalamata, which the hillbilly guy in Ano Verga had mentioned on our visit to that mountain village. Riveting eye-witness accounts of the battle feature in the book *Tell Them We Were Here*, written by a veteran of the battle, the late Edwin Horlington. He believed the evacuation of allied troops, described as "more dangerous than Dunkirk", was a disaster, with top-level blunders by the British leading to thousands of troops being left behind and captured by the Germans.

But it wasn't just the allies who suffered. Many Greeks also lost their lives in this battle, fighting with the allies to save the region from German occupation. A retired businessman in Megali Mantineia, called Miltiades, told us a heart-rending story of how his Kalamatan grandfather took his own heroic stand against the Germans. During the battle, as well as the ground troops advancing from the north to the city, the

Germans sent in the Luftwaffe to attack British ships trying to evacuate the allies, who were massed on Kalamata beach. As German planes flew low over the city, Miltiades' grandfather grabbed his single-barrel shotgun in a moment of rage, ran out to the garden of his house, shooting at advancing aircraft, but was killed instantly in a retaliating burst of machine-gun fire.

Harry's plan for the 70th anniversary was something that was absorbing more and more of his attention and while it was inspiring, he admitted it would be a challenge to pull off the involvement of the Red Arrows, despite his contacts. He asked us to help him with the publicity if, and when, the time came and we said yes, though we didn't really think it would eventuate. Bettina did, however.

"When Harry sets his mind to something, he's like a Jack Russell with a bone," she said with a wink.

Apart from his astounding knowledge of this historic battle, Harry was also an expert on surviving in modern-day Mani. It was Harry who set us straight about the British expats in the village and how to deal with their often funny attitudes. After a carafe of his favourite red, he once told us: "Don't worry about the expats. They're wankers, the lot of them!"

@@@@@@@

If anything can illustrate how complex and contradictory Greece is in August, it's the fact that in the middle of this hot, crazy party month comes the second most important religious day of the year outside of Easter. The 15th of August is the feast day devoted to the Assumption of the Virgin Mary, known in Greek Orthodoxy as the *Koimisis tis Theotokou*, literally the "falling asleep of the God Bearer", and her ascension into heaven.

From seven in the morning, when the church bell started to chime, and Jim had another attack of tinnitus, the congregation began to arrive. As this day is a public holiday, with many Greeks returning to their family villages for a lunchtime feast, there was a mix of people from as far away as Athens: affluent matrons with big hair and designer jewels, handsome young couples, smartly dressed, dipping outside to answer mobile phones. And there were village families as well, the elderly members looking demure and well pressed, like old roses kept for eternity in a heavy book.

There was a buzz about the place at 8am when we arrived. Devotees were milling about the icon of the *Theotokos*, more commonly known in Greece as the *Panayia* (Virgin Mary). They stopped to kiss its glass surface, the wooden ledge below the icon piled high with flowers and small metal *tamata*, votive offerings, symbolising a wish, a prayer for the item embossed on the tiny plate, whether it be a wedding dress, a graduation scroll, though most featured babies.

Robert Downey Jr was in good voice, dressed in a gold embroidered robe, hurling the heavy incense censer on its silver chains out towards the congregation like a man possessed of a magic, smoking yoyo. Clouds of pungent rosemary-scented incense billowed over our heads.

Jim had decided, after several minutes of crowd trauma, to retreat outside to a group of men huddled in the forecourt taking turns to nip into the *kafeneio* for a reviving ouzo or a cigarette. Left to my own devices, I squeezed along the central aisle. That's when I saw Foteini in the middle of the women's section, summoning me with a wave of her arm, a black shiny bag hooked over it.

"Sit here," she called in a hoarse whisper, indicating the small wooden chair she'd just vacated, its legs grating across the tiled floor. I felt like a senior on a bus being offered a seat. Did I look unwell?

"No, I'm fine," I said, quickly perusing the area around the empty chair. The usual line of old women on their high-backed chairs came suddenly into sharp focus, their eyes staring keenly at this exchange between Foteini and the *xeni* woman. Foteini was attempting now to squeeze between two tight rows of chairs to reach the aisle, bumping every set of knees along the way.

When she finally made it, she was hot and flustered, her forehead glistering with the effort. She kissed me extravagantly on both cheeks. I could smell oranges and rosemary and a curious aroma I would describe simply as 'fresh air', for all her time spent outdoors. She told me she had wanted me to sit in her chair so I could enjoy the service better. I thanked her but said I really was fine in the aisle.

"*O'ti theleis, Margarita.* Whatever you want," she said, squeezing my arm, her eyes flickering towards the high-chair women. I wondered if Foteini's offering-of-the-chair gesture hadn't been planned to impress the women somewhat with this blossoming friendship, or even to offer me more legitimacy in this conservative rural outpost than a newcomer would otherwise have. Despite the simplicity of her life there was a complexity even about Foteini that I was just beginning to sense but couldn't completely grasp because of my inadequate Greek.

Foteini was wearing her smart black suit, a simple brooch pinned to the lapel, her hair pulled back in her favourite tortoiseshell band. I smiled to myself. Almost the last time I'd seen her she'd been showing me a goat's dirty bottom.

We were pushed further down the aisle now as more people surged into the church. Foteini was in front of me, fending off the crush of people like an armoured vehicle. The service was unusually long and devotional, with two extra chanters in attendance. The heat and the high emotion of the day conflated with the chanting, incense, and the fixed gaze of heavy-lidded saints in frescos to produce a strange anodising effect on my brain. When I shut my eyes my mind seemed to be floating upwards to a plateau of calm. Was this perhaps the cunning ploy of this ancient Byzantine service to draw the congregation ever upwards with the ascending God Bearer, Mary?

Whatever the origin of this long soporific state, I was enjoying it immensely until I was snapped back down to earth by Foteini. She had reached behind her back during the service and grasped my hand, holding it tightly for a very long time. I could think of nothing else then, not even the divine Mary as she slipped skywards like a runaway hot-air balloon. To be gripped by Foteini's calloused, rustic hand felt like being lovingly embraced by a 1,000-year-old olive tree. For the time since I arrived I felt the outer layer of my foreign-ness begin to peel away, just a tiny bit.

Later that day, Jim and I were invited for lunch at the home of one of Foteini's neighbours. Eftihia lived in a modern two-storey house with her mother Pelagia and her brother Yiorgos. A long table had been set out on the terrace of the house that was deeply shaded under a thick vine sagging with fat bunches of succulent grapes. It was a welcome refuge in the blistering 40 degree heat of August for the dozen or so people already crowded round the table. Greek family lunches are a gloriously convivial and enervating occasion, especially on a national feast day like this one.

Eftihia means happiness in Greek and it suited this woman's personality perfectly, with her round smiley face, curvy figure and glorious black eyes. Her laughter was rich and deep and we often heard its uplifting tones rippling across the olive groves. Eftihia was a smaller version of her mother Pelagia, who had an ample build and the family characteristic of thick, black wavy hair, almost untouched by grey. When the two women sat side by side, which was very often, they were like two voluptuous bookends.

Eftihia and her visiting siblings moved in and out of the nearby kitchen, ferrying platters of food: Greek salads toped with slabs of feta cheese drizzled with fresh green olive oil, mounds of garlicky beetroot, boiled *horta,* leafty greens gathered from the hillsides, lemon potatoes and stacks of still-sizzling, deep-fried courgette fritters, plates of barbecued meat, and lastly, chilled carafes of Yiorgos's homemade wine with its flavours of melon and honey.

Like most Greek women, Eftihia liked to see guests eat as if they were all pregnant with triplets. Greeks simply cannot understand people who pick at food, but as a Greek friend once explained to me, this had something to do with the widespread starvation people here suffered during the Second World War and the fear of ever suffering it again. If you are lucky enough to have the food, you simply have to eat it.

Anxious that Jim and I would waste away before the end of the day, Eftihia was on a mission to fatten us up. When I took some of the Greek salad as a starter, she scolded me for the tiny amount on my plate and proceeded to stack it higher from one of the many platters spread down the centre of the table. There is no point in arguing with Greeks intent on this form of extreme hospitality, so I left her to stack, except for one element of the salad.

I shouted above the din of nearby conversation: "Not too many roof tiles for me, Eftihia."

Guests stopped what they doing and stared at me with quizzical faces, including Foteini, who was seated at the other end of the table, about to set to work on a stacked plate of potatoes and *horta*. Eftihia laughed heartily.

"Margarita, I think you mean *kremidia* (onions) not *keramidia* (roof tiles)."

The rest of the diners joined in the laughter, though it was more appreciative than mocking. All Greeks seem to love a language mix-up, as even they say they get their Greek wrong at times. I'd just fallen foul of a fiendish pair of Greek words that almost sound the same, like the night at a local taverna where I'd asked for "moussaka with a side helping of window shutters", instead of beetroot, since the two words are similar, *patzari* for beetroot and *patzouria* for shutters. At least the blunders made people laugh and they somehow never forgot you, replaying your Greek mix-ups again and again when you next met them, which was strangely gratifying.

It was a long, leisurely lunch that passed without any other linguistic or culinary tangles, until Yiorgos, who had been busy attending to the barbecue, made a certain discovery.

"Margarita and Jim, you haven't tried the *tsikles*."

I'd seen them, of course, piled on a plate in the middle of the table, their small bodies pathetically frail. *Tsikles* are whole pickled birds, usually thrushes, with the heads left on. This is a delicacy in the rural Peloponnese and every autumn you can hear the thump of rifle fire on hillsides day and night as local farmers bring down the birds, as well as hare and rabbits. The Mani turns into a war zone and in village supermarkets at this time you will see boxes of ammunition stacked behind the check-out counter beside the cigarettes. Yiorgos also liked to hunt, and these birds were his proud catch.

Jim and I exchanged nervy looks when the bird plate was pointed out, but mercifully this was one dish that Eftihia wasn't about to foist on us, even though it was she who had pickled them expertly in oil, garlic and herbs.

"I don't like them," she whispered across the table, and Pelagia nodded in agreement. But Yiorgos was adamant.

"You must try the *tsikles*, Margarita," he said, then adding in English, "They beeeutifool, my friend."

"I didn't know you could speak English," I said to him, feebly trying to deflect his attention.

"Yiorgos learns all his English from television," said Pelagia, laughing, her big shoulders hunching up and down.

"I spik a leetle...from cowboys films. Favourite thing. Yiorgos is cowboy eh?" he said, with a quaint exaggerated American accent, as if John Wayne had been crossed with Zorba the Greek. Except that Yiorgos, with his soulful black eyes and drooping black moustache, looked more like a handsome Mexican bandit than a cowboy.

Yiorgos and his family were among the kindest people in the village, with a compelling story. Their father had originally come from Altomira, Foteini's village, but moved to Kalamata for work when the children were small. The family were living in the historic quarter of the city when the devastating earthquake of 1986 struck and their house was wrecked beyond repair. But the saddest twist of fate had been that Eftihia had been due to take up a much-coveted job in one of Kalamata's biggest, commercial operations employing thousands, the Karelia Tobacco Factory. The job was to start the day after the earthquake struck. Now, without a home, and Eftihia's father taken ill, the family left the city and moved to

Megali Mantineia, where Pelagia had been born, later building a house on family land.

When her father later died, and with only a small farming income, Eftihia never married and neither did her brother. It is still the custom in rural areas of Greece that when a sister is unmarried, often the brother will remain single as well, in order to support her. These were generous, vital people who would share with you whatever they had, even in the midst of the crisis, asking nothing in return. On my many visits over the year to Eftihia's house I would bring her a small gift. She would shake me gently by the shoulders and say: "You don't have to do that, Margarita. *I agapi paizei rolo* (love plays a role)." The love between friends was more important than the gifts, she would say.

My attention was snapped back to the *tsikles* when Yiorgos said: "Come, my friends, try one."

My heart sank. Jim and I had tried every kind of food in Greece but I drew the line at the tiny birds. Until now. Everyone's eyes were on us, willing us to sample a bird, and it felt like one of those bush tucker trials on *I'm a Celebrity ... Get Me Out of Here.* Okay, time to take the plunge.

"How do you eat them?" I asked.

Eftihia put one on my plate with a resigned shrug. I pulled some of the flesh away from the brittle ribcage and chewed gingerly. It had a gamey but not unpleasant taste. Everyone looked gratified that I liked it. Foteini, who had sat strangely silent all through lunch, suddenly became animated and clapped her hands, saying loudly, "Bravo, Margarita!" as if I'd passed some difficult initiation ceremony.

"Beeeutifool, eh? Now you, Dimitri," Yiorgos said to Jim.

Jim gave me a thin smile. "Here goes," he said, reaching across to my plate and pulling a shard of brown meat away.

One burly man nearby, a cousin of Eftihia's, who confessed to a passion for *tsikles,* seemed determined to show Jim the pack drill. He plucked a bird off the central plate and then, in one swift movement, bit its head clean off and chewed it, making a dull crunching sound that seemed to go on forever. Jim and I looked nervously at each other.

"You eat the whole thing. The bones are soft," said the man, his eyes imploring us to follow his lead.

"No way," Jim whispered to me.

I caught Pelagia's eye. She gave us a sympathetic smile. "That's enough of *tsikles* now," she announced loudly to the table with matriarchal authority, and everyone returned to their own dining experience.

"More wine at least," said Yiorgos, getting up from his chair and bringing the carafe over, filling our glasses and slapping Jim on the back. "Well done, my friend...eating birds...is beeeutifool!"

Yes indeed, August is a strange month.

11

Between a rock and a large place

"WHY are you going to Monemvasia?" said Angeliki. "We've got 25 churches in this village alone. You don't need to see more churches than that."

That was true, the village had churches tucked away in fields, in gorges, on hilltops, and one in a cave. Most were kept locked and only visited on the saint's feast day, after which each church was named. But Monemvasia had more pull than just its heritage listing and Byzantine churches.

"This is work," I told her.

"You don't call having a holiday within a holiday work, do you?" she said with an impish grin.

"Since you've put it that way.... probably not."

"Are you taking Vassie with you?" she asked.

"Of course."

She rolled her eyes. "That's about all they're lacking now in Monemvasia. They've had Turks, Venetians, pirates, starvation. Now they're getting Vassie...praise God!"

When we came to the Mani, as well as touring this unique area, we also planned to see some of the more outstanding places in the two other peninsulas. Monemvasia is half way down the east coast of the (right-hand) Laconian peninsula and is one of Greece's least-known attractions, mainly because Greeks like to keep it for themselves. Often described as the Gibraltar of Greece, Monemvasia is a soaring monolithic rock, 1,000ft high, that was sheared away from the mainland during a devastating earthquake in 375AD. Its only fortified town of

Kastro is a compelling mix of Byzantine and Venetian architecture, and so well restored in the past 30 years that it feels like you're time-travelling to another age.

We both received a commission from different publications to write a travel feature about Monemvasia, and on the strength of this we could have blagged a complementary stay in one of the Kastro's expensive boutique hotels, but because we had to take Wallace we had to book private accommodation instead, somewhere that would take a dog. Leaving Wallace behind on tours or assignments was always going to be a worry, as not everyone can cope with a Jack Russell. This was why, in Scotland, we always sent him back to Brigit's farm to be with his own loopy family of dogs. But here, dog lovers were hard to find.

Desmond and his wife June had agreed to look after Wallace once when we were offered a commission in early summer to write about the salubrious new Costa Navarino hotel and golf complex, near Pylos, on the west coast of the left-hand prong of the three peninsulas, near Navarino Bay. We were curious to see it as it had been panned by environmentalists during its construction phase because great numbers of old olive trees had to be cleared from the land, though many were later replanted around the site. And there were concerns about the dizzying amounts of water needed to irrigate the fairways of the golf course.

Part of the concern was the fact the hotel complex is close to an environmentally sensitive area, including the famous horseshoe-shaped cove called Voidokoilia, which has pale sand and silky water and is impossibly romantic. And also within flapping distance is the renowned bird-watching centre in the Gialova lagoon, where 245 species of birds have apparently been sighted. Perhaps Egrets, I've Had A Few should have been taken up as the hotel's signature tune.

The resort offered us a two-day stay at the Romanos Hotel, which lived up to the hype of being nothing short of a Hollywood film set, with luxurious pool areas bordered by lush, water-guzzling gardens. Most of the guests staying in 2010 were Greeks, mostly from Athens, in the days when they still had money. But the Russians and Middle-Eastern visitors were the most lavish spenders. On a tour of one of the 'presidential villas', beside the long sandy beach, the glamorous PR woman told us that it cost 10,000 euros a night and that recently a Saudi princess had hired it for 10 nights, bringing her own chef along.

After a refreshing stay at the hotel, we returned to Megali Mantineia to find that Wallace had been the house guest from hell. When we went to pick him up, Desmond had the tired, grey look of a man who's been up all night trying to calm a colicky baby. Which was not far from the truth, as Wallace had woken the couple up about every 15 minutes after one o'clock in the morning with a round of screamy barking as patrons at a nearby popular taverna departed noisily at regular intervals.

Another stay with Desmond was out of the question, but after scouring the internet we found only one rented house on Monemvasia where dogs were welcome. The 12th century restored house was on the Kastro and owned by a Greek businessman called Stelios, whom we spoke to over the phone when we booked. When he asked if Wallace was well-behaved we said "of course", hoping that screamy barking and knee-capping people at the front door might just qualify as exemplary behaviour, especially at a time when holiday bookings in the country were beginning to dwindle.

But this was our only choice of accommodation in the Kastro at least, and in all the stories we had read about

Monemvasia, the authors had stressed you must stay on the rock itself, rather than the mainland, to get a feel for the place.

@@@@@@@@

We made the four-and-a-half-hour drive down through the Mani passing the harbour town of Gythio, overlooking the Laconian gulf, with its tiers of renovated neoclassical buildings in gelato colours. It has a semi-circle of harbourside fish tavernas with freshly caught octopus hanging outside, as if to dry, on washing lines.

For all its quaintness, Gythio's strength seems to lie mostly in its position and the fact that it's a springboard to other places. Yet it had an illustrious past, founded by two gods, Apollo and Iraklis (Hercules), and was once the main port for powerful Sparta. It is also steeped in ancient legend and sexual intrigue. It was on the nearby tiny island of Marathonisi (now called Chranai) that the greatest romantic tearaways of all time took refuge. After the Trojan prince Paris stole minxy Helen from her husband Menelaus, the king of Sparta, they spent their first steamy night on the island, a getaway caique anchored nearby. Helen's flight to Troy later sparked the Trojan War.

From Gythio we drove across the head of the Laconian gulf and down through the peninsula, perhaps the most untamed of the three with a remote, pared-down beauty.

Laconia takes its slightly tough, uncompromising aura from its capital city Sparta, further north in the Evrotas valley, with its long, pugnacious history which explains why this important Peloponnese city has fewer ancient sites than any other Greek city, its budget eaten away in ancient times by long battles with the neighbouring region of Messinia, and the protracted Peloponnesian Wars.

Stelios, the owner of the house we were renting on Mon-emvasia, lived and worked in the nearby modern town of Yefira on the mainland, which is connected to the rock by a narrow bridge on an isthmus. We were to meet him in the small parking area outside the main wall of the Kastro, where we would have to leave our car, walking into the town through the huge stone gateway leading into Monemvasia (*moni emvasis* in Ancient Greek means 'one entrance'). Wallace bounced up and down in greeting, in his usual fashion, on rubbery legs. I don't think Stelios was used to dogs, definitely not Jack Russells, and tried in vain to ruffle the fur on his head every time Wallace reached the peak of his jump, and eventually gave up.

Beyond the entrance to the Kastro, with its thick wooden doors (scarred by bullet holes from historic skirmishes), no vehicles are allowed and along its narrow cobbled pathways, there are few reminders of the modern world: no overhead power lines, no visible TV aerials, mobile phone masts or modern street lights. Things like the internet, Facebook and Twitter have vanished up their own cyberbums.

Thirty years ago, much of the town lay in ruins, but with World Heritage status and renovation grants, the 40 Byzantine churches, and the mansion houses and Venetian palaces, have slowly been returned to their former grandeur (some of them dating back to the 11th century), though with very strict planning rules. From the mainland, the Kastro isn't visible as it faces south towards the Myrtoan Sea and that was the general idea when it was first built by a Byzantine emperor in the 6th century AD. Serious fortifications were built in successive centuries to defend the rock from invaders such as the Franks in the 13th century, Turks in the 16th century, Venetians in 17th. The Turks held the rock again from the early 18th century until it was finally recaptured by the Greeks during the Greek War of Independence.

Stelios was a genial guy with an Australian background, like many Greeks in this region. Although born and brought up in Melbourne, he went to Monemvasia in his twenties to renourish his Greek roots and to take over several of the old houses that had belonged to his family, including the one we were renting. He was slightly rotund, with the chilled-out look of an Aussie koala bear and an accent to match.

The property was a traditional, two-storey stone house close to the lower sea wall, with a large sitting room/bedroom upstairs, with windows on two sides that overlooked the sea. With the rock's distinctive pearly light, the room could have been straight out of a Rembrandt painting, and Stelios had enhanced the atmosphere by decorating the place with some of the family's traditional old rugs, furniture and prints.

The downstairs area was darker, with a huge stone fireplace and high windows but definitely felt like it was leaning more towards the 12th century – and certainly the plumbing did – but it had some nice touches, like the guards' room with the miniature domed ceiling and brackets on the wall to hold firearms, as defence here was once a serious issue. There was a real chill about the lower room and it wasn't just the evidence of damp on the walls. Wallace was still on his lead but kept pulling towards the stairs and the upper floor, whining.

"He seems a bit nervous," said Stelios, clamping his big hand finally over Wallace's head and ruffling his fur. "Will he be all right here, if you have to leave him to go out in the evening?"

Maybe Stelios was having second thoughts now about having a dog in his ancestral pile.

"He'll be fine," I said. "He won't mess the place up. Don't worry, he's not like that."

Stelios nodded sagely. "Dogs sense things, don't they, and I have to admit there's definitely a vibe here. I've felt it. There's a lot of history here. I mean, look at this old wooden hatch."

He pointed to a long wooden panel in the floor under the stairs which was quite a few centuries old. He told us that many of the historic homes here had these hatchways leading down flights of stairs to secret passageways that ran under the town so the inhabitants could escape from invaders. Most of these routes led to the Portello, not far away, a fortified sea gate in the outer wall leading to a narrow stone pier, where boats were tied ready to spirit the inhabitants to safety.

Stelios told us stories about his ancestors and how they survived here during terrifying attacks down the centuries by interlopers keen to get their hands on this rock that sat on a strategic trade route in the Mediterranean. He had heard the stories as a child from his grandmother, sitting in front of this same fireplace.

The house was wonderfully atmospheric, yet there was something slightly creepy about it as well, not helped by Stelios's stories about Turks chasing people along dark, dank passageways, and we woke up several times during the first night, hearing things creak and bump. Although we put Wallace's bed in the upstairs room, not far from us, some time during the night he crept on to the bottom of the bed and raked the covers into a burrow, presumably so we couldn't see him.

On the second night a furious wind came shrieking across the sea and a set of windows that I was sure had been closed tight came bursting open with such a force it felt like we were about to entertain a helicopter landing. We woke up terrified, and Wallace started running around the room, skating about the floor boards, bunching rugs into piles, and barking loudly, the way he does with thunder. After 10 minutes of this I feared the whole of Monemvasia was awake by now, ready to pull up their hatches and escape to the Portello.

Jim jumped out of bed and secured the window. By the time he got back to bed, Wallace was already in it again, burrowing his way under the covers, as if answering finally to the Jack Russell impulse to plunder fox holes at midnight. We yanked him back out and sent him back to his bed, but he wouldn't settle and kept getting up and roaming about the house.

"I hope this isn't going to be a repetition of our holiday on the isle of Skye, don't you?" Jim said, with a nervy jangle in his voice.

We had once gone for a holiday to the Scottish island and rented a 200-year-old converted croft house in the desolate north-west corner. The owner had told us that at one time, a family of 13 had lived in the house, with just the one bedroom, which was still the main bedroom in the house. In this tiny room there was an old-fashioned raised box bed with a wooden canopy above and a wooden step ladder for climbing aboard. From the minute we put our bags down in the room, Wallace didn't like it and I also felt a chill sensation around the old fireplace near the bed. During the first night we were woken by a frenzied scraping of nails on wood and heavy breathing.

"What the hell was that?" said Jim, waking up from what he explained was a nightmare about being locked in a coffin. He was sweating with anxiety. I reached for the small torch I kept under my pillow in case of a night-time scramble to the toilet. I switched it on with a shaky hand and saw two black, terrified eyes staring at me from the top of the steps. I screamed, then realised it was Wallace, trying in vain to get on to the box bed. The next minute he lost his balance and fell backwards down the steps and gave up, legging it out of the room, never to return. And in the morning we found a big pee puddle by the front door, which is unusual for Wallace, as he normally has a bladder as fortified as the Aswan Dam.

In Monemvasia, we lay awake sleepless for an hour or so, listening to the wind, and the waves crashing against the rocks down by the Portello.

"At least it's not a box bed this time, but there's an atmosphere all the same. Do you feel it?" said Jim.

I did, until Jim started to explain a complicated theory of monolithic rocks and how they have special energy fields around them that can trap the cataclysmic emotions of past events, only to release them back into the atmosphere when 'geo forces' are in their optimum co-ordinates. That's when I fell asleep, only to be awakened the next morning by bright sunshine and a dog on my head. Wallace had excelled himself this time and was lying on the pillow behind my head, breathing hot air in my ear.

"What's going on with you?" I moaned as I got out of bed and padded across the room to open the window shutters. My feet connected with something cold and wet. I looked down at one of the lovely old Greek rugs.

"Guess what? Wallace has piddled all over this rug. Unbelievable!" I said.

Jim shuffled across the floor, arms akimbo, the male position for asserting dominance over domestic chaos.

"Hmmm. He must have been really scared last night."

"Why couldn't he be scared over hard flooring or vinyl. Why must it be over ancestral rugs. Maybe he sensed a spooky presence again, like in Skye," I said.

Jim poked his toes around the end of the rug, where some of the threads were coming loose.

"It's a bit old this rug, anyway," he said.

"Old but priceless. No-one makes these rugs any more. This one's probably worth 1,000 euros or more," I said, contemplating its rich ethnic design with bands of colour, mostly reds, browns and pinks. It was rather fetching, despite the pee stain.

"I saw stripy rugs like this on the way into Yefira yesterday," said Jim.

"Don't be daft. Those were factory-made copies meant to look like traditional ones. These are really fine and made on an old loom, an *argaleios*. No-one works the looms any more," I said, sounding like some smug folk rug specialist.

I got dressed and took the rug downstairs to the bathroom and decided to wash out the pee stain carefully in the shower recess. It was the type of rug without a pile and quite thin but closely woven. When I'd finished with it, it seemed to be worse, leaving a grubby watermark. What the hell! I plugged the recess, filled it with warm water, and pushed the whole rug in.

Jim appeared at the bathroom door. "Don't know why you're going to all this trouble. You could have just wiped it. It's dog pee, not the Ebola virus."

He took a step closer. "Oh my God. The colours are running."

"Don't be ridiculous," I said in a panicky voice, crouched in front of the wet rug, wringing my hands together, like Lady Macbeth murdering furnishings.

The colours hadn't run completely but fixed themselves into fudged bands of red and brown like a Rothko painting. Some of the original hues had given up the ghost entirely. We carried the dripping rug to a tiny courtyard behind the kitchen that caught the afternoon sun. We made a pact not to go out and obsess over the rug until it was properly dry and I prayed that it would, by some strange miracle, end up looking like an ancestral rug again, but very much cleaner. Then we went out to explore Monemvasia.

You can't appreciate how unique the Kastro is until you climb up to the plateau at the top of the 1,000ft-high rock, along a zigzag path that leads through another wooden gate at the top, peppered with more bullet holes, and look down on the town below, with its Tuscany-hued roof tiles, church towers and domes. On the plateau above is the impressive 12th century church of Agia Sophia and there are traces of an old citadel and the ruined walls of early settlements now lying like bones among the dry grass and swathes of purple cyclamen.

Once, this area, and the Kastro, supported some 50,000 people, though most of its food supplies came from the mainland, if not its wine, which was famous in the Middle Ages. It was exported to Britain, where its name *malvasia* was later corrupted to malmsey. Life dwindled on the plateau through the centuries and the last resident descended to the Kastro in 1911.

The Kastro was impenetrable and the Venetians once bombed the citadel, from a distance, to overcome its residents, but it was never taken by fire power alone. The Venetians and the Turks managed to starve the residents out by cutting off food supplies across the bridge. The Venetians took Monemvasia in the 17th century and populated the Kastro with Cretan and Albanian workers, who helped in the building boom of that era, creating remarkable churches and mansion houses which have been renovated in the past few decades, turning Monemvasia into a coveted place to live, although few residents stay all year round.

It's hard to blame them. In the winter, waves crash over the sea wall and a wild wind screams about the narrow laneways. Despite its obvious beauty, this is one of those rare places that resonates with the weight of history and the tang of violence, enough to make even a Jack Russell wet his pants.

On the afternoon of our last day we decided it was time to check the rug. However, the minute we opened the back door I could see it was still a mess of colour, but at least it was dry.

Jim smirked. "Stelios won't notice, honestly, unless he worked for Carpet World in Motherwell in another life."

"He will notice. It's a family heirloom. He's had this carpet in the family since he was a kid. His grandmother probably made it. You don't forget how things look when they've been around that long. He'll want us to pay him compensation."

"Take it out of Wallace's allowance," Jim said.

"You won't be laughing when Stelios sees it."

"Okay, I promise I won't laugh."

We took the rug upstairs and put it back beside the coffee table. Stelios came to the house the morning we were due to leave to collect the money for the let as arranged. When he walked in, Wallace was hiding under the bed, ashamed. Stelios did a casual walkabout in the sitting room, perhaps checking that all the heirlooms were still in place. He looked at the rug for what seemed an eternity, the melty bands of colour, and scratched his forehead. Jim and I exchanged tense looks.

"You must be very proud to have these wonderful old rugs and things," I said, with a nervy catch in my voice.

Stelios shrugged. "Most of these rugs are modern. I got them from a shop in Yefira. I wouldn't put expensive rugs on these floors."

Jim was stifling a hearty giggle. He coughed instead.

"So they're not Greek then?" I said.

"Oh no. Most of these are made in China."

'Well done China', was all my addled brain could think of.

Stelios helped us back to the car with our bags, said goodbye and told us to come back again some time. No mention of

Wallace. We drove away back across the bridge to Yefira and the road home.

Now when someone says Monemvasia I don't really think of Byzantine churches, passageways to sea gates, romantic ambience you can cut with a scimitar. I think of carpet trauma and the trouble that Wallace got us into for the umpteenth time in his tiny terrier life.

12

Does my bum look big on this donkey?

"I'M going to be on television – tonight," said Foteini, leaning into the car window. She'd been riding her donkey Riko along the road into the village when we passed. We waved out the window but didn't stop. We were in a hurry to get home after the long drive from Monemvasia but when I looked in the rear-view mirror and saw her trying to goad Riko into a gallop, which clearly he wasn't up for, despite having nothing much on board that day, I decided to stop. She vaulted off the saddle, running up to the driver's window, gabbling about her TV debut. I had visions of Foteini in a new kind of reality programme; an extreme make-over show. From Goat Farmer to Glamour Girl in One Week.

Which is not as strange as it sounds, as Greek TV stations have bought the format for all the same reality programmes screened in Britain, like Big Brother, Dancing with the Stars, and a curious home makeover show where builders during their lunch break don't sit around eating bacon sandwiches and moaning, but get up and perform Greek dancing amid the rubble in hard hats.

"I've been filmed by a local television station this morning. Me and Riko," said Foteini, slightly breathless.

"What station?" I asked.

"Don't know."

"Why did they want to talk to you?"

"Don't know but they asked me where I was going with my sacks of *haroupia* strapped on to Riko."

"What's *haroupia*?"

She screwed up her face. "How do I explain what *haroupia* is when you don't know what *haroupia* is." She plunged her hand into the pocket of her trousers and handed me some hard black objects.

"These are *haroupia*," she said, her blue eyes brimming with satisfaction.

They looked like broad bean pods that had recently been the victim of a botched cremation and we later learnt they were dried carob pods from the many trees that lined the main road.

"What do you do with these?" I asked.

"Feed them to the goats."

Poor sods, I thought, and wondered how their dental work was faring.

"So that's what the TV crew wanted? You, Riko and, em, black pods."

Jim stared at the pods and pestered me for a quick translation. He shook his head.

"Must have been a slow news day on the TV station, that's all I can say."

"What time is it on tonight?" I asked.

"Don't know," replied Foteini.

"Do you have a TV?"

"No. I'm planning to go to Sotiris's taverna to watch it."

"Come and watch it on our television instead. We're having pizza tonight. You like that, don't you?" She didn't know what pizza was. "Come anyway, you'll like it."

She took Riko the donkey over to the other side of the road to mount it. Foteini was a stocky, muscular woman from all her physical labours and she had a backside that even Jennifer

Lopez would envy. She marched Riko to a long, low outcrop of rock, clambered on to it, and then did something amazing. She leapt backwards off the rock, describing a spectacular arc in mid-air, her legs tucked into the sitting position, her arms flung out. She landed with uncanny accuracy on the wooden saddle, with a mighty thud.

"Wow. I bet the TV network didn't get that," I said sniffily.

"Definitely a slow news day," said Jim as we drove home. "Why would a Kalamatan news crew come out here to get footage of a farmer carrying bags of burnt pods on a donkey? It doesn't make sense, unless they're trying to encourage everyone in Greece to get back to their old rural ways in case the country finally collapses."

He had a point there as we had heard stories from the villagers of Greeks going back to their ancestral olive groves to rework them after leaving the trees wild for years, even though there wasn't much money any more in olive oil production.

"Farming people like Foteini who work on their own and carry stuff about on a donkey, and also ride it, are pretty unusual," I said, feeling some wind in my sails now. "That's why they wanted to interview her. That's why we wanted to talk to her in the first place, don't you remember? And why we're in Megali Mantineia as well – lured by the promise of rural authenticity."

"Okay, okay. I agree Foteini is unique, to us. But surely not to most Greeks?"

I disagreed, remembering the village woman out collecting *horta* on the day we met Foteini. She had described Foteini as a 'traditional woman', saying there was probably no-one like her now in this part of the Peloponnese. Some old farming guys kept donkeys and pulled the laden animals along by a rope. You rarely saw them riding one. Young farmers, who often ran other businesses as well, like tavernas or shops, had the small brightly-coloured tractors that seemed to be fashionable. There was a kind of tractor envy in this area and men would roar up and down the main road showing them off. We often saw a bevy of them parked at the bottom of Goat Lane, while the guys were hanging round the unofficial abattoir. I wondered if one day we might see a woman driving one. But it wouldn't be Foteini.

⊚⊚⊚⊚⊚⊚⊚

At 7.30pm there was a loud screeching noise that sounded like a cat being propelled through the air. A face was pressed against the glass door.

"Come in, Foteini," I said, opening the door.

Before she did, she flicked the side of her hand towards Cyclops, who was flattened against the front balcony railings, his one eye laser-like with fear.

"*Tha fas xilo*," she shouted at him. A folk saying that literally means, 'you'll eat wood', or otherwise, 'bugger off!'

Foteini came inside, wiping her shoes on the mat. She was wearing dark trousers with a heavy plaid shirt on top, and a blue patterned headscarf. We had just cooked a large pepperoni pizza in the oven and I was cutting it into fat slices. Foteini watched with hungry eyes.

"That's the thing you mentioned? Peeza?" she said, toying with the word, pulling faces.

We put the pizza on the coffee table in front of the TV and balanced plates on our laps, eating the pizza slices with our fingers. We gave Foteini the best chair, one that Desmond had raked up at the furniture sale of a quickly departing expat. We offered her wine but she said she only drank soft drinks.

We hunkered down, a comical looking threesome no doubt. Jim was surfing through the local TV news channels while he ate his pizza. Foteini ate her first slice in a few deft bites, offering appreciative noises, licking the tips of her fingers when she'd finished, so I kept delivering more slices to her plate. It was as if she hadn't eaten for weeks.

Jim surfed some more. We had to sit through news footage of shops being boarded up in Kalamata due to the failing economy; priests blessing school children about to start their new year, and a story about a curious village north of the city where dozens of earth tremors had mysteriously been arriving every day since early summer, but no footage yet of Foteini.

"I'm sure your piece will turn up soon, Foteini," I told her. She shrugged, seemingly unconcerned about her TV debut.

We chomped our way through the whole pizza in record time. I put a large bowl of fruit on the coffee table, with small plates and knives. I knew she was passionate about fruit and she quickly picked up an apple, peeled and cored it with a deft hand. After that she picked up a banana, peeled it, then got up and walked to the sink. She discarded the peel on the draining board, and then did something very odd. She washed the peeled banana thoroughly under the tap, returning to her chair. Jim and I grinned at each other.

"Foteini, why do you wash bananas when they have a thick skin on the outside? They can't be dirty."

She stopped chewing a moment and gave me an exasperated look, like you would a child asking a ridiculous question.

"I have to *wash* them. Kostas the grocer, who comes by every week in his van, says bananas come from *xena meroi*, foreign places."

"Lots of fruit comes from foreign places now," I said.

"I know that, but bananas come from places that are VERY foreign, and I've been told that monkeys eat them there. Pah! Imagine that?"

"But not the very same bananas, surely?" Jim and I started to laugh, which was unavoidable really.

"Why are you laughing?" she said, breaking into a smile herself.

"No reason. Don't worry."

She quickly moved on to the late-season figs, peeling the skins carefully off, but mercifully not washing them. We surfed and surfed for about two hours and told Foteini that TV stations don't always use the footage on the day it's taken. It could be used weeks from now.

"It doesn't matter," she said getting up and brushing the front of her trousers because some of Wallace's fur had stuck to them. In her world, goat hair was acceptable, dog hair not. "I've had *kalo fagito*, good food, thank you," she said, then used a kind of folk expression, "*alla i parea sas me hortase*", but it's your company that has filled me up. With that she left, probably not realising she was the first goat farmer in the village to have ever had a British-style TV dinner.

We asked around the village for a few days afterwards to find out if anyone had seen Foteini's screen debut but heard nothing, and we started watching the local news in the evenings more thoroughly than anyone should have the heart to do, as Greek TV news reporting was often tedious, with the same clips shown over and over again in quick succession, as if to make a better point. We finally gave up when, a week or so after returning from Monemvasia, Jim came down with 'man flu', the kind of bad cold that makes a fellow seek the solitude of his duvet for a week like a yogi in a cave, counting his spinal chakras, and rejecting all sustenance – even wine.

In Jim's case, it was five days in bed with Stephen King and his latest novel, a huge tome of around 900 pages, possibly the longest novel ever, that made *War and Peace* seem like a ferret fight in the bottom paddock. But while Jim was languishing in bed, I had to carry out the designated 'man jobs', like heaving rubbish bags across the road to the giant bins.

Rubbish bins are a sore point in Greece. They are huge ugly metal constructions with lids that are often too heavy to crank open and shut and which, consequently, many people leave in the open position, encouraging plagues of cats. Usually these bins are on the edge of villages but here, for reasons we couldn't fathom, they were right in the middle of it, and no-one seemed inclined to move them. There was a fourth bin as well that was upended because, as the story goes, it was struck one day by a truck and left where it fell, its wheels pointing to the sky.

With Greece experiencing the increasing wave of austerity measures mainly aimed at the public sector, with jobs being axed and pensions cut, there were a series of general strikes during the year, in which garbage collectors were included. And there were now threats of more action, all of which made bins in Greece a very dirty subject.

Having bins right across the road from Spiti Mou had been its worst feature. Even in early summer, the smell often drifted across the road and Jim had become an unofficial bin minder, patrolling at least once a day for an errant pushed-back lid.

That particular day in late September, the temperature was about 30 degrees and when I reached the bins I noticed the smell was much ranker than normal. Further up the road, Leonidas the farmer, wearing blue overalls, was fixing his small orange tractor. He got up when he saw me approaching and said something I didn't quite catch, something like "don't....lid" but it was too late. I lifted up the lid on the last bin an inch or two, and fat blowflies fizzed out through the gap. I dropped the lid and covered my face.

"What the hell's in there?" I asked.

Leonidas came striding up, frowning. "There's a cow inside."

I shook my head. "Sorry, for a minute I thought you said cow. Please excuse my poor Greek."

His blue eyes twinkled slightly, not with mirth. More sympathy for our poor house location. "I did say cow."

"A whole cow?"

"Not a whole cow exactly. The bones."

He paused slightly to see how I was taking it so far.

"BONES in buckets. Bloody HELL....!!!!." I said petulantly in English. I think he caught my drift. He sighed, the blue eyes were downcast.

"One of the farmers down the valley has been slaughtering cows and putting carcasses in bins, like this one, and it might be a few days before the garbage truck comes around again. The other villagers don't like it either, but he keeps doing it."

I started to feel faint and suddenly recalled the scene in Goat Lane not long after we arrived, the two men standing around the pale corpse of a goat, knives flashing. We had seen that same scene in August, the day of the Feast of the Assumption, with farmers preparing for family get-togethers, and while we had never got used to the idea of neighbourhood abattoirs at least we never saw the animal remains.

"Why can't this farmer dispose of the bones properly?" I pushed on, trying to imagine what 'properly' would mean in Greece now with poor waste disposal methods and no money. I started thing about how in Britain today you can't put anything suspect in a bin without the threat of prosecution, or the latest move by councils to hide cameras under lids. But now I would have killed for some bin-cam.

"The farmer should take them somewhere else, and I am going to talk to this man," said Leonidas, rubbing his oily hands down the front of his overalls. Just as he did that I was reminded of Paul Newman again in a scene from the film *Cool Hand Luke*, where he's serving time, working by day on a chain gang, and looking impossibly fit.

"Don't be alarmed. I promise I'll talk to the farmer today." And he took the bag of rubbish I was holding and slung it into one of the other bins and walked back to his tractor. Leonidas had a nice style – kind, dignified as befits the elder of the village church – yet beneath the calm, handsome exterior you had the impression he could kick ass when need be.

"Very good," I said to myself, rather more uplifted than previously.

I returned home and pushed open the gate to find Desmond was in the courtyard, unpacking a DIY patio table, a set of instructions in one hand and a heap of wooden planks on the ground. When we first looked at the house with the Kalamatan agent, it had been empty, and Desmond had promised to have the basic furniture in place by the time we arrived. Other bits and pieces came later, brought from his own village house in a large wheelbarrow or in the back of his car. Some furniture had come from his basement, including one sofa that was so mouldy it should have been accessorised with gas masks. We asked him if he could find us something better. The next and final sofa was a small purple Ikea number, donated by an elderly couple who were having a new one shipped from London. And so we took the garish piece and put it in the middle of the main room, where it sat like a grumpy plum.

One of the items Desmond gave us early on was a striped sun umbrella made of papery material, like an origami experiment in sunshades. It was fine for about a week, then one morning we found it completely shredded, as if it had been attacked in the night by a flock of ravenous, apocalyptic parrots. Desmond's concept of 'furnished house' was amusing at times, but the bucket problem wasn't. He was wielding a screwdriver now and cursing under his breath and I knew he'd be in no mood for dead cow stories. But I told him anyway.

"This is Greece, what do you expect?" he said, using his favourite expression, and holding his arms out rigidly, in the Greek way, which usually means don't ask/blame/pester me. "I've been here 10 years now. I've just learnt to look away when I see something I don't like."

"Whatever!" I said, turning on my heel and walking back into the house, hoping Jim would be more receptive.

He was still in bed, burrowed right down under the duvet, still reading. Wallace was curled up beside him.

"You won't believe what's in the bins. It's straight out of a Stephen King novel actually."

He dragged his eyes off the book long enough for me to explain about the cow bones and how Leonidas had promised to sort it. Then he went on reading.

"Well, what do you think?" I asked.

Hmmmm," he said, looking slightly green.

Jim is always a team player. Clearly he was sicker than I thought. I would have to take a different approach.

"Cow bones in a bin. Now what would Stephen King have done with that?" I asked.

His eyes flickered towards me. "Stephen King turns death into dosh. Lots and lots of it. Whereas we must rely on a local farmer to sort out this environmental threat."

"Well, we're lucky we've got Leonidas to help us. No-one else will, it seems."

Jim sat up straight in the bed, more animated now. "Leonidas is a nice man but he won't be able to do anything. You know how hard it is sometimes to get Greeks to change the way they do things. Look at the whole business with the economy, trying to get people to pay their taxes." Then he slumped back into the pillow, exhausted, like a balloon that's been popped.

Greeks don't like any kind of authority and rules, and I admired them for that, and the Greek lament, 'Look, we gave you all Socrates, and em…Nana Mouskouri. Cut us some slack here'. When they find a regulation, they want to shoot it down.

"I think I'll leave you with Stephen King and take Wallace out for a walk. I need some fresh air," I said.

I walked Wallace up to the top of the village, past the shop and along the main road, where the view towards the gulf is glorious, especially on a sunny day. It was at times like this that you had to remind yourself that despite the occasional frustration of living in Greece, with its bureaucracy, its maverick attitudes, and especially the disregard for the environment, there was still so much to love. As I walked Wallace back to the house past the Good Heart, I saw a figure leaning over the terrace wall above.

"Margarita," said Angeliki, in her girly voice. "Come up and give me some *parea*."

"I've got Vassie here."

She shrugged extravagantly. "That's okay, Margarita. Bring him up. We've got bigger things to worry about these days than noisy cucumbers."

13

Heart and soles

ANGELIKI was sitting at the edge of the cabin. Ilias was installed at his usual table in front of the TV, smoking and watching the news. They looked despondent.

"How's everything going?" I asked her.

"Not good, Margarita. Things are quiet," she said with a shrug.

"Not so many customers now?"

"No. And August wasn't as good as we expected. August is our last chance to make a good profit for the year."

This situation was repeated all around the village and across the Mani as Greeks, who normally enjoy eating out regularly and celebrating name days in big family groups at tavernas, were now having to tighten their belts, so that even though August had seemed lively to us, it was nothing like previous years. How would these small businesses cope from here on, especially with more business taxes on the way and harsher legislation for collecting VAT?

"Where's Jim?" she said.

"He's in bed with a bad cold."

She relayed this information to Ilias, who turned away from the TV and laughed heartily, offering a risqué explanation as to why Jim was really lying in bed, exhausted.

"I hope Jim's feeling better soon," he said, with a wink.

"Don't worry. *Nomizo tha zisei*," I told them, roughly translating the English for "I think he'll live."

They both stared a moment and started laughing. "I think he'll live", is not an expression that's commonly used in the same way by Greeks, but sometimes by doctors, in a similar bantering manner to the English, to allay a patient's fears. But my use of the expression seemed to have tweaked the couple's funny bone. That was to be the start of a crazy repetition of the expression, or versions of it, by Angeliki and Ilias almost every time we went to the *kafeneio* or walked by on the road. They would lean over the terrace wall and ask how you were, adding: "I hope you'll live."

They both had a devilish sense of humour, and although Angeliki had been helpful with my Greek from the day I first met her, she loved to tease me over my mistakes, like calling Wallace 'a cucumber'. One night at the *kafeneio* I told her: "I love your golden worms." She tossed her head back and laughed so much that tears rolled down her cheeks. I had said *skoulikia*, worms, instead of ear-rings, *skoularikia*.

Sometimes, when my Greek was so messy it was like scooping up road kill, she would look at me in exasperation and beep me loudly on the tip of my nose with her thumb and index finger. It never failed to make me smile.

All the villagers, however, were mostly generous in their praise of my language endeavours, no matter how dire they were, saying: "Greek is hard, even for us." And just about every Greek I have ever met uses this expression: "For every Greek noun there are five different words." And then they will hold up five fingers, though I've seen variations of this. Sometimes it's seven fingers, sometimes three, depending on their concentration level at the time or whether or not they've been the victims of industrial accidents.

Before I left, Angeliki got up from the table and went to the kitchen, bringing back a plate of newly baked honey biscuits for Jim and a small box of lamb bones "for Vassie". He smelt the lamb, tail wagging, and put his paws on her knees in his excitement. She let out a tiny scream.

"Just because I give him lamb, it doesn't mean we're engaged!"

"But you do like dogs just a little bit, surely? Cute little dogs like Wallace?"

"Not really," she said, stubbornly sticking to her beliefs. "What are dogs? They don't have real feelings, apart from hunger and cold, things like that."

"Of course they have feelings," I said, trying to wind her up a bit.

"Prove it," she said, leaning back in her chair, folding her hands over her lap, challenging me to come up with a story.

"It's not something you can easily prove," I said, wishing I'd never broached this thorny subject. I knew one thing at least, that anyone who has had a dog in their family will know they feel and understand much more than we think they do. How deeply that goes I guess we'll never know – until they can talk.

I had a funny little story, one with an ending that always made me smile, but there would have been no point sharing it with Angeliki. She'd have thought that both the dog and I were crazy.

After my mother died, nine months after getting Wallace, I never doubted that he sensed our sadness, and the emptiness of our Victorian house in Scotland. Wallace responded by becoming overly territorial and possessive, as one dog psychologist had explained to me. But he also reacted in playful ways. A cynic would say the playfulness was random, just part of his puppy development. And I'm fine with that, but Wallace used to do things that were beyond easy explanation, but which I suppose were right for the exceptional time we found ourselves in.

One day he devised a new game, probably meant to amuse himself while we were at work, but it certainly delighted us. Brigit had described Wallace as a 'grazer'. He liked to eat small bits of food all day so we always left a bowl out for him with dried food, like tiny 'biscuits' in various shapes and colours. One evening when we came back from work we discovered he'd planted biscuits in the downstairs rooms, the laundry, kitchen and dining room. He'd placed them in the corners of all the rooms, sometimes just one biscuit, sometimes a small pile, though we couldn't figure out why, only that when we collected them up he'd run around wagging his tail, very pleased with himself.

One freezing winter morning, I was dressed, ready for the drive to Stirling station for the Glasgow train, through a heavy fall of snow. Apart from the bad weather conditions, I was dreading the day ahead as the paper where I was doing casual writing shifts at that time was going through a period of painful restructuring and the atmosphere was always tense. The country may have been entering a political renaissance, but its home-grown newspapers were teetering on a Dark Age, with takeovers, budget cuts and falling advertising revenue, which reflected world trends. They were also starting to reduce their feature sections, so that while I still coveted a full-time writing job in Scotland, it never happened. I spent nearly 10 years as a freelancer, which would have seemed like career death to some, but I grew to love the independence, keeping my own hours and choosing subjects that inspired me for once, rather than section editors.

But on that particular winter's day, I knew I was in for a long slog and it was tempting to call in and say I couldn't make it through the snow, which was more or less true. I was in the laundry, where we kept the walking boots, and swithering over what to do. I pulled out the ones I always wore in the snow and when I put the first one on I felt a small hard object under my toes. I shook the boot out. A small brown dog biscuit fell onto the floor. It was heart-shaped. Wallace was scampering around beside me.

"Did you put that there?" I said, laughing. He wagged his tail. It was a small silly incident, but it instantly put me in a good mood and I decided to make that arduous journey to work. I told all my jaded colleagues about it, even producing the heart biscuit from my coat pocket as comic relief. Only the most hard-bitten journalist failed to raise a wee smile.

The game with the biscuits continued for some time after that and we found them in various shoes each morning, sometimes three or four biscuits at one time, and I came to look forward to shoe retrieval in the laundry, plunging my hand in to see what biscuits lay inside, always hoping for the hearts and always enjoying Wallace's fizzy reaction. A mindless game? Probably. But I always like to think that Wallace had an uncanny urge to make us smile.

If I'd explained that story to Angeliki now she'd have said: "Margarita, it was just a dog biscuit after all."

And I'd probably have replied: "Eight different biscuit shapes in the box ... and Wallace picked the little brown heart."

@@@@@@@

As I left the *kafeneio* with Wallace, a face peered over the terrace wall above.

"Regards to Jim. *Elpizo tha zisei.* I hope he lives," said Ilias.

"I'm sure of it," I said, waving at him.

Wallace picked that moment to do one of his crazy hand-stand pees in the road, which brought Ilias to near-hysterics, as he had never seen this trick before.

"He should be on television...*Greece's Got Talent*. Better than all the other *vlakes*, dimwits, on the show," he shouted down to us.

As I walked home, I felt light-hearted. More so when I saw Leonidas by the side of the road again, his tractor parked nearby. He smiled and walked towards me.

"Good news, Margarita. I've just spoken to the farmer on the phone and he assures me that he won't put animal bones in the bins again. He knows it was very wrong."

Just like that, a problem that you might imagine would be as difficult to remove as a Greek rice pudding stuck to a shag-pile carpet was now out of the way in a few hours. I was so happy at the outcome, and impressed, I grabbed Leonidas's arm and squeezed it. I considered offering him a honey biscuit, but he was sweet enough just as he was.

"Thank you so much. That's very good of you," I gushed, just as another small orange tractor roared past with two chirpy village boys riding high. They gave us a nod of interest, and at the same time I had the impression a curtain was twitching on our kitchen window opposite.

I said goodbye and thanked Leonidas again and crossed the road. When I went through the front door, Jim was about to go down the stairs, carrying a glass of water, on his way back to bed and Stephen King.

"You won't believe it, but Leonidas has sorted the problem with the bins, just like that," I said, snapping my fingers.

"So that's what the cosy chat on the road was all about?"

"You were spying from the side window, weren't you? You're supposed to be sick."

"I am sick, but the male of the species is never sick with his eyes shut."

"Ah. You're talking in village riddles now. Here's another one. The male of the species must endeavour not to draw a testosterone veil over every encounter he sees."

Jim squinted. "What does that mean?"

I pushed the plate of Angeliki's biscuits towards him.

"Have some honey biscuits. You need them."

He uncovered the plate and took one.

"Are you not feeling any better?"

There was no reply.

In my Greek language notebook that night I noted down all my newly acquired vocabulary, everything to do with rubbish and agricultural waste disposal. And I boned up on other useful Greek phrases, just in case: "Can you tell me if there is also a cow's head inside? How many dead goats do you think are in there?" Whatever else I couldn't say in Greek, at least I could do filth quite well.

14

Hook, line and stinker

"**D**ID you imagine when we first came to Greece that one day you'd be driving to hospital and I'd be sitting beside you welded to a plastic fish?" Jim said in a thin, wiry voice.

"Not for one single minute, my sweet."

How would I when we had woken up that October day with the temperature hovering around 30 degrees and the sky as blue as a Santorini church dome. We had gone to one of our favourite coves that morning on the strip of coastline south-west of Kalamata, taking Wallace along for a swimming treat. The area was called Paleohora (meaning 'old capital') as it had been settled from ancient times. Homer had mentioned this area in the *Iliad*. It once had monasteries and a castle on the cliff top.

After the three of us swam around the cove, I settled into a beach chair with a good book. Jim pulled a small pouch from his beach bag with fishing gear in it. That's when the day slid into the abyss. This was a new hobby/obsession, the kind that men grasp in the blink of an eye and won't let go of. It was the red plastic fish lure that gave me a bad feeling. With its ugly two sets of triple hooks hanging from its belly, it lived up to its name. Since Jim found it lying on a beach months earlier, it had shadowed us, sitting on tables, bookcases, even on bedside cabinets, the hooks twitching, reminding Jim to buy some accomplices – the fishing line, the small reel the Greeks call a *karouli*, to which the evil lure is attached and cast by hand into the sea.

On that beach, on a perfect autumn day, I was thinking how good life was at that moment, and then I looked up and saw the evil lure dangling from a bloodied finger.

"It was my first throw," said Jim mournfully, sounding like a man who's just gambled away his wife on a roulette wheel in Las Vegas.

I looked at the finger. The hook was in deep. "I can't pull it out. I've tried," he said.

And that was how we came to be driving towards Kalamata Hospital, as we were told early on by other expats that most medical problems would have to be sorted at the hospital because there was no medical centre within easy reach in this north Mani region, and the concept of the GP, which Greeks call a *pathologos*, is not so common, outside of Athens.

Jim had cut away the reel but the lure was fixed to the hook with a metal ring so it had to stay and he struggled to get dressed. I knew he'd regret the choice of gear today, the torn denim shorts and the white T-shirt with the Scottish map on the front and the words Mad Jock on Tour. It was a farewell gift from Scottish friends and now spattered with droplets of blood.

As I drove towards the city I was full of dread for our first hospital visit, as we'd heard horror stories from expats about their medical experiences. Desmond told us how he'd fallen out of one of his olive trees during the harvest and went to hospital, where a broken arm was diagnosed but the radiologist completely missed his fractured collarbone because she'd been too busy watching a Greek soap on a nearby TV set.

We found a place in the hospital car park and left Wallace in his travel harness on the back seat. Kalamata Hospital looked better than expected – clean and orderly. Nothing like hospitals we remembered in Scotland, with smokers outside dragging their intravenous drips behind them. No argumentative prisoners brought into the waiting room, manacled to burly prison guards like I'd seen once in Glasgow. When Jim showed the receptionist his dangling fish lure, she smirked and pointed us towards the main treatment ward, a big airy space with many examination beds, mostly empty. We were seen straight away by a young female doctor, who spoke good English.

"Where are you from?" she asked, as she looked at the hooked finger.

"Scotland."

She gave the T-shirt a derisory glance, which didn't augur well. A young male doctor joined her to perform the 'removal' with a big set of wire cutters and industrial-sized green pliers. Jim was pale. When they were about to grapple with the hook, I asked if Jim could have a small shot of local anaesthetic. Men are too proud to ask.

"It won't make any difference," the female doctor said.

"He hasn't had a drink, if that's what you're thinking," I said, wondering if perhaps Jim's diverting outfit implied he was a boozer just off the plane and staying in the tourist resort of Stoupa, further south. Maybe they didn't give a local if they thought you'd been drinking.

The lure was quickly clipped off with the cutters, and binned, never again to snare the souls of wannabe fishermen. The male doctor now drove the hook through the finger using the pliers, which looked painful. Jim was squirming but it was me who was feeling faint. Again I asked if he could have a shot of local.

"Why inject another sharp thing into the finger?" the female doctor snapped at me. And I understood in a blinding flash why the Greeks had managed to invent logic, and not us. It was so simple. Why hadn't I thought of it? She seemed perplexed by the constant harping on about anaesthetic.

"You haven't got a heart condition, have you?" she asked Jim, and my eyes willed him to say 'yes' but his mind had gone blank.

After another toe-curling push of the hook, the whole thing was over finally, the finger bandaged, some paperwork attended to and we were out the door. At least it had all been quick.

"The moral of the story seems to be no matter what you go to hospital for here, tell them you have a heart condition and you get all the drugs," I said.

"Yeah. Should have thought of that. Still, it's out now," Jim said, holding up a massively bandaged finger that looked like he now had a white ping-pong ball rammed on the end of it.

"At least the evil thing got binned," I said.

"But will it stay binned? Will it not turn up on another beach sometime to tempt another innocent guy?" asked Jim.

"You've been reading way too much Stephen King."

When we reached the car Wallace was fizzing with anxiety, like an over-shaken lemonade bottle, and licking the inside of the window, for some odd reason.

"He's broken out of his harness," I said, opening the door.

"Good God, even Houdini couldn't do that!" said Jim.

It wasn't until a week or so later, when we were telling a Greek acquaintance in Kalamata about Jim's experience in hospital, that we discovered what may have been the reason behind the lack of anaesthetic.

"It's all because of the economy," she said, shaking her head sadly. "I've heard stories in Kalamata that the hospital is running out of certain drugs because it doesn't have the money to pay drug suppliers and the items have been stopped. And the situation can only get worse."

It was the first chilling reminder that the economic crisis was now beginning to have a direct impact on people's health and well-being.

@@@@@@@

At the end of the summer, one of the English language newspapers in Athens ran a story about how Greeks were dealing with the economic crisis so far. One politician was quoted as saying that if it wasn't for Greece's incredible natural beauty and its climate, it would be a hellish place to live right now and people would be severely depressed. Others, he said, would feel so frustrated there would be a rush for the exit door. This proved to be the case not long after that, especially among the country's youth, with a quarter of them unemployed, and rising.

We were also distracted by Greece's beauty and easy lifestyle. We asked ourselves how things could be so messed-up while the sun was shining and it otherwise felt great to be alive. For the first six months in Greece we didn't feel any real impact from the economic crisis, apart from higher petrol prices and food bills, with VAT rising to 23 per cent on many items. But we had personal experience at least of how the rest of the world perceived the Greek crisis when it was time to knuckle down and produce more newspaper features.

Apart from the travel pieces we were writing, we had also planned some property articles, as homes in the Peloponnese were good value compared with many other parts of Greece, and we had lined up a couple photogenic homes for sale in the Mani, as case studies. While a few property editors had expressed interest in the features just before we left Britain, they had now changed tack. The property editor of one London broadsheet told me bluntly: "Look, Greece is now a basket case. Do you seriously think I would encourage my readers to invest in holiday homes there?"

Yet with prices to beginning to fall there was never a better time to buy in this region, and the number of properties on the market was increasing as expats started to panic over the crisis. However, as one English woman explained to us, the selling of expat houses in this part of Greece tended to go in waves.

"There's a seven-year itch here. British people buy houses and about seven years later, they want to go back home. It's got nothing to do with the crisis."

During the property boom in the UK, from around 2004, many expats had been lured to the Peloponnese by opportunistic and cunning Greek property developers, who placed advertisements in some British newspapers, promising 'cheap' land and house packages in spectacular locations. Many retired expats were persuaded, selling up in Britain, often with enough money to keep a bolt-hole back home and buy a new Greek home. To be fair, some of the expats ended up with fabulous homes, but most ended up paying over the odds for their piece of paradise, often buying houses with building flaws, inaccurate surveys, or illegal extensions that were only discovered much later.

In one case, the land that one English couple bought in the Mani was found to contain archaeological relics, which held up the completion of the build indefinitely. Most expats, however, had been philosophical, believing that when they finally got bored with Greece at least they could sell up and return permanently to the UK having made a huge profit. That was before the global downturn of 2008.

One retired couple put their home up for sale after seven years, saying the task of assimilating into Greek life had been more punishing than they expected. They told us that before they came here they had a dream of retiring either to the Norfolk Broads, or Greece, two places that couldn't be more different. They chose Greece, but were now considering their other option. They had an amusing catchphrase they used whenever the subject of their house sale came up.

"The Norfolk Broads are calling us," they would trill.

"Funny, I don't hear them," Jim said one day after the catchphrase was used once too often.

With lack of interest in Britain for property stories, we concentrated on other topics. In October, I was asked by a Scottish newspaper to write a feature about Scots living in the Mani and to spice it up with some insights into expat life. "Try to get under the skin of the expat," I was told by the commissioning editor, and was given a long list of uncomfortable truths I had to uncover about expat life, including "Don't they feel guilty about leaving their ageing parents/children/jealous friends/pets behind?"

I told the editor I would do my best to get subcutaneous with the expats, knowing full well I would never be able to write the kind of story he wanted, unless I was planning to evacuate Greece immediately. Finding Scots in the Mani had proved difficult because there were so few of them, for reasons I couldn't fathom, apart from the fact most direct flights for years had only come from Gatwick or Manchester. The search proved frustrating and time-wasting and I began to wish I'd never taken on the commission, and after the story appeared in the New Year I would feel that regret even more keenly.

Perhaps the lack of Scots in the region explained the issue of Greeks not knowing much about Scotland, apart from the fact it produced whisky, that sometimes men wore skirts and its greatest hero went about with a blue face. Some people knew about Mel Gibson's take on William Wallace from the movie *Braveheart*, as it was shown on TV on all the Greek national holidays. The Greeks who did know a thing or two about

Scotland identified with the Scottish cause at least. "You had the English for centuries, we had the Turks," they would say.

But it was the older rural Greeks who hadn't a clue where or what Scotland was. And some of them struggled with the rest of the planet as well. One afternoon I was strolling around the village graveyard looking at its ornate, inscribed head-stones. Family graves in this country are often a fascinating snapshot of a whole family's history, with framed photos of the deceased inside the marble and glass case fashioned into the top of headstone. As well as photos, you might see a favourite drinking glass, amber worry beads, a child's toy. If the deceased was musical, there might be, for example, an old *baglamas* (tiny bouzouki).

I began a conversation with an elderly widow dressed in black attending to her husband's grave.

"Where are you from?" she asked. I told her Scotland.

"Where's that?" she said.

"Above England?"

"Where is England exactly?"

"It's all part of Great Britain."

"I don't know where that is." So I drew a map of Britain on the dirt path, showing the coast of nearby France and Holland, to put it in context.

"But where is France and Holland?" she said.

I looked at my watch, wondering if I had time to replicate the world map for her. She looked apologetic, and I stifled a smile.

"I don't know where anything is," she said with a shrug. "I've spent my whole life in this village. This is all I know."

I looked at the lovely olive orchards around us and the sea beyond.

"That's all you really need to know then," I said and bade her farewell.

The Scots I eventually found for the feature were all very different from each other but the urge to escape former lives was a common thread. One man had reinvented himself as an IT professional in Greece and after several decades in the Mani had many gritty stories to tell. He explained how the first wave of British expats here were generally an insular lot who sat in seaside bars all day drinking and moaning about Greece. "Why can't these bloody Greeks get Christmas right?" complained one elderly Brit, referring to the fact that Christmas is a muted affair here.

But much of what he told me was unusable because it would have offended British readers, not to mention most expats in the Peloponnese. The hard part was getting contemporary insights into the expat soul that I *could* use. To do that I was forced to immerse myself more in the crazy world of the expat, something I never wanted to do as the whole idea had been to live as Greek a life as possible while we were here.

For the sake of research, however, we went to some events in Megali Mantineia like the Film Club, launched by a well-meaning group of expats to show outdoor films now and then, and 'contribute something to local life', as they put it. On an evening that threatened rain, we went to the playground of a now-defunct village school for an outdoor screening of *Alice in Wonderland*, the Gothic version by Tim Burton, with Greek subtitles. Seats were arranged in front of a roll-down screen and a DVD projector. There was a small group of Greeks and only five kids, though the village only had about 12 children anyway. The expats and the Greeks sat more or less separately.

Many Greeks walked past the school during the film show, just out of curiosity. Foteini was one of them, dressed in her wellies and a big jacket. She stopped at the gate, stared in wonder at talking rabbits and cats. Perhaps it was the lack of talking goats on screen, but she soon scurried away. Half way through the film, rain began to fall but because it was so fine it was decided to keep the film going. Yet one by one the Greeks began to leave, perhaps glad they had an excuse.

"Another disappointing turnout," said Desmond afterwards, with an uncomprehending shrug.

"Maybe they don't like the subtitles," I offered.

"You don't need subtitles with *Alice in Wonderland*, surely? Rabbits, tea parties, funny hats. What's not to understand? No, it's always the same really. We started the film club a few years back as a way of getting the Greeks and expats together and to do something for the village, especially the children. For the first film we ever ran, we picked a Greek one so the villagers wouldn't be put off by subtitles. Despite that, by the end of the evening all the Greeks had fled and it was the expats who were left, scratching their heads over incomprehensible Greek."

He laughed but you could sense that deep down he thought the situation more tragic than funny. And I guess it was.

The other event we attended was one that Desmond had told us about early on, the expat lunches organised regularly by a neighbour called Nigel. Now living permanently in the Mani, Nigel was a convivial, middle-aged guy and a keen amateur chef who liked to have people over at the weekends to sample his creations.

The lunches were usually themed, and this one was Chinese. Outside, in the back terrace, there were around 30 other expats squeezed around a mismatched collection of tables, under shady umbrellas, where the temperature was already hovering around 34 degrees. There was hardly a soul under 60, and most were quite a bit older, which made it feel like a cheery senior citizens' outing in a British pub beer garden during a heatwave. Some of the expats were from the village but others had driven here from all over the Mani, and even the Messinian peninsula opposite, as Nigel's lunches were apparently famous in the region.

They were already hoeing into sticky mounds of barbecued spare ribs and sweet and sour pork, returning to the dining room for seconds – and thirds – where rows of dishes were laid out on long tables, and the women helpers in aprons were fanning away squadrons of flies. Some of the expats we met over lunch were initially wary when we told them we were journalists on a year's adventure.

"You're not here to write some filthy pack of lies about expats for the *Daily Mail* are you?" said one pensioner, waving a chewed spare rib at us to make his point.

As the afternoon wore on and the plastic bottles of local wine were consumed, people seemed less bothered, or simply forgot we were journalists and candidly told us their back stories. It didn't take long for a similar pattern to emerge. Nearly all of them seemed to be escaping from some uncomfortable aspect of Britain, whether it was the bad weather, career disappointments, or broken marriages. Most of the expats were entertaining enough, some were brave, like the retirees who had come here to settle permanently, despite having serious health issues. Many were now having to cope with the chaotic health system. We heard more tales of heart conditions, gall bladder operations and fuming prostates than was quite good for us – that was even before the very un-Chinese-like dessert arrived, the banana trifle.

While it all seemed quite amusing at first, after a few hours a quiet melancholy settled in. Although the expats wouldn't admit it, most seemed rather homesick, as if they had marooned themselves here and it was too late to go home again. British food, above all, seemed to offer more than physical sustenance, it was an instant connection back to a familiar landscape, which I suspect was why they were all here. So whenever Nigel was putting on one of his themed lunches – whether it was Indian, French, fish and chips, or bangers and mash – expats came in their droves.

In one afternoon Jim and I had heard enough stories to fill a dozen features, and some of it was damning of expat lifestyles in the sun, but again, I wasn't going to be able to use most of it unless I wanted to wake up one morning with a donkey's severed head under the duvet. In the end, I wrote what I thought was an entertaining piece, with a few truths about expat life in the Peloponnese and a light-hearted dig, mainly at the large enclave in Stoupa further down the Mani. Here, expats stuck doggedly to a more British style of life, spending a great deal of time socialising together and pontificating on local expat internet forums.

It wasn't the hard-hitting piece I could have written, in fact I thought it was pretty tame. At least no-one here could possibly take umbrage. But what I knew about expats then could have been squeezed into one of Nigel's pork and sage bangers.

15

Olive envy

"YOU'RE not going to help Foteini with her olive harvest, surely?" said Adonis, the president of the village *syllogos*, council, when we were sharing a drink with him one night at the *kafeneio*.

"We're doing it for the experience. It might be something we'll write about one day," I told him.

"*Po, po, po!*" he said, waving his hand around. "You'll be sorry. Foteini does it the old-fashioned way with a *katsoni* (stick), beating down the olives on to ground sheets, sorting them by hand. You won't survive a day, I tell you."

Jim and I exchanged nervy glances.

"What could we do? She told us she has no other help. It's a lot of work for someone her age."

"The problem for Foteini is that everyone is doing their olives at the same time and no-one can spare much time to help others. Not like in the past, when we had bigger family groups in the village and more time on our hands," he said.

Foteini had mentioned her harvest weeks before when she told us her *Barba* Lambros had died suddenly. *Barba* means uncle but it is also used as sign of respect for an older man. Lambros had been more of an old friend and helped her with the harvest every year, and now he was gone. She was distraught. Along with a few people in the village, who offered her a bit of help here or there, we promised a couple of days work for nothing, just to see what olive harvesting was all about.

But I couldn't help remembering Adonis's words when we turned up on the designated day in winter at Foteini's *ktima*, the nearby peaks of the snowy Taygetos like a tray of baked *kourabiedes* (Christmas biscuits thickly covered in icing sugar).

Foteini came to the gate looking like Rambo in a headscarf. "*Kalimera paidia* (good morning children)," she said, kissing us on the cheek, using one of her terms of affection.

She was wearing layers of clothing topped with another of her thick plaid shirts in muted shades. She wore wellies and had a leather holster round her waist that held a small hacksaw. She gathered up her other implements, several long sticks, a small axe, a bag of provisions, and untied Riko the donkey, who was standing nearby with a pile of empty sacks over his back.

"Is that all the equipment, then?" I asked, hoping Adonis had just been pulling my leg after all.

"What else do we need?" she said, looking puzzled.

"Nothing," I said meekly as she pulled the donkey off to a nearby field, with us trailing along behind.

Already, early in the olive season, we'd seen families at work on their trees with the modern equipment, the petrol-driven combs on sticks that whirr gently to release the olives, and it all looked quite easy, but the way we were about to do it was the equivalent of helping a British farmer harvest fields of wheat with a scythe instead of a combine harvester. But at least we would get a feel for olive harvesting, which is an institution that dominates life in the Peloponnese from November to February.

All the Greeks in our village had olive orchards of various sizes, which they had inherited from their ancestors. Some had more than 1,000 trees in orchards on the outskirts of the village. Foteini had about 200 trees, many of them growing into a nearby ravine, which were difficult to access and meant that each year she only managed about half, and had no money to pay proper workers.

The Messinian region is one of the richest olive-producing areas in Greece, with some 16 million trees, producing around 10 litres of oil each. The fat purple Kalamata eating olives (grown from a smaller number of trees) are known the world over. Every spare piece of land in this region, even within the city itself, is given over to these delightful trees.

Olive oil production dates back to the Mycenaean era. The important Mycenaean site of Nestor's Palace, north of Pylos on the far west coast of the southern Peloponnese, was once a fabulous two-storey pile built in 1,200BC with frescos and tiled floors. Little remains of the palace now but a ruined storage room has rows of earthenware pots that once held olive oil, a testament to its enduring popularity.

Greeks have a passion for olive trees because they provide so much: food, medicine, animal fodder, firewood. But mostly I think it's their almost human shape – the thick, curvy trunk, the bushy branches sprouting upwards like sticky-up hair. To see these trees massed together in a sunny orchard, their branches dripping with fat clusters of crimson olives just before harvest, is an image you never forget.

From ancient times the number of olive trees a family had was a sure indicator of wealth and success. It still is, and every November the obsession with olives begins, and a kind of 'olive envy'. "Mine are bigger than yours!" "His are as small as sultanas and won't produce enough oil to lubricate a creaky hinge." And there is endless bickering about the best way to harvest: the new methods, or the old way. Some just preferred the old methods. Leonidas had about 800 trees and could afford the new equipment but he preferred to use a stick, saying it damaged the olives less.

It was our task to pull the olives off the branches, which meant raking them down with our (gloved at least) fingers and letting them fall on to the ground sheets that we spread around each tree in turn. It was Foteini's job to climb up a rickety wooden ladder, the lower rungs of which had split at some point and were patched together roughly with bits of metal and twine – her own innovation – and saw off the branches with the most olives and leave us to remove them, which meant we were folded over like Taco shells for half the day. But she had the dangerous undertaking on the makeshift ladder.

"Aren't you worried those rungs will snap under you one of these days?" I asked.

She gave me the exasperated look Greeks reserve for foreigners who haven't yet cottoned on to the national sport of brinkmanship. And in a few words she summed up Greek philosophy better than Plato could ever have done.

"Pah! I'll worry about it if it happens."

Jim looked at the ladder and shook his head.

"Don't even think about doing ladders on this harvest," I told him, remembering the last time he'd tumbled off one and ended up with a wrist full of metal.

"Don't worry – Eddie's already had a word in my ear," he replied.

Eddie was a recent daft invention. After two broken wrists in the past, and various other small accidents since, including the fish hook, I had become exasperated with Jim, saying that, like most men, he was incapable of thinking rationally before plunging into risky exploits. So I invented Eddie Edit for him, a small invisible gremlin that was supposed to sit on Jim's shoulder and edit out potential disasters.

Jim agreed to consult him before doing anything that involved ladders, hammers, Marlin fishing, anything basically that had 'death wish' as a sub-plot. And so far it had worked like a charm and Eddie had become something of a silly game between us – our imaginary friend.

Crazy us? Yes, of course. We were having an adventure in the Mani, a part of Greece that even Greeks still describe as 'wild' with a wave of the hand and a "*Po, po, po!*" (bloody hell) in a time when Greece was suffering economic suicide. We were in an olive orchard with a woman in wellies wielding a hacksaw at ancient olive trees, on a lethal ladder. Crazy – yes please!

Foteini climbed high into the trees with no fear, walking out on branches that could easily have snapped, except that she knew every tree by heart and which branches were healthy and safe, and which were not. They were like the children she'd never had. At one point, maybe just to wind up the timid *xenoi* a bit, she treated us to an impromptu concert, climbing up to the top rungs of the ladder, her head poking above the tree top, clapping her hands and singing a repertoire of folk songs in a remarkably sweet voice.

After she scrambled back down the ladder, ready to move the plastic ground sheet to the next tree, she slapped me playfully on the shoulder, telling me she had *kefi* that day, using a word that's much loved by Greeks as it means 'high spirits' or 'good humour', a state of mind that is normally characteristic of this race.

Adonis was right – the harvest was hard, punishing work but there were moments to savour. There is something deeply satisfying about clawing your hands through a branch full of juicy olives and having them rain down on you before they plop on to the ground sheet, then rolling them into a fat pile. And the view from the orchard was easy on the eyes – the Taygetos mountains, and crowning a nearby hill, the ruined walls of romantic Trikotsova castle, and to the left of us the broad scramble of Kalamata city. With a group of friends and family harvesting on a sunny day, and plenty of banter to pass the time, Greeks say there is no better way to spend a day.

Desmond also persuaded us to help him one day in the small orchard below the house and because he had a bad back, and is generally accident prone as well (without the benefit of Eddie Edit), his very fit wife, June, climbed their 20 or so trees and pruned them, while he sat in the middle of his ground sheet on a plastic chair like an olive oligarch, directing the operation, moaning every time his gimlet eyes spotted an olive pinging into the undergrowth, sending you off to retrieve it. He also combed his olives out so slowly and painstakingly it prompted one cheeky villager to comment that when Desmond was harvesting, he looked like a hair stylist at work with plenty of time on his hands.

Foteini's harvest was progressing well on that first day. After doing about eight trees, we stopped for a lunch break by the shed, where the legs of the plastic chairs were now set into mud, but at least the hornets had gone. Foteini's orchards and goat enclosures used to belong to her grandfather, who, like her, had been born in the mountain village of Altomira. The village is 2,800 feet above sea level, too high for growing olives trees, and most people kept animals, or grew almond trees and wild pears. It was the custom in higher-altitude Taygetos villages for people to spend the summer there and then move to villagers lower down, or on to the plains, in the winter to start the olive harvest in family orchards.

When Foteini was young, she helped to look after her father's 150-strong goat herd in Altomira and in the winter the animals, along with mules and donkeys, were brought down the mountain side on the Biliova, one of the oldest and longest *kalderimia,* donkey tracks, in the Mani. They went to her grandfather's fields to graze, in Megali Mantineia. The family lived in a tumbledown house nearby, which was now abandoned. In the summer they went back up to Altomira. In the mountain village it was a tough existence for the family – her parents and younger brother, living in a rough stone house with no electricity or running water and very little furniture.

The village of Altomira is a glorious mountain eyrie, with lush green pastures, alpine flowers and staggering views of Profitis Ilias, the highest peak of the Taygetos. It once had a population of around 100, enough to support two tavernas, a *kafeneio*, a shop, a small village school, and a priest. These facilities have gone now and the churches are only open on saints' feast days. Today, the village has a tiny population of around 20 residents, mostly farmers, which can swell to 80 in summer with Greek holidaymakers returning to their renovated family houses, or holiday homes. In the winter, only a few hardy souls stay on, and one day there will probably be none. Foteini told us she had to sell her family house in Altomira a few years ago and it went to an Athenian couple.

"I got nothing much for it. It needed work, but you should see it now though, all new, as if we never lived there," she said, pointing up towards the bare peaks in the distance that enfold, and completely hide, Altomira. "We'll go up there in the spring. We'll take some fruit and some *paksimadia* (traditional long-lasting baked bread), and off we'll go."

We had become used to hearing this refrain, but each time we tried to set a date for the excursion there would be the usual excuse: "I can't leave the goats, I can't leave Riko. One day, one day."

Foteini's family left Altomira for good in the mid-1980s, the parents too old and tired to keep making the yearly migration. They locked up the house and left it as it was, bare and neglected for lack of funds. With her brother as well, they moved to Megali Mantineia, where a kind family member gave them the village house she still occupies, even though it was just another neglected stone property. They set about making a new, permanent life there and grazing their goats in the fields that Foteini still owns.

But while it was meant to be the start of an easier life, it was the beginning of three disastrous years, when her parents died and her brother was tragically shot dead in the village when an argument with a man from another village got out of hand. The man was jailed for his crime. We later discovered that her brother had been shot outside the old stone house she lived in and it perhaps solved the mystery of why Foteini didn't invite strangers there.

Perhaps the only glimmer of hope in her life had been that during these first years in the village, Foteini finally got married – in her early forties, late by Greek standards. The marriage was arranged by a kindly relative but it proved to be an imperfect union with a man who was much older, a widower from a nearby village with a grown-up son, and sadly the marriage produced no children of their own.

Foteini was probably lucky to have ever married at all though, considering that in mountain villages after the war, young men started to leave for work in the city, and only a few eligible men were left. A new bitumen road was built to Altomira by the council in the 1980s to ease the lives of its residents, but tragically, it was stopped a few miles short of the village and the rest of it is still a dirt road full of hairpin bends, covered in scree in parts and treacherous in the winter, meaning that Altomira is still a remote, but beautiful, outpost.

"I can remember the day I left Altomira with my family in 1985 when we were all still together. It was in March, but it was a day like today, grey and cold. I don't like these kind of days now," she said.

Foteini didn't like to talk much about the details of her marriage, or the death of her husband 15 years after they married, or her stepson, out of respect for them and their families, or about the details of her brother's death, which devastated her, and was the only murder in recent history in Megali Mantineia, a fact that villagers still talk about in hushed tones.

Violence in Mani villages in the past hasn't exactly been rare, starting with the punitive raids by the Turks during the Orlofika revolution. In the 1770s, the Maniots planned a campaign against the Turks, for the whole of Greece, with the help of a small group of Russians. The campaign failed, however, and the Mani came under fierce attack by Turkish insurgents, though they never got a proper foothold in the region. In a cave on the side of the Rindomo Gorge, the southern boundary of Megali Mantineia, there was one infamous slaughter of villagers by Turks in 1769.

Villagers (mainly women, children and old people) had taken refuge there when they heard that the Turks were advancing on the area. The mouth of the cave was narrow and some 30ft high, blocked with stones in the lower half, leaving a narrow entranceway. The Turkish soldiers heard some of the children crying, scrambled down the steep side of the gorge, getting close enough to the cave to lob a sulphur bomb inside, forcing the villagers outside, where they were then slaughtered.

Megali Mantineia also suffered during the German occupation of Greece in the Second World War, when troops raided the village, and during the civil war afterwards, as did the whole of Greece, when communist groups, who had led the resistance against the Germans, now fought against the government army for more political dominance but were crushed by 1949. In the Mani, communists hid out in mountain strongholds and atrocities were carried out by both sides. Many villages, even today, are still strongly allied to either the left or right.

Many farmers in the Mani, like Foteini, have suffered hardships but what made her different was the fact she relied on no-one else to make her living. While she was in her mid-sixties, few younger people could match Foteini's stoicism or brute strength. Later that day, after stripping some of the sawn branches bare, she lashed them together in a fat sheath and threw the lot over her back to take to the main *ktima*. Jim rushed to her aid, but she waved him away. He looked over at me with a helpless shrug of his shoulders.

She asked us to lead Riko, who had several sacks of olives strapped to his back, and we walked part of the way along the main road, with Foteini in front, carrying her bundle. Villagers drove by and beeped their horns and waved, as if seeing Foteini carrying these loads was commonplace, and no wonder film crews had come to capture these incredible feats.

But for one dislocated moment I felt I was in a destitute corner of Africa, where women still carry tall water jars on their heads for miles or do unimaginable jobs to eke out a living, yet this was modern, albeit debt-ridden, Greece and this was a part of the Mani where people also had chic villas hidden in the hills, some with swimming pools and most with fabulous views, where they could afford to hire the best labourers to do their olive harvest. How could these two different worlds slide past each other without friction?

When we got home on the afternoon of the second day we collapsed on the bed, exhausted.

"How does she do it?" said Jim. "Every day for months."

"We only helped her for two days. It's a drop in the ocean, isn't it?"

I kept thinking of how much she thanked us for our paltry efforts. She had promised us that after she collected her oil from the nearby olive press, she would give us a large tin of it and added: "In the spring, when I make my *mizithra* cheese from the goats' milk, I'll give you some."

"Good," I had said to her, trying to sound grateful, but feeling faint. *Mizithra*, a soft white cheese, not unlike feta but much less tasty, is made by just about everyone who has goats and was our least favourite cheese. Just thinking about its rich, fatty goatiness sent my cholesterol intergalactic. I felt sick.

"We must accept it. She'd be hurt if we didn't," I told Jim.

"I think she'll forget all about it by spring," he said.

"No, she won't forget," I said, with great confidence.

And here's the thing: when someone promises you a special food treat, it will always be the one thing you hate the most (goat's intestines, birds' heads, monkey's brains), that you will definitely be given – in spades.

16

Frescos and frenzy

WE pushed open the stout wooden door and found ourselves in a space that felt like a dungeon – musty, almost pitch dark, with bone-biting cold, despite it being a mild winter's day. The fact this church was reputed to have wonderful frescos seemed impossible, and the atmosphere was unwelcoming. We had developed something of a passion for Byzantine churches in the Mani and had found many with a cold, forbidding air, often due to neglect, but nothing as creepy as this one. Wallace, picking up on spooky vibes as usual, didn't like it either. Five minutes after we got there, he was straining at his lead to get out.

Christianity came late to the Mani but when it finally arrived, the Maniots went into a frenzy of church-building, creating some of the best examples in southern Greece, many of which date from the 11th century. Some of the frescos in these churches were even said to have been created by well-known icon painters of Mystras. Once a fabulous town built on a hillside not far from Sparta, this was the last outpost of the great Byzantine Empire. Mystras had some of the era's finest churches, and in turn, attracted icon painters from all over the Byzantine world, including Konstantinopolis (modern-day Istanbul).

The smallest church we had seen in the Mani was the 11th-century Agios Yiannis, the size of a large phone box, built high on a rock in the middle of an olive grove, with some original frescos, badly faded. Most churches created after the

Byzantine era ended (15th century) maintain a Byzantine style in their buildings and frescos. Many churches are permanently locked because of their valuable frescos, and finding a key holder can be a trial. In villages, the key will be held by the local papas who is never there, but is either asleep in his manse, in another village, or living in a monastery on the top of a mountain, 10 miles away. To find a church open, with memorable frescos in good order, is good fortune indeed.

We had been told that this church of the Panayia of Chelmou was unlocked yet contained some lovely, well preserved frescos dating from the early 18th century, though some of the old monastery ruins near the church were probably a century older. Few people ever went there, as it was difficult to locate from the road, and well concealed on a wooded hillside overlooking the Taygetos mountains, not far from the famous Rindomo Gorge.

We were warned that it would be very dark inside, so we took a few dozen tea-lights and candles because we planned to take photographs for a piece we were writing on our website, charting our adventures in Greece. We quickly set to work placing the tea-lights around the sanctuary and on the altar, a massive stone slab on a plinth. As the candlelight increased, the effect was dazzling – perfect frescos in strong colours burst into life, and up above, in the dome of the apse, the fresco we had come all this way to see, a beautiful woman with a serene, enigmatic smile, her arms stretched wide. We stood motionless, looking up in wonder at this fabulous image that had hitherto been smothered in darkness.

Neither of us spoke until Jim broke the silence, rubbing the back of his neck.

"I think I've just invented a new medical syndrome," he said.

"What's that?"

"I call it fresco neck. It gets me every time we visit a Byzantine church."

"I know just what you mean," I said, smiling and holding the back of my head as well, all the better to gaze at this fresco and take in all the detail.

This was a beautifully preserved depiction of the *Panayia Platytera,* a classic pose of the Mother of Jesus with her arms spread out, 'wider than the heavens', supposedly offering love and protection to all who stand before her. We had seen versions of this in other churches, but this was a powerful depiction in excellent condition. And below this, every bit of wall space was covered in frescos of saints and apostles.

This was a church, however, of two halves. The sanctuary was well preserved and enchanting and we took many photos here in flickering candlelight, while the main part of the church, with its high cupola above, despite the addition of light from some hand-held candles, remained cold and creepy. We had tied Wallace up to the door handle so we could keep an eye on him but he wasn't happy and whined, keen to get back out into the sun. At first I thought he was just cold, but later I was sure he'd picked up some unpleasant vibe here, as he had so many times before on our travels. Jim and I hurried along the walls, like a pair of bumbling tomb raiders, lighting up different frescos as we went, finding some gems but also some macabre frescos, like a saint being devoured from the feet up by a whale.

Greek Orthodox churches depict scenes from the Bible – the birth of Christ through to the Day of Judgement. They were meant to be instructive for congregations centuries ago who were mainly illiterate. Nothing is as graphic as the grotesque images of hell with unbelievers sliding down ladders through flames into the gaping maw of monster fish. And frescos in the churches dedicated to the Christian martyrs often feature sorry souls being beheaded, dismembered, flayed, torn apart on Byzantine racks, yet maintaining a regal calm.

Patrick Leigh Fermor, in his book *Mani,* in a chapter on icons, talked about this "orgy of martyrdom". He wrote: "A mild and benevolent composure in the faces of both executioner and victim robs their impact of anguish and horror ... They do not demand that you should participate vicariously in their torments."

This composure seemed to be the case in this church until we came to the last fresco. What lessons the Byzantines had in mind with this we found perplexing. On the right of the front door we lifted our candles and jumped back in fright at the life-sized creature with a grisly, horrifying face, with only the whites of the eyes showing and a gaping mouth with long, blood-tinged teeth. This was a cross between movie villain Freddy Krueger and the kind of image Mr Bean might have knocked up when let loose among Byzantine paint pots. In another setting it might have been funny.

"That's gross," said Jim, rushing off to snuff out all the candles. "Eddie Edit tells me we should vacate ASAP."

Although the camera was low on battery power I thought I'd have enough for one last shot – of the hideous ghoul. I was wrong. Even when I turned the camera off and then on again, which sometimes squeezed a bit of life from the battery in this digital camera, I got nothing. Not only that, the camera jammed into the zoom position and, most curious of all, never worked again, and we had to buy another camera. Hexed by the ghoul?

I unhooked Wallace, who was now shivering with anxiety. We rushed out and Jim banged the door firmly shut.

"How could a church have that exquisite fresco of the *Panayia* and then that hideous creature, all in one place?" I said.

167

"Maybe he was like the club bouncer," replied Jim, bending the rules of Byzantine iconography.

While Jim was packing up his rucksack, Wallace was fizzy and pulled me straight over to a low stone wall, where there was a thick patch of moss, and started barking. Just when I thought I'd seen all of Wallace's crazy stunts, here he was, barking at moss, except that it wasn't moss – it was moving. I took a step closer and froze when I discovered the 'moss' was in fact an undulating mass of caterpillars crawling nose to tail over the stone work. But, oh dear, they were no ordinary caterpillars – these were the ones we had been warned about. "If you ever see them, run for the hills," Desmond told us once, and I began to understand why few people ever came up here.

I pulled Wallace well back from them and waved at Jim to get his attention.

"The pine processionary caterpillar," I whispered hoarsely.

"Why are you talking like David Attenborough?" said Jim.

"Very dangerous," I rasped, pointing at the hairy critters.

In the pine trees above we could see the tell-tale candyfloss nests where the caterpillars sleep during the day, while they do most of their feeding at night, like hairy vampires. They form colonies of up to 400 and kill pine trees by stripping off the greenery. They are harmful to humans and pets because their tiny hairs are barbed and if you get one in your mouth, or breathe one in, you're almost history.

"Is there anything cheery at all about this place?" said Jim, putting on his rucksack.

We legged it down the hill and back to the car, parked near the gates of a small factory building. In the factory yard, a man sat on a plastic chair, facing the hillside, smoking a cigarette, as if he'd been waiting for us. He got up, opened the gates and walked towards us with a quizzical expression.

"I saw you from my house in the village when you parked your car."

His eyes flickered over the rucksack. "Have you been up to the church?" he asked, stubbing out his cigarette in the dirt. We nodded.

"What did you think?"

We told him we thought the place was spooky.

"It is a bit. Once it was a monastery and most of that's in ruins. But did you see a small house up there?"

We nodded.

"In the locked basement of the house there is a narrow passageway that runs all the way from there to a secret crypt beneath the church, where the monks sometimes had to hide."

"Hide from what?" I asked him, though my mind had conjured up two things straight off – ghouls and caterpillars.

"Everyone," he said expansively.

These foothills had been infamous from the 17th century as a hideout for *kleftes*, bandits, on the run from clan warfare, vendettas, or for not paying local taxes, which was a distinguishing factor of the maverick Maniots of the past (and still is), together with a general hatred of rules. The factory man also revealed that his family, who had lived in the nearby village of Kendro for generations, had told him stories of the exploits of Messinian-born legend and freedom fighter Theodoros Kolokotronis. Before the War of Independence in 1821, Kolokotronis had supposedly hidden out in the now-ruined tower at the top of the hill above the church, plotting the overthrow of the Turks. It may have been a rural myth but it gave this rather creepy place slightly more cachet.

Had Kolokotronis also hidden in the secret crypt when marauding Turks got too close? Our friend couldn't say.

"I only know that the monks fled there in times of strife and many would have stayed for weeks. I have heard that some may have died down there. They were old men."

It made me shiver. The place was haunted by more than legends.

"The dog was frightened in the church," I said, as if to confirm its unsettling aura.

He gave Wallace an arch look. As if Greeks care about the sensitivities of dogs.

"If you come back again, I can take you down to the secret crypt," he said.

Pass, I thought.

He was an affable but odd kind of guy and I was still wondering why he was hanging about. I looked at the factory again and noticed a metal sign hanging on the front fence that I was sure hadn't been there before. It had 'for sale' on it.

"Is this your factory?"

"Yes. It's a cheese factory, or used to be."

"Mizithra or feta?" I asked impishly.

Jim shot me a curious look – as if I'd totally lost the plot.

"Everything ... but now I am forced to sell."

He didn't volunteer why. We didn't ask.

"You don't want to buy a cheese factory, do you?"

"Not really," I said, bemused. Of all the crazy ventures we might take on in the Peloponnese if we had a mind to, owning a cheese factory wasn't one of them.

Jim cleared his throat and I could tell he was stifling a hearty laugh, as I was. The man looked very downcast. I almost felt sorry for him and cursed myself for a lack of interest in cheese. We said our goodbyes and piled into the car.

"Do you think that's why he was waiting for us, to tout for a sale?" asked Jim.

"Who knows? That whole place is odd: Freddy Krueger with the dentures from hell, crypts and caterpillars, a broken camera, and a strange man selling a cheese factory. What would Stephen King have made of it?"

"A thousand pages and another pile of dosh," he said.

When we got home and tried to download the pictures we'd taken in the church before the camera jammed, they seemed to have vanished into the next dimension. Even the ones of the beautiful fresco in the sanctuary were gone. Eaten up by the evil ghoul? But worst of all, Wallace seemed off-colour that night and wouldn't touch his dinner.

"Do you think he breathed in some of those pesky caterpillar hairs?" I said.

"I'm sure it's not that. You kept him well back," replied Jim.

"It only takes one tiny hair apparently to cause havoc."

"You worry too much about Wallace, do you know that?"

"No I don't," I said, getting out the special medical kit I'd brought for him with all his various tablets, his eye drops, ear drops, skin cream, tick-removing implements, flea collars, combs, brushes. Worry? Me?

I gave his coat a good brush and checked him out for caterpillar hairs. I didn't spot any, but what I did find was much more worrying.

17

Wallace meets his match

"HOW is killer machine today?" asked Angelos the vet, as we lifted Wallace on to the examination table a couple of days later.

The nickname had come about after Wallace had put on a feisty turn while being examined the last time. Now he seemed a lot more subdued, even as Angelos pulled back his thick fur to examine the two hairless lumps on his back which I discovered when we returned from our church excursion. I had seen the lumps a few months earlier but they were much smaller then.

"I think they are okay, probably just a skin condition," said Angelos, giving us a cream to rub into Wallace's back for a week. "If the lumps don't improve, you must return to the surgery. Rrrright?"

The cream made no difference and so we went back. When Angelos examined the lumps the second time, he discovered that a large area of skin around them had also thickened, which he wasn't happy about. He took a scraping from each lump and from the surrounding area and checked them out under a microscope, as he had specialised in animal skin conditions. He wasn't pleased, saying the cells looked abnormal.

"What are you thinking, that the lumps are cancerous?" I asked.

"I don't know, but I'm going to send the biopsies to our laboratory in Thessaloniki and get them checked and then we'll know."

"What if it's cancer?" I asked.

"You know, I don't think it is," he said, his brown eyes looking sympathetic.

"But if it is?" I am the kind of person who likes to know what I'm up against.

"Then you would have to take him to Athens for special cancer treatment. We don't do that here. And it would be expensive."

The possibility that Wallace might get sick in Greece hadn't crossed my mind. We had been more worried about medical dramas ourselves as we had only basic medical cover here. But this was something we hadn't expected. Whether it was our anxiety or not that prompted him, Angelos changed his mind and decided to take the lumps out as soon as possible and send everything up to the laboratory in Thessaloniki, northern Greece, just to be sure.

When we turned up later that week for the procedure, Wallace was quickly anaesthetised and we were allowed to watch at the beginning while a large section of his back was shaved. Angelos pulled a section of skin up between his fingers to show us how the area had thickened.

"This is very curious. I don't know what's going on here, but we'll find out soon enough."

It wasn't a long procedure and after the lumps were removed, Wallace was given six stitches. With his back shaved and the wounds doused in a brown antiseptic solution, and uncovered – because Angelos said dressings wouldn't stick on an active dog like Wallace – he looked like he'd just done five rounds with a Doberman. The bad news was that the results would take two or three weeks, or more, because the lab would be shut over the Christmas/New Year period. Angelos saw my distressed look before we left and patted me on the shoulder.

"Don't worry, killer machine will live. Rrrright?"

As we left the vet's surgery, passers-by stared at him. Seeing a Jack Russell was novel enough in Kalamata but one with a shaved and stitched back was a curiosity, and when he stopped at the corner of the street to do a handstand pee on a car tyre (nothing stops Wallace) he drew a few amused stares.

Wallace always slept in the bedroom. In the summer we put his bed in front of the floor fan, and in the winter, in front of the electric fire. It was always freezing in the bedroom, and the exposed stonework on one wall made it feel like a dungeon. There were curious deep holes in the blocks of stone that Desmond described as a "natural feature", but which I feared were habitats for more nesting scorpions and other critters. I had managed to plug most of them up with balls of Blu Tack.

After we put the lights out that night I felt Wallace jumping on to the bed beside me, whimpering. I left him there as I guessed the poor little guy was in a fair bit of discomfort and I kept putting my hand on his head to reassure him, ruffling his fur, and at some point he fell asleep. Unlike me. I wriggled and turned until early in the morning, when the first of the chained dogs in the village started howling. I kept wondering what we would do if the lumps were cancerous. What would treatment be like here? Would it be best to go back to Scotland?

We had come to Greece for a great adventure, a chill-out year. We hadn't brought poor Wallace here to succumb to cancer. But there was another factor in his illness that nagged at me. Wallace was a tangible link back to our early days in Scotland, when my mother was still alive, and Wallace in his daft, delightful way had made her laugh. Losing Wallace would feel like losing a dear old friend. I shed a few tears that night and when I got up the next morning I felt worse for knowing that it would be weeks before we got the biopsy results.

We went out for our morning walk and just as we opened the gate and stepped on to the road, I saw Irini, the little girl who had stood so many times watching Wallace play in the courtyard below. Irini never said very much because of her learning difficulties but had a gentle disposition and the most remarkable eyes I'd ever seen in a child. Big, brown and penetrating. When she asked you a question she stared at you hard, as if she was looking into your soul. It was both amazing and unnerving. She walked straight towards us, staring at Wallace's back.

"*Skilos?*" was all she said, pointing at the wounds, her big eyes looked terrified. She didn't need to say any more.

"*O skilos einai arostos* (the dog is sick)," I told her.

She put her hand to her mouth and stared. She bent down and touched Wallace's ear lightly with her long fingers, then turned and ran back up the road to her house at the top of the village, without looking back. She probably got the fright of her life.

When we walked past the *kafeneio*, I saw Angeliki leaning over the wall, staring at us curiously.

"What's happened to Vassie?" she asked.

I told her and she came down the steps on to the road, looking carefully at his back but never getting too close.

"It's not a beautiful sight, is it?" she said.

"No, not really," I said.

I told her how long the biopsies would take. She waved her right hand around in a windmill gesture, the way Greeks do when they want to express disbelief or outrage, and I feared it meant "this is Greece, it's bound to take longer".

"Come by later," she said, "I'll have some lamb bones by then. The dog will like them."

This time when she said *elpizo tha zisei* (I hope he'll live), she meant it literally and not with any irony. For someone who didn't like dogs much, she was being thoughtful, and I liked her all the more for that.

@@@@@@@

Christmas and New Year in the village were strangely subdued, as they are in Greece, because Easter is the most important celebration, but mainly it was because everyone was out harvesting olives. On Christmas morning there was a knock at the door. It was one of our neighbours bringing us a plate of *kourabiedes* biscuits and a tin of olive oil from her harvest.

Konstantina was a sweet young woman who was also a goat farmer and, with her ageing father and some of her family from Kalamata, harvested olives from their 1,000 trees every autumn. I had often spoken to her as she walked along the road on the way to her small *ktima* in the valley below the village. And in November she had invited us to a *mnimosino*, memorial service, at the village church for her uncle Panayiotis, who had died a year before, and we were invited to the meal afterwards at one of the local tavernas, as is the custom. A *mnimosino* is held at set intervals after someone dies.

The village church was packed out with all Panayiotis's grieving relatives and friends, dressed in black, as if it were another funeral. A small table had been placed in front of the *iconostasis*. It held a vase of flowers and the traditional *koliva* 'cake', a ritual food that dates back to the time of Ancient Greece, and contains wheat, nuts, pomegranate seeds, herbs, dried fruit and spices. The wheat represents resurrection, and all the sweet and sour elements of koliva together depict the cycle of life and death. There was also a framed picture of Panayiotis, a popular character who we knew almost nothing about. Yet, while it felt as sombre as a funeral, the *mnimosino* had an implicit sense of celebration for Panayiotis's former earthly existence, and his new spiritual life.

We left the church afterwards with the rest of the congregation, walking up the road to light candles at the foot of his grave, where the priest held a short service. On the way out of the graveyard, Konstantina and her family gave out small containers with the *koliva* to each of the congregation. This was the first *mnimosino* service we'd been to and we knew little of its customs, but luckily we found Eftihia and her mother Pelagia at the taverna afterwards, sitting at an empty table. They beckoned us over, guiding us through the formalities of lunch and telling us to eat everything that we were served, otherwise it would be bad manners. So there we were, tucking into stewed meat, pasta, feta cheese and salad at 11am – all of which, curiously, has its symbolic role in the memorial ritual.

Robert Downey Jr, the *papas*, was holding court at a long table and seemed relaxed for this serious occasion, loosening the white collar under his black robe, rolling up his sleeves and bantering with some of the young men who were sitting either side of him and hanging on his every word. We mistook the conviviality of it all for a normal lunch gathering. When jugs of wine were brought to each table, I poured wine for those nearby and Jim and I clicked our glasses together with the others, saying, as Greeks always do at a meal, "*Yeia mas*", our health, which sounded suddenly loud and festive because there was a lull in conversation around the taverna. Eftihia's normally cheery face turned pale.

"No," she said in a stage whisper. "Don't say that. It's very bad. You can't make a toast to health when it's a *mnimosino* meal."

A few people turned and gave us black looks and we were suddenly in need of a heart massage, or a requiem mass of our own.

"That's the last time foreigners will be invited to a *mnimosino*," I whispered to Jim.

Eftihia sensed our embarrassment. "Never mind, Margarita. Eat up. Drink up!" Then she moved closer to me, whispering in my ear. "At least you don't have to deal with *tsikles* (picked birds) today, eh?" We smiled. It was an ice-breaker.

And here was Konstantina on Christmas Day, offering us gifts. "My mother was a kind woman. She liked to give things to other people to make them feel good. I want to do the same," she said, thrusting a big five-litre can of olive oil towards us. "It's what my mother would have wanted."

The holiday period passed peacefully and happily enough. Then early in January we got a call from Angelos the vet.

18

Hit with the basil brush

THE phone call was short. It was Angelos telling me Wallace's biopsy results had not come back yet. "How long does he think it will take?" asked Jim when I came off the phone.

I shrugged. "Could be another few weeks. Do you think it takes longer to do biopsies when there's a suspicion of cancer?"

Jim shook his head. "You're being paranoid. You're thinking the worst before it happens."

"There was I thinking domestic animals were unpopular in Greece and now the labs are out the door with work."

"Probably to do with economic cutbacks. But hey, look at Wallace, he seems okay."

Wallace was stretched out nearby, shredding the wrapper from a chocolate bar and tossing the bits all over the floor with glee. I couldn't help but smile.

"And this morning he was doing handstand pees. Do you think a dog does that when he's not feeling well?" said Jim, trying to cheer me up.

"Only in a circus, with no health and safety rules for Jack Russells."

Jim put his hands on my shoulders and gave them a gentle shake, the way he does when he wants to reassure me, but when I looked into his lovely green eyes (that I always said jokingly looked like unripe olives) I could sense some anxiety there, even though he was trying to be chipper.

"Don't worry. Wallace is a tough wee guy. Remember why we called him Wallace in the first place after William Wallace, the Braveheart," said Jim.

I laughed when I remembered how cool we thought it would be to name the dog after a Scottish hero, and Wallace was heroic as a puppy, trying to defend us against house visitors he perceived as the enemy. He could also hold his own against most things, including aggressive dogs twice his size and bad-tempered Scottish tradesmen. The fact that he was now frightened of flies and bees didn't diminish his bravery – much.

But I still had a niggling fear that the lumps were sinister, and if they were, this delay wouldn't help at all. Meanwhile, we just carried on taking Wallace out for his daily walks. When the village kids saw us they'd come skittering over to see his scars, as if he were a war veteran. And they laughed at the funny square bald patch on his back that looked slightly punky. Some of the old people were also intrigued about the drama of the strange white dog. An old woman called Phaedra, who often stood silently on the road staring down at Wallace while he played in the courtyard, approached us on one of our walks. She looked down at Wallace's healing scars and shook her head gravely. I took it to be an expression of sympathy.

"Pah! I've got embroidered cushions my sister made for my dowry years ago, and they still look a lot better than that job," she said, with small tight eyes, like a petulant seamstress. "What's wrong with the dog anyway?"

We told her about the lumps, the biopsies. She waved her hand around in the typical windmill fashion.

"Dogs with lumps now," she muttered, like someone who has not quite seen everything there is to see on the planet, but she's almost there. "Try praying for him. That's about all you can do," she said with a sniff, and walked off down the road, poking its rocky edges with her long *magoura* stick, used more commonly for bashing olives during harvesting.

I had her comments in mind, though, when we went to the special church service for the festival of the Epiphany, or the Blessing of the Waters, one of the oldest and most solemn of religious festivals in Greece, which also commemorates the baptism of Christ by John the Baptist. It was Foteini who had told us first about the service taking place down in the village of Paleohora. When we asked if she wanted to come with us, she said: "I can't – I've got the goats to look after."

If goats could sit quietly in church pews, or at festive tables, without making pigs of themselves, I'm sure she would have brought them along. But this service was in another village and rural Greeks seem to believe that other villages are like other countries, and full of *xenoi*, especially as this one was down by the sea. Robert Downey Jr was taking the service, as he worked between two or three of the local churches.

"Don't forget," Foteini had told us, "to get a blessing from the holy water and bring me back a piece of holy bread."

This was a long, ornate service, in which the priest energetically 'baptised' everyone by flicking a great bunch of fresh basil, dipped in holy water, towards the congregation, the water droplets spinning out over our heads but nearly drowning a poor old guy in the front row. The sight of this tiny old man dressed in black taking out his freshly ironed handkerchief and drying his head made a few people nearby comment sympathetically about his plight, and also make a joke of it. Even the priest seemed to be stifling a smile.

Despite its Byzantine solemnity, I was always intrigued by the way the church services at times had an aura of amateur dramatics about them. The iconostasis, the richly decorated screen that divides the main vault of the church from the sanctuary, has three doorways through which the priest and deacons appear and disappear at certain points in the service and through which the priest will appear, swinging his censer or carrying the gold-plated book of the Gospel. Some scholars have suggested that the *iconostasis* may have its origins in Greek tragedy, from the proscenium arch used in ancient theatres with three doorways.

Yet the solemnity and drama of the services seem to do nothing to curb the craziness of the Greek congregation, and perhaps that is one of its great charms. I had seen the oddest behaviour in churches and I was reminded of an amusing interlude once in the imposing Kalamata Cathedral, or the Church of the *Ipapanti tou Sotiros* (Presentation of Christ the Saviour), built in 1860 over a much older church.

The church contains the reputedly miraculous icon of the *Panayia* holding the baby Jesus which, in the traditional style of these very devotional icons, is covered in a sheet of beaten silver at the front, with only the two faces peeping through. The icon had been housed in the older church and survived after the Turks set fire to the building in 1770. According to local legend, this old icon was found among the ashes of the ruined church and although the back of it was burnt, the front was completely unharmed. The icon, depicting a serene, enigmatic *Panayia*, is also supposed to have given the city its name from the words *kala matia*, beautiful eyes.

We had gone to the church one day to see the icon and sat in front of it beside a smartly dressed middle-aged woman. The church was dead quiet until the *William Tell Overture* started to rise out of her handbag, becoming increasingly loud: a ludicrous, chavvy sound in this quiet sanctuary with pin-sharp acoustics. Like many Greeks in church, she hadn't bothered to switch off her mobile phone and answered the call, shouting what seemed like a long set of instructions for an evening meal. After she hung up, she walked around the church, kissing every icon (an act of penance perhaps) and then flounced out the door.

At the end of the Epiphany service in Paleohora, when the side doors were opened and the congregation started to file slowly down the aisle, we were propelled forward by an impatient crush of people behind us. Through the heads of those in front I had glimpses of a colourful robe, basil leaves, the flash of gold, sprays of water, and guessed this was "the blessing" Foteini had referred to. I was trembling with nerves.

All thoughts of sending up a silent prayer to the Saint of Sick Beasts, whoever that might be, disappeared when our 'turn' came and the soaking basil bunch was bounced on our foreheads, and a gold cross was thrust towards our lips, and kissing it seemed the only means of escape. We then staggered out into blinding winter sunshine. I had water rippling down my face and my mascara was running, but Jim was strangely euphoric.

"I think I liked being hit with the Basil Brush best of all," he beamed. "I'm getting to love the dramatic vibe of Greek church, aren't you? The rituals, the incense…church in Britain is so plain in comparison. I'd call it Jesus Unplugged."

I gave him a terse look. "Sometimes I'd like to unplug you."

Outside the church, a crowd gathered around the baskets of holy bread. "I have to get bread for Foteini," I said, sounding like I was off to the shops.

I couldn't get anywhere near the baskets. Great burly matrons in black kept elbowing me out of the way, and with each attempt I was sucked out to the back of the crowd. Finally, I felt a hand on my arm and turned. It was Leonidas from the village. The blue eyes looked slightly amused. Maybe it was my basil-bleary face and panda eyes.

"I'll get you some bread," he said, giving a loud command to the man dispensing large squares of holy bread, with its warm spicy aroma. And suddenly the crowd seemed to part for Leonidas, like Moses at the Red Sea. I always knew he had clout and here was proof of it. He handed me a bag with many pieces of bread inside, smiled sweetly and told me to follow the other people walking down to the seashore.

A Byzantine fortress had once stood on this high point that juts out slightly and overlooks the gulf and Kalamata, though there is nothing left of it now, apart from a natural opening in the cliff-face, the Portello, down which the inhabitants fled during invasions. From the top, a staircase leads down to a small windswept cove where the congregation was now assembled. Leonidas came into view first at the head of the procession, holding a huge wooden cross aloft, and behind him were Robert Downey Jr and a retinue of church elders. The priest climbed onto nearby rocks and hurled the wooden cross (attached to a rope) into the freezing January waves as a blessing.

This ritual also involved one of the more curious traditions of the Greek Orthodox Church, played out all over the country on this day, when young men dive into the icy water to retrieve the cross. Two teenage boys had been standing by, dressed only in brief swimmers, and when they hit the water, a sympathetic cry went up from the bystanders. Tradition states that whoever reaches the cross first and swims with it to shore will be blessed with great good luck. And he will be stood many rounds of drinks in local tavernas for months to come, in a bid perhaps to reconstitute his manly bits.

A few days after the church service, we both came down with bad colds.

"It's because we kissed the cross in church," said nasal Jim. "Imagine how many people kissed it that morning and how many people had colds. I could hear them coughing and sneezing all the way through the service."

"Maybe the cross should have had a health warning: 'Kissing this cross could seriously damage your health'," I said.

"That's wicked."

If I had known how bleak January would feel at times, I would gladly have stripped off on the Epiphany and dived into the water myself to fetch the cross. In January, it was hard to believe that the country that gave us scorching temperatures, mayhem on the seashore, and the fecund fig, could also be so stormy and bitterly cold, especially when the wind tore down from the snow-capped peaks of the Taygetos mountains behind us.

The Taygetos were first alluded to in ancient times in Homer's *Iliad* and named after the mythological nymph Taygete. Profitis Ilias, at 7,897ft, is the highest peak, topped by a perfect pyramid shape which dominates the Mani region and can be seen as far away as Corinth in the north Peloponnese. It is said to have mystical significance and in July draws pilgrims from around the world, who camp out near its peak on one particular day to await the sunrise the following morning as it casts a perfect pyramid shadow across the Gulf of Messinia.

The Taygetos range has from ancient times been both inspiring and foreboding. The ancient Spartans, with their militaristic outlook, used the bleaker expanses of the mountains to dispose of citizens who were considered a burden (invalids, or even deformed children) by hurling them into the deep, dark chasm known as the *Kaiadas*, near the famous Langada pass, on the road from Kalamata to Sparta.

In January, the mighty Taygetos can make you feel very mortal. The great Greek writer Nikos Kazantzakis, who spent time in the Mani, wrote of the mountains: "Look at the Taiyetos (sic) and your chest expands, petty calculations vanish, you are ashamed of the tiny, meaningless life that you have led."

That particular winter month, I knew exactly what he meant. Sitting huddled around the wood-burning stove in Desmond's house, when it was too cold and wet to go out, I felt very tiny indeed. And there were more than a few times in winter when we thought fondly of our centrally heated home back in Scotland. The storms, at least, were as exciting and mythical as you would expect in the Mani, when it rained 'chair legs' (*kareklopodara*), as they say in Greece. Sometimes the rain shot vertically across the hillside as well, and down on the coast, where tiny hamlets hugged the shore, the bars, shops and beaches that were once thronging with people were now deserted, as massive waves flung hundreds of large sea stones across the coastal road, sometimes closing it for hours.

At least the stove was good and warm once it was cranked up, packed full of olive wood from Desmond's harvest, and we sat in front of it all day in the worst weather, reading. However, finding enough English books became more and more difficult, unless everything was ordered on the internet, which took weeks to arrive by post, so we mostly borrowed books from other expats, and had to stretch our taste in genres.

One day I found Jim curled up on the plum sofa in front of the fire, nursing his cold and being unfaithful to poor Stephen King. Instead, he was reading a chic-lit novel, something about cat walks, kitten heels and coitus. He seemed engrossed.

"Jim, you're supposed to get in touch with your feminine side, not hug it to death."

"Well, needs must," he groaned.

The evenings were also a challenge, with nothing on terrestrial TV, which was all we had, apart from gloomy reports about the escalating economic problems, and a plethora of amusing but puerile Greek soaps that might easily have been renamed something like Carry On Up The Temple of Aphrodite. On many nights we escaped to the warmth of the village tavernas which were all friendly, family-run businesses.

Each of the tavernas had a roaring fire and were bright, lively places where the dynamics had changed from the summer. There were few expats now, as even the so-called 'permanent' ones had now gone back to Britain for the joys of central heating and the Marks & Spencer food hall. Most of the clientele were village Greeks. In the Good Heart, we sat around the *soba* in the cabin, watching television beside tables of Albanians surfing the net on their laptops, while Angeliki surfed the tables, desperate for some diverting *parea*, company.

She always had ideas about how to fill the long winter days and nights. One afternoon, on the spur of the moment, she asked if we'd like to go to a nearby hill village to see her mother, who had been resting up with a bad back. Fifteen minutes later we were driving up through the spectacular pass that cuts through the Taygetos on the road leading south through the Mani. We turned off at the village, where her mother Ourania lived in an old house. Angeliki and four other siblings had been born and brought up there. Ourania was smart and bright-eyed for an old woman, with a plethora of village stories. She was fond of a good joke and, like Angeliki, roared with laugher at my mashed Greek. When Ourania commented on the recent bad weather, I told her "Kalamata had been full of washing machines (*plindiria*) one day" instead of *plimires*, floods. Angeliki laughed so much I thought she'd crack a vertebra, and I could see how bad backs had become a family trait.

The mother apologised for having nothing much in the house to offer us, apart from a large bag of walnuts from her garden, and we spent the afternoon trying to crack them on hard surfaces with little success, whereas the old woman cracked hers expertly by slamming a couple of them together in the big leathery hands that are the mainstay of farming women.

Later that night over dinner, Jim said: "If you'd asked me once what I'd be doing in January 2011 in Greece it wouldn't have been sitting in a village house trying to crack walnuts on a sideboard, and being outdone by a 90-year-old woman."

We also frequented a taverna run by a sweet-natured woman called Chrisanthi (meaning Goldenflower). It had a small dining room that in the winter felt like a Greek family home with Chrisanthi's parents sitting either side of the roaring log fire warming their hands, and her son in one corner, his homework spread over a table. By the front door there was one particular table that was always the haunt of the village farmers, who sat for hours over plates of grilled meat and jugs of red wine, talking loudly about olive yields and the economic crisis. Eftihia's brother Yiorgos was there most nights and while he was a gregarious man who liked a good laugh, as the crisis deepened, he seemed more pensive, as did all the farmers, now suffering with low prices for their olive oil and increasing rural taxes.

In winter, whenever we asked Yiorgos how he was, he would first reply in English with: "Greece has no M-O-N-E-Y!", saying it with great emphasis, holding up his right hand and rubbing his fingers together. It was a comical gesture that made everyone laugh, and yet there was nothing amusing about the reality behind it. The farmers watched the news avidly every night, sometimes arguing heatedly over some new tax or the threat of more wage cuts. The other programmes that caught their attention regularly were the Turkish soaps, which are now strangely popular all over Greece and featuring, as far as I could tell, teary women dominated by shouty men and corpulent, scheming mothers-in-law, with plenty of vendettas in exotic locations.

One night I asked the farmers why they watched these programmes.

"Aren't the Turks still your enemies?"

Most shrugged majestically, trying to distance themselves from the soaps, pretending they were simply eyeball massage while they were gossiping with their buddies. Yiorgos was more forthcoming.

"You are right, Margarita," he said, twitching the ends of his moustache. "Four hundred years of Turkish domination. You'd think we'd be finished with the Turks, but now we are slaves to their crazy programmes."

Everyone laughed. But it was Chrisanthi, when she was clearing away our plates, who told us some of the village women watched these Turkish soaps all day long and were hooked. She admitted she quite liked them as well, for the similarities in their way of life and culture – a fact that many Greeks still don't admit to. These similarities are in music and food particularly, and the fact that Greek contains many Turkish words, just as Turkish has much Greek vocabulary.

When I asked Yiorgos and his friends if they would be happy therefore to have Turkey join the EU one day, his eyes flashed with quiet resentment. "We don't mind seeing them on the TV but we don't want to share a bed with them." The others laughed loudly.

Sometimes in the taverna, the farming banter would end up being rowdy and argumentative, and Chrisanthi would come rushing out of the kitchen, waving a wooden spoon, or sometimes a kitchen knife, chastising them with: "Why does everyone have to shout? The *xenoi* don't shout."

The farmers would look our way and shrug apologetically: "These are troubled times." Or they would come out with an expression that is heard everywhere in Greece, every day, and is like a mantra, delivered with a tired shrug of the shoulders: *"Ti na kanoume?"* What can we do?

I quickly learnt that this expression is indispensable in Greece, and will cover any gap in conversation and answer any mournful examination of life. And it was becoming truer by the minute. In crisis-hammered Greece, what could anybody do?

19

Paradise in freefall

ONE cold January night we arrived early at Chrisanthi's taverna and found it empty, apart from Leonidas the farmer sitting alone at a table, drinking red wine before his meal arrived. He had the healthy, tanned glow of all the olive harvesters who spent weeks in the open in the winter sun working their orchards. Leonidas had 800 trees and was legendary in the village for choosing to do the harvest the traditional way with the *katsoni* stick.

He invited us to sit with him, nodding towards two empty chairs. "I see you've both been here all winter," he said, with a smile that hinted at approval, and also curiosity. "How long will you stay now?"

"Until May," I replied.

"What will you do then? Buy some land, build a house?" That was the usual question in the village.

"We're not looking to settle here, not yet anyway. This has just been a *peripeteia* (an adventure, a break)."

He looked surprised, even though I'd told him all this when Desmond introduced us at the beginning. But most Greeks have trouble understanding foreigners who come to Greece for a long break, especially in these uncertain times.

"Will you stay longer then? Another year perhaps?"

"We don't know. We'll have to go back sometime."

"Why? If you like it here, stay," he said, with that clear-cut rural logic that we'd experienced so many times. Why not accept the obvious, is always the subtext.

He ordered wine for us and poured it into the wine glasses favoured in Greece that are squat, like small tumblers, without a stem. He also ordered some *mezedes,* appetisers: small plates of local spicy sausage, cheese pies and courgette fritters. Although Leonidas must have had a roaring appetite from all his labours that day, he ate slowly and with a certain delicacy for a farmer.

Yet he wasn't typical of local farmers. As well as his role as a church elder, he had a thoughtful reserve about him that set him apart and made him seem a bit mysterious. He was certainly very wise. The pale blue eyes (that seemed to be a feature of some of these village farmers) were more distinctive at closer quarters, even with a few rugged laughter lines. His eyes gave the impression of a man who deflected difficulties. Like the gnarled olive trees in the orchards, the sun, the rain and the mountain winds glanced straight off him. His presence always had a calming effect.

"You make staying on here sound much too easy," I said at last.

"But it can be," he said, pouring a little more wine into the glasses.

The decision to put down roots in Greece had certainly been easy for many Brits. We had met quite a few already who told us they had come to Greece on holiday for the first time ever, fell in love with the country, and at the end of the first week had put a deposit down on a house, with a view to moving out here permanently. One English couple had seen a crumbling village wreck 'with potential' on their first week and had been in such a hurry to put down a deposit on the place (without any checks or surveys), they raided their bank accounts every day, drawing out cash up to the daily limit from ATMs. This urge to buy a house at first sight is such a common occurrence all over the country it prompted one British long-term resident to remark that expats "leave their brains on the baggage carousel" when they go to Greece.

But with the Greek economy in crisis and house prices dropping, it seemed that fewer Brits were being so cavalier about buying tumbledown wrecks, or indeed any houses at all. Our estate agent friend Rochelle told us the number of inquiries from interested Brits had fallen in the past nine months and expats who already had houses in the region were beginning to sell up.

Staying longer was something that Jim and I had touched on near the end of our first wonderful summer. "What if we could have yet another summer?" we'd say while bobbing about in the water at the pristine coves of the Messinian Gulf. Yet we had no idea if we could even afford to stay longer, despite having rented out our apartment in Scotland. We had sold the Victorian house nearly two years earlier because it had become too big for the two of us, and expensive to maintain. We had been fond of the old place and had done a fair bit of work to it, but it was time to be more realistic and we downsized to an apartment as a precaution, in case of dire changes at Jim's Glasgow paper. In the end, that proved to be a good decision when his newspaper rationalised its operations and journalism entered a much tougher, shabbier era.

A year in Greece was meant to be an escape, a life-affirming adventure. But now it was slowly becoming a part of our lives and there was the nagging fear that with Britain still deep in recession, there probably wasn't any work for us to go back to.

"We might stay another year, who knows?" I told Leonidas.

"Would you stay in this village?"

"Probably."

"Or perhaps you will decide on a different village?"

He gave us a meaningful look. I couldn't decide if it was a piece of advice or a prediction.

"We love the village, and the people," I told him.

"Yes, the people are marvellous, but some have old ideas."

"What do you mean?"

He answered with an enigmatic smile. I wondered if he'd ever clashed over some of these old ideas. I remembered a story from one of the village women about Leonidas and how, when he was a young man, he was stunning, with blue eyes and fine features, and many of the village girls had lost their hearts to him. I could see that for a time, in his youth, his good looks and his gentle manner might have put the village in a spin, especially with a bevy of ambitious mothers eager to secure him as a son-in-law.

"You have to understand that we Greeks are difficult people to comprehend sometimes. We are complex. I think sometimes we don't even understand each other and the things we do, so what chance will *xenoi* have?" he said, shaking his head and smiling, showing strong even teeth. "Remember the trouble we had at the beginning with the cow bones in the bins?"

"How could I forget it?"

"That's all I am saying – old ideas, strange ideas. You mustn't fear them, but you mustn't ignore them either. If you do, you can easily lose your way."

I wasn't sure really what he was trying to tell us, or if he just feared for our apparent rootlessness in this alien land. At that point I was reminded of something Socrates had once said: "The only true wisdom is in knowing you know nothing."

@@@@@@@

Any thoughts we had of staying longer were temporarily swept away as January progressed, throwing up more challenges. By mid-January, the story I had written about Scots in the Mani was published in the Saturday magazine section of a well-respected Scottish broadsheet. I thought that was pretty much the end of the assignment. I wasn't expecting any comments from expats in the Peloponnese, as most had no idea I'd even written the piece. However, one evening a friend phoned.

"You should check out the forum on the expats' Mani website. I think you're in for a surprise."

"Why?"

"I think you've upset quite a few of the expats with your story on the Scots."

"You're kidding!"

"I think it was the headline on the story that probably did it: 'Trouble in Paradise'."

My first thought was how anyone here could have seen the piece, as it was not freely available online yet. But my heart sank over the headline. It was a cliché and didn't really reflect the story as much as the standfirst, which I hadn't written, that read: "The heat and lifestyle have made Greece a favourite among expats. But with the economy on its knees, is the dream over?" Of course, if there was one thing I'd learnt about the British expats while we'd been in Greece it was that they couldn't deal with any criticism of their way of life at all, no matter how justified.

The story had been outed by a Glaswegian who seemed to keep a tenuous link with his favourite holiday destination in the Mani by regularly reading the website forum and posting, often provocative, comments on it. He'd seen the article in the Saturday magazine and immediately alerted his forum cronies. Within hours, the forum was buzzing with anxious expats wanting to read the piece online, as it wasn't uncommon for this forum, and at least one other in southern Greece, to pick up on media stories about the region, and discuss them, or pull them to pieces. But in this case, forum members went to extraordinary lengths to read the piece, even signing up with the newspaper for its one-day trial subscription.

Within a few days of the story coming out there were more than a thousand visits on the forum thread and dozens of comments. The reaction was hysterical, often vitriolic, with many comments from a core of seemingly grumpy older men who were enjoying a Mediterranean retirement and didn't like female journalists, in particular, pouring cold water on it.

The negative reaction was mainly the result of me having had a cheeky dig at the expat enclave in Stoupa, a beachfront village popular with British holidaymakers for a few decades and now attracting British retirees and escapees. Its bars and restaurants were their regular haunts. This is the most touristy area of the Mani, and the southern Peloponnese as a whole, but it is a small, confined section of this region.

Despite some of Stoupa's tavernas offering themed nights with curries or fish and chips, I had remarked that many of the British expats there were still desperate for regular deliveries of sausages and pies and other UK 'delicacies' from a foodie supplier in the Mani. This was a well-known fact and most sensible expats at least thought it was hilarious that the sausage express rolled through the Mani once a week for these deprived Brits. Others Brits, however, were angered that I had drawn attention to their home deliveries.

I had also mentioned Megali Mantineia in the story, but as a place where "villagers and expats bump along quite well", and had even included a glowing quote from one respected taverna owner about how the village had benefited from the expats over the past 10 years. Even still, expats here were not happy that I was highlighting their haven in the sun. Some of the Brits in the village blanked us in the days and weeks after the story came out.

It made me think about what Rochelle had told us the day we looked at Desmond's house, when she was trying to put our minds at rest about the expats. "You'll hardly ever see them," she said, "so don't worry." And that was true in a way, yet the few who were more visible in Megali Mantineia made sure their Britishness was felt very keenly by expats and Greeks alike.

Even the Scots I interviewed seemed unhappy. "My friends back home will think I've been a right numpty, making a poor choice of retirement country," moaned one. Another claimed to be outraged by the headline 'Trouble in Paradise' and threatened to fire off an angry letter to the editor of the paper. Could it get any worse?

But the irony in all this was that in the year after the story was published the headline was nothing less than a tragic prediction, especially in May and June of 2011 when Greeks began a series of general strikes and violent protests in Syntagma Square in Athens against increasing austerity measures, the TV footage of which was beamed around the world. By the middle of 2011, Greece would become the most written about and vilified country in Europe. As time went by, no-one bothered much to complain about my story, or the headline.

But I guessed the petulant reaction to the piece also had something to do with the fact that while researching it, I had come across more expat secrets than was probably healthy for me to know, though it wasn't anything they hadn't told me willingly, albeit after a few jugs of local wine. In fact, the candour of some expats surprised me, though it shouldn't have because during my years as a journalist I have come to realise that most people want to talk. They want their 'fifteen minutes of fame' as Andy Warhol famously put it, whether it's talking about their unfaithful husbands, or their 'secret' breast implant operations. In the right mood, few people hold back from sharing their secret anxieties with a stranger, to the point where I often think that journalists are nothing but psychiatrists, without the couch and the outrageous salary.

Not all the expats were as touchy, however. One evening we saw Bettina and Harry in the *kafeneio* and joined them for a drink. Harry roared with laughter when I told him how upset some of the expats were about my article.

"Wankers!" he roared. "Don't worry about them. They're just a pinhead on the radar screen here, and they know it."

But Harry had happier things to talk about than expats. He told us he had received an email from his RAF contacts to say they were seriously considering his request to send the famous Red Arrows display team to town for the 70th anniversary of the Battle of Kalamata. This would be a major celebration in the region, drawing a large number of family and friends of the now-deceased veterans, and most importantly, the last three surviving veterans of the campaign.

Harry, in his mid-seventies, had been in poor health for several years and before Christmas a bout of bronchitis had taken the edge of his normally gregarious personality, but this encouraging news about the Red Arrows had given him an enormous boost.

"More than anything else, I want to see the Red Arrows flying here before I die," he said.

Bettina nudged him. "Don't be silly now, Harry, no-one's dying."

Harry and Bettina had tried more than most expats here to give something of themselves to the village, even if it all seemed slightly eccentric at times. At Christmas, in years gone by, some of the Greeks told me Harry had dressed up as Santa

Claus and went round the village giving sweets to the children. And during the carnival days in the lead-up to Lent, the couple rigged up a generator in the back of a trailer and put on a kind of travelling show for the village, with lights and music playing, again to involve the children. Villagers told me they remembered these shows with great affection.

Some of the more ambitious, though well-meaning, projects they were involved in, along with a few other expats, had backfired, however. They told us how they had tried to raise money through various events to buy a computer, which the village children could use in the now-defunct school house. But they had misjudged cultural attitudes and Greek pride, mainly because few of them spoke enough Greek. When the money was ready to be handed over to one of the village elders, this highly respected Greek, who had a reasonable command of English, appeared to be offended by the gesture.

"Do you think we cannot afford to buy our own children a computer in this village?" he said.

The money was refused and the expats were wary about embarking on any more goodwill missions. Perhaps they had failed to take account of what Leonidas had been talking about in the taverna – the old ideas.

20

Hard times, soft centres

"*YEIA sou, koritsara mou,*" hello my girl, Foteini shouted from her *ktima* gate. No sooner had she opened her mouth than I knew something didn't look right. She had a big gap in her side teeth.

"What happened to you?"

"Ach!" she said, slapping her hand on her thigh and sighing. "Binid brought me chocolates again from London and I ate a hard one and it broke two of my teeth. They weren't up to much anyway."

"Who's Binid? Do you mean Bernard?" I asked her.

She squinted for a few seconds. "Yes, Binid. That's right, isn't it?"

"Yes, why not?" I replied. The name had a certain charm.

"Anyway. The teeth have been taken out and I have to wait before I get something sorted."

"Do you have a good dentist?"

She expelled air forcibly through her lips. "She's good but expensive. I'll have to pay maybe 1,000 euros to get this fixed." I imagined that would be all Foteini's savings.

"That's terrible," I said, looking at her teeth and thinking they were quite good for a farming woman and it was heartening that she took this much interest in her appearance, as most other farmers would probably have just gone gappy to save the money, especially these days.

Teeth were very much on my mind at that time as I'd starting having niggles with my own. Maybe it was the cold weather but several of my front teeth and side teeth started to feel over-sensitive. I instinctively touched my front teeth with my tongue.

Foteini peered at them. "You've got *xena dontia* (foreign teeth), haven't you?"

"What do you mean, that they were treated outside Greece?"

"*Xena*. I mean they're not your own."

I laughed, guessing she meant they looked like false teeth, though I wasn't sure if that was actually a laughing matter or not, and no-one had ever said that before. I explained that the front ones were crowned. She came closer, her eyeballs nearly in my mouth, peering at my teeth, weighing them up from every angle going: "Hmmmm."

"Don't you like them?"

"Yes, but they're still *xena dontia*."

All this talk about teeth was making me nervous. Although I had always had regular check-ups I was phobic about the whole business of dental treatment, especially in Greece.

"Tell Binid not to bring you so many chocolates, or ask him to pay for the broken teeth," I said, jokingly, trying to end the conversation.

She made the big windmill gesture with her hand, meaning 'don't be so absolutely daft'. As it happened, I later saw Bernard in the village and told him about the chocolates and Foteini's teeth. He looked mortified.

"My God, that's appalling," he said. But he was more shocked when I told him that Foteini often gave us some of the chocolates he'd carefully brought back from London.

"I suppose that means she doesn't like them much now."

"Soft centres are the way to go," I suggested.

"She gives us things as well, you know," said Bernard, smiling. "A couple of weeks ago, we were driving past her *ktima* and she flagged us down for a chat. Then she went off and came back with a bag that looked like it came from some bakery in Kalamata with small chocolate croissants inside, slightly squashed."

"Did you eat them?"

"Of course not, darling! They could have been in her compound for weeks!"

"You're wrong. We bought them that morning in Kalamata. I remember the day perfectly. We drove past and stopped and gave her the croissants, as a treat, thinking she'd love them. Obviously she didn't like the look of them at all and tried to palm them off on you."

Bernard shrieked with laugher, and I felt quite amused myself. I started to wonder about the other things I'd given Foteini over the past nine months and what might have become of them. At Christmas I had, on the spur of the moment, decided to give her a red tartan scarf I'd brought from Scotland. It was an expensive Royal Stewart design and I'd never worn it. I knew she liked plaid shirts and thought she'd love this cosy Scottish gift.

"It's not for wearing to church of course," I said, trying to show her I knew the limitations of tartan in Greek culture. "But it will keep you warm in the *ktima* on a winter's day."

After that, I never saw her wearing it, and I alluded to the fact one day.

She squirmed a bit.

"It's the colour, Margarita. Bad things always happen when I wear red."

I stifled a smile. This was either folk nonsense, or her way of saying she hated it, this strange object from a country she couldn't even place on a map. After that I started to gaze intently at people around the village in winter trying to spot the tell-tale Royal Stewart flapping around their necks. 'A gift from Foteini'. Yet it appeared the scarf had vanished.

I had gone to the *ktima* that day mainly to take her some oranges from Desmond's trees, as these sweet oranges that ripen in winter were one of her favourite fruits. She hung the bag of oranges on a rusty nail outside the shed and went inside to make coffee. She brought it out on the usual tray beside a round loaf of wood-fired village bread, the kind that now made my teeth ache just looking at it.

Foteini sliced off a massive chunk and on this occasion, however, she pulled off the crusts and put the soft bread on a plate. She then poured green olive oil over it (from her own harvest) and I could smell its powerful fruity aroma from where I sat. Then she added a culinary twist I'd never seen before in Greece, she liberally showered the lot with sugar.

"Is that your lunch?"

"Of course," she said, surprised at the question.

I said no more. Foteini ate whatever was on hand generally, and never very much. One night before Christmas she had rung me at home. She had our number and often rang in the evening when she saw our light on from across the way, just to wish us good night and *kalo ximeroma*, good sunrise, a quaint Greek expression.

On this occasion she told me she'd just had her dinner.

"What did you have?" I asked her.

"*Yiaourti*, yoghurt."

"Is that all?" I said.

"Noooooo, of course not," she wailed, offended. "*Efaga yiaourti me meli* (I had yoghurt with honey)."

I waited until I'd hung up and fell about the house in hysterics.

At the *ktima*, as she chewed her way through the bread concoction, she asked: "Where's Dimitris today?"

"He's got a cold."

"Ah…and what's happening with Vassie?"

I told her Wallace had to wait a few more weeks for the biopsy results.

"Don't worry. The *skilos* will be all right."

"I don't know."

"Yes he will."

"Why are you so sure?"

"Dogs don't get cancer, that's all," she said very decidedly.

I knew that wasn't the case, but I preferred her take on things. When she finished her lunch, I got up to go.

"Stay. It's good to have *parea*. I'll make more coffee." She got up before I could protest, bringing another *briki* back and the freshly washed cups. She refilled our water glasses from the tap.

"Do you like living in the village, Margarita?" she asked.

"Yes, of course."

"Is it better than your *patrida*, homeland?"

"In some ways."

"How long are you here for now?"

"Til May."

"And then what?"

"I don't know yet."

"Maybe you'll stay longer? Maybe forever. Help me with the olives again. Give me more *parea*."

"I thought Greeks didn't like making plans. You've just planned the rest of our lives out."

She laughed. "It's good to have friends, Margarita."

She turned away and looked towards the road, as she always did, watching the passing cars, seeing who was driving them.

"I had a break-in here at Christmas, did I tell you? Someone climbed over the top of the fence and took away my *kazani*."

She looked towards the road in disgust. The *kazani* was the old metal cauldron she used to do all her washing, set high off the ground so a good fire could be lit underneath. Scrap metal had suddenly risen in value during the economic crisis and these kinds of thefts were becoming more common.

"Why don't you get a dog here? Put it on a chain like everyone else does?" I said, slightly ironically, as we hated the practice of keeping dogs this way. At least she would have been kind to it. She treated her animals like gold dust, especially the donkey Riko, which she would often caress and lavish with kisses and endearments. She never left the donkey alone in the *ktima* and when she rode it home every night she hid it safely near her house where no-one could see it from the road.

"Dogs cost money," she said. "There's vet bills to pay and medicines to buy. I don't have that kind of money. Not for a dog anyway. What did you pay for Vassie to have his operation?"

I told her the amount and she nearly choked on her last piece of bread.

"Where did you get Vassie, in Scotia?"

I told her how we had bought Wallace in Scotland after we arrived from Australia with my mother. That seemed to open the door to one of those Greek conversations where every relative in your family must be accounted for, their ages, their children and so forth, though in my case there wasn't much to say because I didn't have much family left to worry about.

"You know, Margarita," she said, looking serious and tapping my knuckles with her big solid hand. "You and I are very much alike."

"Alike?" I asked, thinking I'd misheard the Greek because, after all these months, I still had trouble with her dialect and had to ask her to repeat so many things.

"Yes, you and me. We don't have close family. And no children."

"But you're not alone, Foteini. You have Eftihia nearby and she looks out for you. As for me, I have Jim…Dimitris."

"Yes, of course. And God be praised for that," she said and crossed herself vigorously. "But you know what I mean, Margarita."

When we first met Foteini on the road outside, when we'd just looked at Desmond's house, I never thought we'd become friends, as we had absolutely nothing in common. And yet, despite all the obstacles, including the struggle with language, this slightly bizarre friendship had flourished. Now here we were, huddling round a plastic table in a scruffy compound, on a Greek hillside in mid-winter, contemplating the idea that we were 'alike'.

I shook my head. We weren't, of course. Yet when I looked at her strong face, the blue eyes, the generous smile, there was such warmth and humanity about this stoical woman, with all her heartbreaking struggles to survive. It touched me deeply, and unexpectedly, almost as if I was ashamed of my more comfortable, carefree existence.

I felt my eyes prickle with tears. She looked surprised. I got up, took my glass to the tap and topped it up again, taking a big gulp, and went back to my chair, trying to overcome a trembling lower lip. I sat quietly and said nothing and neither did Foteini, for a long time, twisting her big hands around in her lap, and biting on her lower lip.

Finally, she slapped her hand on her thigh, sending up a puff of dust. "Ach, it's the *skilos*, isn't it? You're upset because of him. Pah! Crying over a dog. He'll be all right. I know it."

I nodded. But it wasn't about Wallace. I wasn't sure what it was about, or whether it wasn't just an accumulation of disparate thoughts weighing me down.

"Foteini, you're not alone," I said, recovering my composure. "You have many friends in the village. You're popular, with the *xenoi* as well. There's no-one like Foteini, they say."

"Do they really?" she said, delighted, like a small child. It shifted a decade of toil from her face. "And they're right, too. When I die, there will be no-one left like me, who does everything that I have to do: the goats, the olives, the firewood, shifting everything about on the donkey. No-one does that on their own now, but me."

She said it without a trace of self-pity. For Foteini, it was a simple fact.

"You're right, Foteini. When you die, one day, many years from now, it will be the end of something unique, the end of an era. Know what I mean?"

She didn't answer, and got up suddenly from her chair.

"Come and see all my *katsikakia*, kid goats."

We went up the muddy path to the goat enclosure with its ramshackle *mandri*, the small pen in the corner, where the kids were kept. It looked like a nativity scene, with a dirt floor and an old wooden feeder filled with dried grass. She had five baby goats there, born just before Christmas, sired by the *tragos*, the handsome billy goat with big twisty horns, that she laughingly called Iraklis (Hercules).

The kids were small and sweet, different colours. She picked up a couple of them in turn and gave them a hug, as if they were puppies. Beyond the *mandri,* in the paddock that skirted the edge of the gorge, the shy goat herd stood in a nervy huddle, watching us closely, and towering over them all was gimlet-eyed Hercules – not a shy bone in his body. Foteini picked up another of the kids, a tan and white one, and kissed it extravagantly on the head, something she would never have done with a dog.

"This is Samaro, my favourite. I won't sell it on at Easter," she said, turning her head and making a kind of pretend spitting noise three times, "*Ftou, ftou, ftou*", to ward off the evil eye. Then she implored me to do the same. The belief in the evil eye, or *vaskania* (evil spells), is still strong in Greece and goes back some 2,000 years. Greeks believe that bad luck comes to you when others look at you or your possessions with envy. And by doing one of a number of things, like spitting or carrying the ubiquitous blue-eye glass charm seen everywhere in Greece, you might be spared a curse.

After we had dispensed with spells, I decided to take a photograph of Foteini with her goat as, along with my Greek dictionary, I always carried my camera with me. I took a photo of the two of them and promised to give her a copy, which I did, returning with it a few days later. She liked it so much she told me she was going to frame it and keep it in her house.

Crazy? I know, but not any crazier than Brigit with her family dog portraits on the wall, or me worrying about Wallace's health, which only increased over January, with still no word about the biopsies, weeks after they had been sent to the laboratory. It was a time when Jim and I began as wonder as well if this dream of a blithe existence in the sun wasn't just another kind of Greek myth.

21

Messing up in Messene

THE Spartans never really cracked Ancient Messene, and neither did we. This fabulous archaeological site north-west of Kalamata, spread out in a lush plain beneath Mount Ithome and Mount Eva, had once been a great city that enticed the warring and acquisitive Spartans again and again, but proved to be their nemesis. While it hadn't crushed us as sorely as the Spartans, after several assaults on it during our year in Greece, we began to feel we weren't fated to see it.

The first time we went to Ancient Messene, in the summer, we took Wallace with us because we got the impression from its tourist website that, with free entry, anyone could come and go. We also assumed there were no attendants on duty, but we should have known better. When we got there we found a small wooden building by the front gate and attendants.

"Can we take our small, well-behaved dog along?"

"No dogs," said a lemon-lipped attendant, pointing to a set of rules on a massive display board nearby, in Greek and English, that stated, among other things, that no dogs were allowed on the site, "only guide dogs". And no amount of pleading would do the trick, so we retreated to the car, slightly bemused, however, at this odd ruling.

"Why the hell would anyone with a sight problem that required a guide dog want to visit a sprawling archaeological compound like this, dodging fallen columns, ditches and cracked marble flooring?" said Jim, shaking his head. "Only a masochist would try it. For a blind person, it would be a bit like an Ancient Greek version of It's A Knockout, without the water features."

The second time we tried to get into Ancient Messene was for a free summer concert to commemorate the 85th birthday of music legend Mikis Theodorakis, to be staged in the majestic 2,400-year-old sports stadium. Our big mistake was setting out too late for the 8.30pm start. And what we hadn't reckoned on was the popularity of this man, even now, and the fact that in these days of economic cut-backs, Greeks couldn't refuse a free event. But it was one of those times when you couldn't get the measure of the situation until you were there, so we set off.

It wouldn't be Glastonbury, at any rate, with rows of portaloos, catering, and ambulances standing by for the fainters. Portaloos were very much on my mind as I am the kind of person who will want to go to the toilet mostly when there are none around. The portaloo anxiety was ramped up to the max when we finally turned off the main road towards Mavromati, the village built on the side of a hill overlooking the ancient site. We came across a tailback, snaking along a rural road for miles, with many impatient Greeks abandoning their cars in fields and farm tracks and walking into Mavromati. When we got to the village, the narrow road was choked with cars and tour buses and there was a fizz of Greeks tooting horns, arguing and manically shoulder-shrugging as if it had suddenly become an Olympic sport.

"Even if we could park here it will be hell trying to leave later," said Jim, "It will make your pee anxiety seem pissy in comparison, if you'll pardon the pun."

"I say we retreat, Jim. If the Spartans failed, so must we."

This was now our third attempt on Ancient Messene. On a cold January day, it seemed like the perfect distraction, but we had Wallace with us again because we didn't want to leave him at home, festering over his health problem. We had a plan though. We would each take a turn at minding him in the car, while the other one dashed about the site, trying to see as much as possible in half-an-hour or so. It would be like cramming for an ancient history exam. We stopped in the car park facing the site and the attendants' cabin near the front gate. We ate our packed lunch in the car, discussing who would mind Wallace first.

"It won't take long to rush around the ruins and there seem to be no other visitors about," I said.

"Yeah. Dead quiet, so maybe they'd bend the rules for once and let us take Wallace in. What d'you think?" said Jim.

"Nah. Greeks and dogs. You know the score."

"Honestly, for a nation that doesn't like rules, the Greeks sure can stick to some ridiculous ones. It's bizarre," said Jim, having a little strop.

I sighed. "What would a Spartan have done?"

"You mean apart from invading the site, killing the government attendants and setting up a Spartan garrison in the middle of the sports stadium?"

"Yes, besides all that … remember we read in our guide-book how cunning the Spartans were during their attacks on Messene. Remember one hilarious stunt where a few young Spartan soldiers infiltrated an important symposium of Messenians, dressed up as women, with knives hidden up their skirts, intent on a murderous overthrow," I said.

"Ha! Who says the warring Spartans had no sense of humour, eh?"

Jim went deadly silent then, staring hard at the entrance gate, as if mentally calculating how best to manoeuvre a military tank through it, and then eyeing up the attendants' cabin. He reached into the back of the car for the rucksack that we always took on excursions and which now had the remains of our lunch inside.

"More lunch? I haven't finished my first sandwich yet," I complained.

"Listen up. Your story about Spartans in frocks has given me an idea."

"You're not going to dress up now and have a daft half-an-hour among the columns? Where's Eddie Edit when you really need him?"

"Forget Eddie. He's got bigger fish to fry today. I've got a plan. We're going to smuggle Wallace into Ancient Messene in this," said Jim, pointing to the rucksack that was now on his knee.

"You've flipped."

"Well, it's easier than taking it in shifts to mind him. And sod them, it's a daft rule! This place has been standing for over 2,000 years. It's had worse to deal with than Wallace and his crazy handstand pees. Now here's the thing. I've been watching the cabin and there seems to be only one attendant in there and she rarely comes out. I'll have Wallace in the rucksack and we'll walk in together, but you'll go over to the cabin window and distract the woman so she doesn't get a good look at the rucksack. Ask her something, and while she's talking I'll just saunter through ahead of you. You can't see most of the site from the entrance, so once we're well inside, we can let Wallace out of the bag."

"Wouldn't it be easier if we just left him in the car for an hour, in his harness, attached to the seatbelt jack?"

"Remember when he did that Houdini thing at Kalamata Hospital, when he managed to slip out of his harness? Next he'll be hotwiring the car on his own. Anyway, it's not fair to leave him on his own. That's why we're all here together."

"Okay. But there's only one big problem: how do we get Wallace to stay quiet in the rucksack and not start barking?"

Jim thought for a minute. "It sounds a bit gross but we'll put him inside with the last chicken sandwich. Then we'll zip the bag at the top and leave him a little air hole. He'll be busy eating. You know what he's like about chicken."

Wallace always had a thing about chicken because Brigit, his kind but eccentric breeder in Edinburgh, fed all her puppies with roast chicken, which was a disaster for feeding programmes later. It explained why chicken was the only food that the fussy Wallace liked unequivocally. He was so besotted with chicken that we had broken every rule in the dog-rearing manual by using the word 'chicken' on occasions where danger loomed and every other command was flatly ignored. We would shout 'chicken' very loudly, and he'd come straight away, without fail. I turned around and looked at Wallace on the back seat. He was panting. He'd definitely heard the 'chicken' word.

"Poor Wallace hasn't even got over his operation yet. He doesn't know what the future holds for him and you want to smuggle him into an important archaeological site in a bag. It will be worse, far worse, than peeing on ancestral rugs."

"Don't worry," said Jim, soothingly, "He'll be okay in the rucksack. Remember the time we carried him in it when we were hill walking in Scotland and he hurt his paw and was limping? He was good and quiet then."

"What would they do if they caught us with Wallace?"

"Call the cops, put us in the cells for the night. Feed us two-month-old mizithra cheese and village bread."

My teeth started to ping. "Ach, let's go for it!"

If nothing else, at least we'd have a bit of a laugh. In January in Greece, you can get like that, wanting a laugh, any laugh.

"Let's try him out in the rucksack first," said Jim, unzipping it and taking things out. First we threw in a couple of Wallace's dog biscuits and lifted him inside the bag, which was roomy. He didn't like it at first but when he caught a whiff of the biscuits, he squirmed around inside to retrieve them, thinking it was a new game, better than hiding biscuits in shoes.

I wasn't totally convinced, but Jim seemed confident and I guessed it was a bit of a boy thing, and probably because he'd finally given up the chic-lit and was reading espionage novels now.

"Okay. Get ready to leave now. Get all your stuff. As soon as we unwrap the chicken sandwich and drop it in we've only got a few minutes or so to get through the gate and on our way," he said, checking his watch at the same time, as if this was a finely tuned military raid.

We got out of the car and locked it. Jim put on the rucksack with Wallace in it and I dropped in the chicken sandwich, torn into several pieces, which was the messiest part of the plan, and zipped up the bag, leaving the air hole. The minute the sandwich hit the bottom, Wallace was down there like a deep-sea diver and the bag was wriggling like mad, then all went quiet. I could almost hear his lip-smacking enjoyment over the chicken. We walked quickly through the main gate, Jim stood to one side while I went to the small cabin window. I remembered the attendant from the first time we came here, but assumed she wouldn't recognise me after a summer of foreign visitors. I asked her what time the site closed.

"Are you together?" the woman said, pointing to Jim.

"Yes?"

She looked at him with narrowed eyes. "Can I ask what's in the rucksack the man is carrying?"

"Just lunch things," I said in a nervous, squeaky voice. I glanced at the rucksack and thought I saw the edge of it was wriggling. Maybe she saw it as well.

Jim sensed the hitch, aware that Wallace was growing restless, eager for another chicken soother, so he started walking down the dirt track that led between broken columns and the outlines of ancient buildings.

"My husband's impatient...big archaeology fan. Been reading all about Ancient Mess..."

"Okay," she said, cutting me off. "But you must be back by 3.30 when the site closes."

I turned and legged it down the track, smiling to myself. When I caught up with Jim I could hear Wallace starting to whine and the zip was coming further apart at the top as he tried to get his snout into the cool air. Jim walked faster. The site sloped down to an old amphitheatre and from there it was a short walk to a cluster of olive trees. Once there we were safe, out of sight of the entrance cabin. We let Wallace out of the bag and did a few high-fives.

"It worked," said Jim, smiling triumphantly. "Wallace conquers Ancient Messene."

On this site in the 10th century BC, a settlement was founded by Queen Messene, daughter of King Triopas of Argos (the Greek city, not the shopping chain), who built the Altar of Zeus on nearby Mt Ithome. The area has also been described as the stomping ground of Dionysus, son of Zeus. The bad boy of Greek mythology, Dionysus was the god of wine but has variously been described as the god of cross-dressing, luvvies, orgies and hangovers.

By the 8th century BC, when Messene had become a significant city, the Spartans began to cast their eyes over it for a possible conquest and this was to be the start of three major wars between the Spartans and the Ancient Messenians that eventually the latter won with the help of Athenian troops. The city of Messene was rebuilt on a grander scale in 369 BC by Epaminondas of Thebes and it was surrounded by five miles of thick perimeter walls, with watchtowers, parts of which are still standing today. And to make up for lost time with the Spartans, the Messenians went mad with their building programme, erecting temples, theatres, and a sports stadium and gymnasium to stage games in honour of Zeus. The city continued to flourish until the Goths overran it in 395AD and it lost all prominence in Greece, finally falling into ruin, buried under olive orchards.

Excavations began on the site in 1897, but many of its sacred buildings were only uncovered from 1986 onwards by revered archaeologist Petros Themelis. Only recently had a fence and entrance gate been added. Our vet Angelos, with a keen interest also in archaeology, told us that before the fence went up it was possible to drive around the site, which Kalamatans regularly did for sport, in old bangers, stopping to pick up bits of scattered antiquities along the way. The idea of mad Greek drivers navigating around ancient columns probably explains why so few of them are still standing.

We strolled through the ruins with the help of a Peloponnesian guidebook, navigating around sanctuaries, assembly rooms, and the imposing large Asklepion, dedicated to Asklepios, the God of Healing which, like most of the buildings, was now mostly floors and broken columns. In the west wing of the Asklepion, in the atmospheric 'cult room' dedicated to Artemis Orthia, we propped Wallace up on the stone slab where once a statue to the great goddess Artemis stood and took his photograph.

"Perhaps Asklepios and Artemis will cast a bit of magic Wallace's way," I said.

"Now don't start thinking about biopsies again. You're not to...."

"Shh! There's someone moving around over there among the olive trees."

Opposite the Asklepion ruins I thought I'd seen a figure dressed in black hovering behind a tree.

Jim turned. "I can't see anyone."

"Let's move on."

So we continued past the Bouleuterion assembly rooms, where the councillors of the independent Messenian cities once gathered. We passed the Hellenistic baths, where the charge for a soothing dip in this tiled sanctuary was the equivalent of a penny. At the Sanctuary of Demeter, again I had the sensation of someone following us, a brief flash of black, a rustling behind trees. When I turned round, again there was no-one there. It was early afternoon by now and we had an hour-and-a-half to go before the site closed, so we went quickly to the grand sports stadium, at the farthest end of the site, where the Theodorakis concert had been held in the summer.

The sports stadium has an impressive colonnade along the top level with over 100 re-erected columns. The restored stone seating below is set in a sweeping horseshoe shape, with some fancy seats like thrones on one side, designed for ancient celebrity guests. We sat on them, gazing out across the expanse of this near-perfect stadium with its arena and a backdrop of hills. The serenity was sublime, but not for long.

"I think I'll go down and test the acoustics," said Jim, perhaps inspired by the Dionysus connection here and the fact that he was also the god of theatre and acting daft.

Jim leapt down on to the arena and stood in the middle where, after a few false starts, he managed to recite a murderous chunk of Macbeth, though I thought that a little something from Sophocles might have been more fitting. The words rolled out across the stadium, loud and menacing. Wallace moaned on the end of his lead, eager to join in the theatrics, but I held him back. I couldn't afford to have Wallace sprinting around the arena like some ancient wannabe going for gold, though he'd probably earned it having suffered the indignity of riding pillion with a chicken sandwich.

While Jim was toying with imaginary daggers, I thought I heard a crackling sound and when I turned around I saw it again, the dark figure. This time it was standing confidently on the top tier of the stadium, silhouetted against the grey sky and the stone columns. It was a man in black, yammering into a walkie-talkie. Jim cut his performance and walked back to the thrones with a grim face. The man sprinted quickly towards us. He was wearing a black puffer jacket and woollen hat, pulled down over his forehead. He looked furious.

"You don't bring dogs here. It is forbidden. You have broken rules," he said in halting English.

We apologised profusely. "He's only small. He hasn't done any harm," I said.

"The dogs are bad for the marbles," he said.

I assumed he meant if they urinated on them.

"Our dog has respected your marbles. Don't worry," I said facetiously.

"How do I know?" he said.

"You've been following us the whole time."

"I want to see what activities you are doing."

He looked at Jim now. "I heard the talking down there. Are you actor?"

"No," said Jim.

"I did not think so."

"Ouch, that hurt," said Jim, screwing up his face.

"You bring the dog in that?" said the guard, pointing his walkie-talkie to the rucksack. We nodded.

"Stavroula at the gate, she called me, told me you have something in your rucksack, something living..."

Jim and I looked at each other and starting giggling, as it all seemed a bit absurd now.

"You think breaking rules is funny?" he said, moving over to the rucksack and pulling it open to peer inside. Maybe he thought we were also stealing artefacts as well, but all he got was the aroma of dog and chicken. "You crazy people...and your dog. You must go now. I don't make trouble this time. Don't do again."

Was he kidding? Getting a Jack Russell to sit quietly in a rucksack once was lucky, twice would be Guinness Book of Records stuff.

"We're very sorry."

"Okay, okay. I get that. You go now."

He strode away quickly along one of the tiers of seating, talking loudly into his walkie-talkie.

"We nearly pulled it off. At least he didn't threaten us with the cops," said Jim.

"We've got to get past Stavroula yet. And incidentally, now I think of it, how did you think we'd get Wallace past the gate again with nothing to keep him quiet in the rucksack this time?"

"Ah, I had a great plan for that as well..."

"I don't want to hear it...we've overdosed on crazy this afternoon."

It was getting darker, with the threat of rain. We walked silently past the temples, sanctuaries, baths, the Asklepeion. Everything looked a bit sinister and cold now, with no sense of lives gloriously played out here, no hint of triumph. Only the wind had a presence, twirling leaves around empty spaces. I was in no mood for an altercation with Stavroula.

When we got back to the entrance gate, with Wallace on his lead, she shot out of the cabin, her hands on her hips, looking fierce.

"I knew you had something in the bag. And I remember you from the summer. You came here with the dog before. I told you then, no dogs allowed." She inched forward as she spoke. "You did not listen and ..."

Wallace had had enough of this Messene mess-up. He went mad, letting off a round of screamy barking. He was straining on his lead and we couldn't get him to shut up, but Stavroula was intent on finishing her lecture, shouting over the noise.

When Wallace wouldn't be quiet there was only one thing left to try. "Chicken, CHICKEN!" I yelled, and Wallace finally gave up, sniffing the air for sandwiches.

Stavroula gave up, too, and marched back into the cabin. We legged it out of Ancient Messene and threw ourselves, exhausted, into the car.

"Well, that all went down well in the end," said Jim, starting the car and looking a little imperious. "Many have come to Ancient Messene but few have triumphed like the small white dog, Margarita."

"I don't know about triumph, Jim, but the Spartans would see the irony, I'm sure. And Dionysus, too."

ᘒᘒᘒᘒᘒᘒᘒ

The end of January gave us many more bitterly cold days, the snow sticking resolutely to the highest peaks of the Taygetos mountains. Yet on the odd days when the sun was shining and there were no clouds in the sky, it was possible to sit outside at midday for an hour or so.

On one of these days, near the end of January, I was sitting in a chair in the middle of the courtyard, enjoying the sun, and reading, when Jim came outside with Wallace in his arms. He stood in front of me, looking very serious indeed.

"What's wrong? Is it news about Wallace? Tell me."

"The small white dog lives!" he said, his green eyes suddenly crinkling with mirth. "The vet has just called. Good news, the biopsies were fine. No cancer."

I leapt out of my chair, screamed and exchanged a few high fives with both of them and then danced around the courtyard, Wallace following me, performing a series of Masai warrior jumps. I didn't see Pericles at first until I stopped dancing. He was standing up on the road, leaning on his stick, like he had the first day we moved in, staring down at us with a slight smirk on his face.

"Don't rush around too much. Remember those bombs." Then he walked on down the road without another word. I looked at Jim and laughed.

"We're in the Mani, living with wild men, women and critters, and there are expats in the undergrowth who will commit mayhem if they can't get a pork pie and mash. Why do we care about bombs? And by the way, what else did Angelos say?" I said.

Angelos had told Jim the lumps that were removed were benign and that the cell changes and the thickening of the skin were probably caused by a previous skin infection of some kind that had gone unnoticed. But there was no reason to think any other lumps would appear.

"See. I told you everything would be fine. This wee guy's got plenty of petrol left in his tank," said Jim.

We stayed out in the courtyard playing ball with Wallace, who seemed unusually energetic and did a few dozen more Masai leaps in the air. Of all Wallace's crazy behaviour, I loved the spirited leaps best of all, when they were done purely for the hell of it, like now. They were his way of celebrating his own life force to the max, and it was a joy to watch. But just when we seemed to be turning a corner, something happened in the village to change the mood entirely.

22

No weddings, one funeral

THE phone rang late one night, early in February. It was Desmond, telling us he'd heard Harry had died suddenly, early that morning, after spending a few days in hospital. We were shocked. I instantly recalled Harry's words in the *kafeneio*, that he wanted to see the Red Arrows flying over Kalamata before he died, and now his dream would never come true.

"Unfortunately, Harry's death wasn't so unexpected," said Desmond. "He'd not been well for a few years and his doctor warned him to take things easy and not drink too much, but Harry was the kind of guy who liked to live life to the full. Hard to argue against that."

The funeral was to be held a few days later and several of the Greek women, after hearing of Harry's death, had gone up to the yurt on the morning he died with some provisions for Bettina and to sit with her for a few hours, as is the custom with deaths in villages. Harry's death, the first expat death in Megali Mantineia, had saddened the Greeks as much as anyone, as most of them remembered the warm-hearted gestures the couple had made in the village.

Yet Harry and Bettina had very much lived in the moment and hadn't made any real plans for what would happen if one of them died in Greece, and while some of their children were on the way from Britain, it was touching the way the Greeks took control of matters and sorted out the difficult problem of burial, securing a place for Harry in the nearby cemetery, where the villagers' families had long been buried, even though he wasn't Greek Orthodox. This was a huge gesture of friendship on their part.

The funeral was a small family affair, with a simple burial and grave in the corner of the cemetery, but Bettina had invited everyone in the village up to the yurt later for a wake, or a 'party' as she described it to expats and Greeks alike.

"That's what Harry wanted. He wanted a party with everyone there and music and singing. And I want to abide by his wishes," she said.

While the Greeks were invited, few of them went, as the idea of a 'death party' is alien to the Greek Orthodox religion, where people go into a protracted grieving process after someone dies. As wakes go, it was quite the strangest one I'd ever been to, with expats from all over the Messinian region crammed into a huge American-style yurt, like a circus tent, but charming in its way with hard flooring and windows with views. The smaller Mongolian version served as the bedroom.

The wake had started out predictably enough, with plates of food spread out on the dining room table, a row of boxed local wine on one end of it and expats walking around the circular room, a glass of wine in hand, looking ashen-faced, some of them giving vent to their own anxieties about growing old in a foreign country and, worse, dying in it as well. At least one couple at the wake, who weren't in the rudest of health, already had their house in Megali Mantineia on the market and were now more eager than ever to sell up and go.

The few Greeks who did eventually turn up at the wake, mainly from Kalamata, were unsettled by the atmosphere as well. I had spent some time talking with a well-educated, middle-aged woman called Sofia, who had known Harry and Bettina for several years and had come to show her respects, even though she admitted she had often been mystified by their strange lifestyle, not to mention the custom of the wake.

While we were talking she was interrupted by one of the Greek youngsters from the village. He was a rather sweet but nervous 13-year-old who had been fond of Harry and had cycled up the hill now to see Bettina, but once he got to the yurt it was clear he was out of his depth with this British tradition and he seemed to have something on his mind. When he realised Sofia was Greek, he made straight for her and after a rapid burst of conversation, he rushed out the door again and cycled back to the village.

When I asked her what it was all about she said the boy had been to the graveside and was upset by our different burial methods, somewhat basic compared to the austere marble tombs of the Orthodox Greeks.

"I just explained to him that foreigners have different customs when it comes to death," she said.

I winced slightly when Sofia said that, aware of how British expats must sometimes appear to Greeks, with their casual and often hedonistic lifestyle, and their poor interest in religion. It was a cultural difference that would never be resolved and something that Harry would never have obsessed over.

At least Bettina seemed composed. "Do you think you'll feel like staying on here, alone?" I asked her, like so many other expats had that day.

"What else should I do?" she said with a shrug. "I love it here, and Harry did as well. He would want me to continue on. And I'll be busy in the coming months dealing with the organisers of the Red Arrows display."

"Is it really going ahead?" I asked her.

"Haven't you heard? The day before Harry died, he received an email from the British Defence Attaché in Athens to tell him the Red Arrows flypast, and a naval presence, had been approved finally. You can't imagine how thrilled he was, knowing he would get his final wish," she said.

I was heartened by the news and admired Bettina's spirit. Despite the couple's unconventional and slightly chaotic life, on what they loosely termed an ecological site, with only a generator which often broke down, Bettina and Harry's story had been inspiring. How that story might look in future years, I couldn't tell.

Later in the evening, when the few Greeks had left, the party shifted up a gear with music and singing – or down a gear, depending on your point of view with wakes. One 70-year-old expat with a late-life interest in drumming brought along a small drum set and a former teacher living in the village brought her guitar and sang. There were tearful moments when the pair performed *Summertime*, which was apparently Harry's favourite song. But things went down the slidey slope after that with tight-throated versions of *Let It Be* and *There are Nine Million Bicycles in Beijing*. It began to feel like that scene in *Four Weddings and a Funeral*, where one wedding features a couple doing a retro-folk music routine in church, with actor Simon Callow pretending to be sick.

After several hours, with the torment of death on foreign soil winging around our heads, I started to feel ill myself, or at least melancholy. I went to get a glass of water from the kitchen, which was a small stone block separate from the yurts and filled incongruously with nice old French furniture. I found Nigel there, the organiser of expat lunches in the village. He was standing alone near the sink, pulling the ring-top off a can of beer. As soon as he saw me he gave me a withering look. I filled a glass of water from the tap and turned quickly to go. But not quick enough.

"I read your story about Scots in the Mani. I didn't like your bitchy comments about Brits wanting their British food."

"I wasn't having a go at you, Nigel, or your lunches. I was talking about the expats in Stoupa – you know that."

"I've got a lot of friends in Stoupa," he said, taking a swig of beer. "Do you know what people are saying about you down there?"

"No, what would that be?"

"That you are the most dangerous woman in the Mani."

I stared at him, stunned. He was joking, surely. But in his eyes there was scant amusement.

"Really?" I said.

"Yes, really."

Rather than being annoyed I was actually quite chuffed with the description. As a small, slight woman with curly hair, I have always sought to be more assertive, and here I was being described as a lethal minx. Wonderful!

"Why am I dangerous then, Nigel? Just because I've spilt a few beans about the expat lifestyle? Are people in Stoupa so thin-skinned?"

He was quiet for a moment, sipping his beer, and I made my way to the door, not eager for an argument with Nigel, at a wake of all places. He didn't want to let the matter drop, however.

"You two have come here for the year to write horrible things about expats for British papers."

"That's not true, Nigel, not at all. We came for an adventure basically, but we've never hidden the fact that we'd also write stories about the Mani. We write about what we experience, that's all."

He gave me a harsh look, lobbed the beer can into a waste bin and left. Jim came in a moment later, just as Nigel was striding back to the yurt.

"Everything okay here?" he said.

"Yes, fine."

I decided to tell him later about my chat with Nigel. Jim is a mild-manned guy, a complete gentleman, but I feared he might take umbrage over it, with so much heightened emotion in the yurt that evening and after all the boozing.

"Come on," he said, "Let's get out of here. This whole thing is doing my head in."

"I wonder what poor Harry would have made of it all, eh?" I said, washing up my water glass and looking round the rustic kitchen a moment, with its stone walls covered in old photos and other memorabilia from the couple's long, peripatetic life.

"Harry would have laughed. He'd have swigged another jug of wine and said, 'Wankers, the lot of them!'"

We said goodnight to Bettina and walked down the dirt road towards the village. It was dark, with only a few twinkling stars to guide our way, as we'd forgotten to bring a torch. Half way down, we jumped out of our skins when a small black mule, tied to a tree on a long rope, suddenly appeared beside us, braying loudly in our ears and all the chained dogs in the vicinity started barking. It was a mournful sound like a Greek chorus.

"Nothing is ever really normal here, is it? Or predictable. Not to us anyway," I said, still feeling slightly stunned over my exchange with Nigel in Bettina's kitchen.

@@@@@@@

After weeks of bitter weather, there was finally some intimation of spring at the beginning of March. The sweet-scented almond trees in Desmond's garden began to bloom, and Greeks say this is the first sure sign that summer is around the corner.

There is a popular poem by one of the country's greatest modern poets, George Seferis, called *Ligo Akoma* (A Little Further), that draws together, with a just a few lines, two ideas: the awakening of spring, and the indomitable spirit of Greece. Never did the poem, so perfectly translated by Edmund Keeley and Philip Sherrard, seem more pertinent as now.

"A little further
We will see the almond trees blossoming
The marble gleaming in the sun
The sea breaking into waves

A little further,
Let us rise a little higher."

The first leaf buds were also beginning to sprout along the skinny branches of the mulberry trees, the ones that Leonidas had so expertly pruned in the autumn. There were wild orchids, irises and poppies on the hillsides, and the wild leafy greens called *horta* began to appear everywhere. This endless variety of greens may comprise wild asparagus, dandelion, dill, oregano and fennel. They are gathered, boiled, doused in olive oil and lemon to produce astonishing sweet and tangy flavours, a dish that will be made again and again throughout the long Lenten period of Greek Easter. And all the farmers now had agile spring lambs and kid goats in their enclosures.

With Easter just around the corner, we started to think again about the year ahead. The idea of returning to Scotland in May, when the weather is often no better than early winter in Greece, didn't appeal to us. The more we considered our future, the more desperate we were to stay in Greece, especially since the first year had gone so fast. But money was the main issue. We hadn't had as many journalistic commissions as we hoped, partly because we had been distracted by the hot summer months and also because many publications were refusing to have stories with a Greek theme.

It was as if Greece was suddenly a dirty word, and the country was to blame for all the trouble it found itself in. In some respects it was, but the focus had not yet intensified on the greedy European banks who had rushed in to offer the country loans in the past decade that they knew Greece could never repay, signing it up for fiscal dependency and misery, like drug pushers turning novices into hard-core junkies.

"If we're going to stay, we need to generate a lot more income from journalism, or else hope that Desmond's mulberry trees will suddenly sprout money," said Jim.

"We don't have to renew the lease until mid-April. Surely something will turn up by then?" I said, not quite believing it would.

But fate did intervene, with an unexpected piece of news given to us through a journalistic contact that an upmarket British travel company was beginning operations in the summer of 2011 in the southern Peloponnese and that they were looking for staff here. It seemed like a bold move, setting up a new operation in Greece in the middle of a crisis, when tourism numbers were generally down on previous years and there were regular threats of industrial action.

After so many years working in journalism, it was Jim who liked the idea of trying something different and contacted the company's head office in London. The firm was looking for just one person who could help to oversee the operation and produce information packs for each of the company's stylish villas in the southern Peloponnese. It seemed an ideal job for a someone with journalistic skills and Jim hastily applied. He was told the company would make its decision in early April.

"If I get the job we can just about afford to stay another year," he said.

We were now in the lap of the gods.

23

Aphrodite's miracle
and a day of revolution

WE heard the tinkling of the bell before we saw him. Then the bicycle swished past us, the wheels crunching over the dirt road. He turned around and smiled, mostly at Wallace, trotting along beside us on his lead. The boy had an angelic face, big hazel eyes and light brown hair. He could only have been about eight or nine, dressed in shorts, T-shirt, sandals, but wearing a cream-coloured woollen scarf around his neck against the slightly colder air of the mountains. He roared ahead up to a bend in the road and came cycling back towards us.

"Are you looking for a church?" he asked.

"How did you know that?" I replied.

"Everyone is looking for it," he said.

I thought he was being precocious – the search for religion in a wider sense. We were looking for a specific church that we'd seen signposted in the square when we parked the car in this small village, hugging the north-west edge of the Taygetos mountains, with a clear view over the whole of Kalamata city below.

We had woken up to a warm spring day and having resolved to see as much of the region as we could, in case we had to leave after the first year, we set off towards the mountains, one of our favourite haunts. Perivolakia (meaning orchards) is one of a cluster of villages on this part of the mountains and has a charming, authentic feel about it. Its central square has a natural spring overhung with giant plane trees.

We set off in search of the church of Agios Yiannis, the signposts indicating it was along a ridge above the village, which is where we were walking when the boy rode past.

"Do you want to see the church of Agios Savvas? It's much closer than the other?" he said.

"All right, but shouldn't you tell your family first?" I said, thinking how novel this situation was and that if we were in Britain an eight-year-old innocent wouldn't be cycling off to a remote church with strangers.

"It's okay. My grandmother will have seen you passing the house. She knows," was all he said.

Knows what? I thought. So we followed this engaging little boy as he powered ahead of us towards the bend in the road again, the ends of his scarf flying out. Then he returned and repeated this manoeuvre several times, seeming to be a very restless soul. Finally we arrived at a very small church. He left his bike on the road and led us to the unlocked church door. The church was fairly new, whitewashed on the outside, with a pretty blue dome. There was enough room inside for perhaps a dozen people to stand comfortably. On a tall wooden stand near the *iconostasis* was the icon of a kindly old saint dressed in a black robe with a ceremonial stove-pipe hat. He was grey-bearded and hugging a red and gold Bible closely to his chest.

"That's Agios Savvas," the boy said with an appreciative smile.

In the huge panoply of Greek saints, Agios Savvas was very new to us and there was nothing much to glean about him here. The boy waited by the door as we investigated the other icons placed around the walls. He was remarkably patient for so small a boy and as we left the church I remarked: "It's a lovely church, but why did you bring us to this one in particular? Is it your favourite?"

"It's *our* church. My family built it for a special reason," he said, in a matter-of-fact kind of way. Jim and I looked at each other in surprise.

"Can you tell us what reason is?" I asked him.

He shut his eyes a moment, arching his brows, the way Greeks do when they don't want to comment, and led us back outside, shutting the door. He cycled back towards the village, ringing his bell over and over, joyously, as if a significant task had just been accomplished. Our curiosity had gone up a gear and we sprinted behind him until he stopped at a neat white house with a vertiginous view from its side courtyard down the mountainside. By the time we reached him a woman had come out of the house as if she had been expecting us.

"Have you been to Agios Savvas?" she asked.

We told her about our chance encounter with the boy.

"This is my grandson Nikitas, and my name is Aphrodite. Would you like to come in for a coffee?"

It was hard not to under the circumstances and gratifying to find this sudden show of the *filoxenia*, hospitality, that Greece was once famous for but which has dwindled largely, even in rural areas. We thanked her and followed her into the courtyard, where a table was placed in warm spring sunshine. We tied Wallace to a side railing and hoped he'd behave himself. Nikitas hovered near him several times but seemed too wary to strike up a friendship, yet instead of Wallace barking or growling as he usually does, he just kept a keen eye on the boy. Wallace and children never really mix. Wallace seems to perceive children, especially very lively ones, as a threat to his precious territory.

Aphrodite served us Greek coffee and an old woman dressed in black, wearing a stout cardigan, appeared in the courtyard and took up a position at the far end, in the shade, where she sat soundlessly toiling over a piece of embroidery. I took this woman to be Aphrodite's mother, as they both had fair skin for Greeks, fine features and large, pale brown eyes. The thing that struck me most about Aphrodite from the beginning was how composed she was. She radiated a sense of inner calm that was almost palpable.

"So you weren't looking for our little church of Agios Savvas especially?"

"Not at all."

"It's just that most people who come to this part of the village are, for very particular reasons."

I told her we had never heard of Agios Savvas and explained that we were exploring Mani villages as part of our year's adventure.

"Your grandson says the church belongs to your family," I remarked.

"Yes it does. We built it a few years ago. We experienced something very extraordinary in this family, a miracle, you could say. Since you are journalists, would you like to hear the story?"

"Of course."

A journalist thrives on those words, 'would you like to hear the story?', but from a purely personal standpoint, I have a soft spot for miracles. Before she began the tale she went into the house and brought back a framed photograph of a lovely young woman with a sweet smile and thick black curly hair tumbling around her shoulders.

"My daughter Melina. The name comes from the word *meli*, honey, and it suits her character very well." She propped the

235

photo up on the table facing us, as if to set the scene. Then she told us her curious tale.

Several years earlier, when Melina was still a young woman, she was diagnosed with a virulent type of breast cancer and had three operations in the well-known Saint Savvas Anti-Cancer Hospital in Athens. Despite the excellent treatment in this highly regarded hospital, Melina's cancer specialist took Aphrodite aside after the last operation and told her the cancer couldn't be completely eradicated and the prognosis was grim. Aphrodite had been staying in her daughter's room to look after her needs, which is common in Greek hospitals, where nursing is not routinely part of the treatment. Although other family members came and went, Aphrodite stayed beside her daughter night and day, distraught, with no comfort apart from prayer.

On the wall of the hospital room was an icon of Agios Savvas, to whom the hospital was dedicated because of his ascetic life and alleged healing gifts. The icon was the same avuncular depiction of the saint that we had seen in the little church. Aphrodite prayed repeatedly, pleading for her daughter to be healed.

"One night while Melina was asleep, I suddenly had a vision of Agios Savvas telling me not to worry and that Melina would be all right. I don't know what the vision was, only that it was as if the saint had stepped out of the icon on the wall and stood before me, like a real person, and it's hard to describe how extraordinary that felt. I spoke to him. I said if he would be gracious enough to cure my daughter of cancer, I would build a church in our village to honour him and invite pilgrims to come and pray there."

After this night, Aphrodite said she strongly believed her daughter would survive and sure enough some days later, before Melina was due to be discharged from hospital, she was given another scan and her specialist was astonished to find that Melina appeared to be cancer-free, though there was no possible explanation for it.

"We were overjoyed and there was a lot of dancing and singing in the hospital ward in the days before we left," said Aphrodite. "The other patients were caught up in the euphoria of this miracle and longing for their own reprieve."

In the following months, Aphrodite and her son, who runs a taverna in the village, raised money to build the small church, with support from the village, and the church is now a local landmark. The family holds a service here every December on the feast day of Agios Savvas, to honour him and give thanks for Melina's recovery and her continuing good health. Melina has been cancer-free in the years following her third operation and she is now married with children of her own.

Agios Savvas was born in the coastal region of Palestine in 439AD. Even as a child he developed a keen interest in the early Christian teachings and entered his first monastery at the age of eight. After many years in several monasteries in Palestine he sought a more ascetic existence and lived in a cave-like cell in the Kidron Gorge, in the desert, near Jerusalem. The hermitage he eventually founded here later developed into the monastery of the Holy Lavra of St Savvas in 478. A man of intense spirituality, Agios Savvas performed many miracles and acts of healing, which accounts for his popularity as a saint, even today.

The time went quickly as Aphrodite recounted her heart-warming story. When we got up to leave, the old lady finally stirred, having sat quietly for over an hour with her needle-work. It was as if she enjoyed being fixed to the sidelines of this miraculous tale, happy to hear it told over and over again.

There was no sign of Nikitas when we said goodbye to Aphrodite at her front gate.

"He'll be out somewhere on his bike. Nikitas feels shy talking to other people about my daughter and what happened, but he's devoted to the church. When people come to the village to see it, he likes to take them there."

We didn't see Nikitas anywhere as we walked back to the car but I had a strong picture in my mind of him racing along on his bike, his scarf ends flying out like wings. I had the fanciful notion that he wasn't a real boy after all but a tiny winged Hermes, the Olympian god of travellers, hospitality, persuasion, and messenger of Zeus, spiriting lost and sick souls to the church of Agios Savvas.

Greece is a country rich in miracles. Hundreds of icons of the *Panayia* all around Greece are said to have miraculous powers, like the icon in Kalamata Cathedral. The mountainous area west of Kalamata has had more than its share of miracles. A short drive from Perivolakia, further back in the mountains, is the remote monastery of Dimiova. It has a famous icon of the *Panayia Dimiovitissa*, also said to have miraculous powers. On the right cheek of the *Panayia* is a mysterious stain dating from the 8th century AD during the struggles of the Iconoclastic period of Greek history, when many icons were defaced or burnt. This icon was also attacked. The face of the *Panayia* was struck with a knife and it was said the gash then oozed with her blood. The stain has remained on the icon ever since.

I later met a local priest, Papa Sotiris, who told me there were many stories of miracles in the villages close to Dimiova. "Everyone has their own special story," he said. But sometimes the miracles have engulfed the whole district. He told me that a few years back when a long, severe drought had devastated crops and livestock, the villagers, in desperation, went to

Dimiova to pray to the *Panayia*. Not long afterwards, it rained heavily for many days.

Miracles or not, one of the great joys of living in Greece was that on every excursion we ever made, we came across fascinating warm-hearted characters, happy to share their food, their time, but most of all their stories.

@@@@@@@@

The greatest story for the southern Peloponnese region, however, is the victory of the Mani freedom fighters who trounced the occupying Ottoman Turks in Kalamata, on March 23, 1821, thus sparking the Greek War of Independence that would rage throughout Greece for the next 11 years.

The Kalamatan offensive was hatched by Messinian-born legend Theodoros Kolokotronis and several clan chiefs from the Mani, including Mourtzinos Troupakis from Kardamili, who formed themselves into a revolutionary army, along with 2,000 Maniot recruits. They began their assault in the square in the old sector of Kalamata, now called March 23rd Square, and where a gutsy re-enactment of this takes place every year. It is street theatre on a grand scale.

The day we joined in the celebrations, the city was frothing with men and boys dressed in traditional *foustaneles* (white pleated kilts) and embroidered waistcoats, and their sturdy black shoes with pom-poms tap-tapped along the pavements. The Bishop of Kalamata, Chrisostomos (Goldenmouth), and a phalanx of black-robed priests descended from the cathedral to the square for a short inaugural service and the celebrations began: the marching of men in *foustaneles*, representing the Maniot revolutionaries, followed by lines of jittery school children, and young women in big skirts and elaborate headscarves.

A scaled-down battle was re-enacted and loudspeakers relayed deafening canon and rifle fire; the sound of men shot and dying; horses squealing; and finally rousing shouts of victory.

And the finale was a spirited cavalcade of war leaders, ghosts from the past, a clutch of antique pistols in their waistbands, charging on horseback through the city streets, watched by hundreds of Kalamatans waving blue and white flags. It was Kolokotronis, however, who had the starring role, wearing his distinctive red helmet. More than a historic hero, the Kalamatan pensioner who plays him every year is a local hero as well, having made this role his own for decades, as long as any Kalamatan can remember, with no signs of him reining back.

Kalamata is a laid-back city, with a chic strip of cafes and tavernas along the beachfront on popular Navarino Street, and a bustling marina. It is a city with great camaraderie, perhaps because of its small population (around 60,000). Kalamatans have shared many hardships, particularly during the Second World War and the Battle of Kalamata in 1941. But most recently, the 1986 earthquake devastated much of the city, most tragically the broad boulevards of stately homes and government buildings erected in the late 19th century, when Kalamata became a major trade centre for southern Greece and was described as the Marseilles of the Morea (the old name for the Mani).

Many of these buildings had to be pulled down after the earthquake and were replaced by the ubiquitous apartment blocks that characterise this city now, though it is still possible to find a few decaying mansion houses here and there with once-elegant wrought-iron balconies and overgrown court-yards, battling on like toothless crones.

Kalamata is the main business centre for this southern region and a cultural hub, with summer music concerts and an international dance festival. It also has all the major health and medical facilities. It was for this reason that I spent many days in March scouring the city streets, looking for a dentist. It was the one thing I had probably feared most during our adventure – dental drama.

@@@@@@@@

I had developed a strange sensitivity in my front teeth during the winter that had steadily got worse. Not quite a toothache, but something I was constantly aware of and I feared it was something I should check out sooner rather than later. But we didn't have a dentist and had no idea who to call on.

Kalamata has many highly qualified health professionals, most of whom work out of surgeries in the apartment buildings that line the main streets. They often have old-fashioned signs on the side of their buildings. With dentists, it is a drawing of a giant tooth, and I seemed to see these giant teeth everywhere I looked. Was it possible there were so many dentists here? In Greece, people tend to see professionals only by personal recommendation. That's the way it has always been done.

I started asking the expats for the name of a good dentist, but the more I queried them the worse my prospects seemed, as many long-term expats at least had teeth like mountain hillbillies. And some Greek recommendations were also to be feared. In late summer, Angeliki at the Good Heart *kafeneio* had recommended a dentist to an Englishwoman who had cracked a back tooth. The woman, called Florence, was building a house in the village and had come out for a month to check things over. It was during the second week that she had her dental mishap and was anxious to get someone to look at it.

Florence saw me chatting one day with Angeliki and asked me if I could get her to provide the name of a decent dentist. Angeliki went one better and phoned her own dentist right away and made an appointment for the next day. Poor Florence seemed terrified, locked into treatment with someone she knew nothing about, imagining, as I did, too, that Greek dentistry wouldn't be up to the standard we were used to.

A week later, when I saw Florence tucking into souvlaki at the *kafeneio*, I asked her how things had gone. She seemed delighted with the dentist and the temporary treatment (she was having the tooth crowned in England when she returned), but she said the equipment was off-putting.

"Remember the old dentist chairs in Britain that stayed upright during treatment? Remember drills with foot pumps? That's what it was like," she said, rolling her eyes.

Now that I was seriously looking for a dentist myself, I decided I wouldn't be tempted by Angeliki's dentist and went on asking around, peering closely at the dental work of everyone I met. Meanwhile, my teeth went on aching.

24

Looking for Mr Molar

I'VE had a life-long phobia about dentistry. I am to dental problems what Woody Allen is to brain tumours. Maybe it's because my teeth got a shaky start in life with a brace during my Scottish childhood. But it was the move to Australia as a child that really sparked the phobia.

Australia in 1960s seemed to be the Wild West of dental professionalism, perhaps because there was nothing remotely similar to good old NHS dentistry. In Australia, dentistry was private and expensive, and prompted my funny Scottish grandmother to remark that in Australia "where there's amalgam, pet, there's always money". Since we moved suburbs a lot in our early migrant years, I had to move dentists regularly as well, which didn't help matters.

There was one sweet old guy who kept dropping fillings on the floor before he popped them into my mouth; the dentist who turned up drunk to an appointment. Yet another had a sadistic method of finding which tooth was troublesome by brandishing a hot prong against each one in the row, going, "Does that one hurt?" reminiscent of the scene in the film *Marathon Man*, where Laurence Olivier is torturing Dustin Hoffman with a dental drill to get information out of him.

Even when I eventually found a better class of dentistry, in adult life, when I also had enough money for expensive procedures, I seemed to be cursed with dentists who kept disappearing. The most memorable incident involved a talented guy called Shane, who had a gentle manner and a surgery decorated with soothing pictures of seals and ship-wrecks. His hobby was deep-sea diving. One day I turned up for a root canal treatment and was told Shane had given up dentistry for diving (not that some people think there's much difference) and was picking over a decayed shipwreck some-where in the Red Sea. I was furious. Where was the apologetic phone call to loyal patients to explain the sudden exit?

Dr Williams, my Scottish dentist, has been the best one yet, and after 10 years under his care, he still hasn't legged it. But there were plenty of other disasters before him, too numerous to mention, and it's a miracle that I still have most of my teeth. But would Greece see them off?

In March, I had run out of options, and it was time to consider a recommendation and stick with it. One expat friend with well-groomed gnashers had told me to use her dentist, a woman on the outskirts of Kalamata. I made an appointment and took Jim along with me for moral support. The surgery looked clean, though slightly on the dated side. She was a tad severe but spoke English at least. She took an X-ray and later stuck it on her old-fashioned light box screen and tutted.

"What we have here is a BIG problem," she said, shaking her head at the X-ray. "For a start, some of the crowns are kaput."

The word 'kaput' was brutal. I was rather fond of my crowns. She might just as well have said that some of my best friends were terminally ill.

"They don't hurt *that* much, not as if I've got an abscess or something."

"They are still finished," she said with a menacing air.

Then she explained what would have to be done: root canals, gold posts, new crowns, even on a tooth that wasn't bothering me. And the price would be 1,600 euros. I gasped.

Then she told me the teeth were infected. I would need to take a course of antibiotics or the treatment may not work.

"Can't I come back after the course of antibiotics and see if there's improvement?"

"That's my advice – take it or leave it," she snapped.

I left it, telling her I'd give her a call some time. I went back to the waiting room.

"I can see from your face it's not good news," said Jim.

"You're right, it's not."

I explained it all to him. "That doesn't sound right. You saw Dr Williams before you left and everything was fine. I can't believe it," he said.

"Well, even if she's right, I don't like her style much and the fee will put a hole in our budget."

"Don't rush into it yet. Wait and see if I get that travel job. If I don't, and we go back to Scotland, you can go straight to Dr Williams."

"But we won't be back for a few months, and what if the crowns are really playing up, it won't do to wait," I said, tooth phobia taking hold of me again.

So I was on the trail again of another dentist. One day at the bank, where we had come to know one of the Greek assistants quite well, I noticed her lovely white teeth.

"Katerina, do you have a good dentist?"

Her eyes widened with interest.

"Yes, of course. His name is Maximus Petrelis, nice huh? I will write down his number and I'll even call him, if you like, to make an appointment."

"Thank you, but you don't need to call him just yet," I said hurriedly. "Does he speak English?"

"He doesn't *speak* it, but he understands quite a bit. Don't worry, you will manage."

Katerina was quite comical for a bank worker and liked a good wind-up.

"Maximus has a very black sense of humour though."

"In what way black?" Visions of the *Marathon Man* movie filtered back.

"How do you say it in English...he has an evil sense of humour."

I hoped what she meant was 'wicked'.

"You will like him a lot."

But I didn't want to fall in love with the guy. My God, I just wanted an efficient tooth man, and a chair that went horizontal. So I made an appointment to see this Maximus and took Jim with me again. In the waiting room, with its closed-circuit TV camera because there was no receptionist, I was in a state of high anxiety. What was I thinking, choosing a dentist who didn't speak English? Was my Greek up to dental discussions?

Jim saw me chewing at my nails and slapped me on the wrist. "For God's sake, you're going to see a dentist, not Dr Mengele."

"Is there a difference?" I said.

From the surgery I could hear a loud, shouty voice and couldn't decide whether the dentist was angry, or telling a joke perhaps. Then I heard a woman's raucous laughter. Jim looked at me with raised eyebrows.

"Somebody's having a good time."

"Laughing gas, Jim."

When the door finally opened, a middle-aged woman came out, laughing still, and Maximus stood at the door, a tall man wearing trendy white clogs and a white medical coat. He had thick curly black hair and sparkling, mischievous eyes. He led me into the room, and Jim waved goodbye. The door was shut and I stood for a moment, not quite believing what I was seeing – dental heaven! Modern gadgets everywhere, a chair that swept down horizontally. Exemplary drills. Not one photo of a shipwreck from an arty angle. I lay back on the comfortable upholstery and relaxed. Thank you, God!

Maximus had a friendly manner but no English, as Katerina had said, and I cursed myself for not boning up on more dental vocabulary. I had another X-ray. I hadn't bothered to explain about the last dentist. After a thorough examination, he told me everything was fine.

"The crowns are not kaput then?" I said, using the other dentist's word.

He laughed. "No, not kaput. They might die another day but for now they're fine."

No major work then. I was so relieved I wanted to borrow his clogs and tap dance across the surgery. The problem, he explained, was gum irritation and he recommended a special dental gel to brush with. The fact that it temporarily turned my teeth brown/orange seemed a small price to pay.

I was then ushered into his adjacent office for the prescription, and to pay. It had all been so painless and easy, and I suddenly gushed in Greek: "Thank you Dr Petrelis for the treatment. You were ....what's the word, very *gentle*," I told him, using *triferos* for gentle. His eyebrows arched up slowly, like cats stretching.

"No, no, *triferos* is wrong. That's very personal," he said.

He scribbled out a receipt. Personal? What the hell had I just said?

"I think you mean *evyenikos*, not *triferos*," he said smiling, as he handed me two bits of paper. But the word *evyenikos*, kind, was not what I had in mind.

I went back to the waiting room and told Jim my good news but, surprisingly, he just glowered.

"That means the other dentist you saw was about to rip you off big-style. Or she's just an idiot. That's appalling. We should ring her back and tell her."

"Oh don't worry about her. I just feel mightily relieved, that's all."

I got out my dictionary, the tattered paperback I always carry about, and looked up the word *triferos*.

"Oh my God, Jim. I've just told the dentist he was loving and affectionate."

Jim roared with laughter and, at the same time, I heard an outburst of mirth coming from inside the surgery. I could imagine that Maximus was telling his dental assistant about my sexy faux-pas.

"You bloody fool," said Jim. "Come on, let's go and have a celebratory lunch. You've found Mr Molar at last. Hallelujah!"

@@@@@@@

In April, Jim received good news from the British travel company. He was to start at the end of the month as the Peloponnese representative. His first task was to write up travel packs for each of the company's villas, with details of what to see and do in the region. It would be an enjoyable part of the job, enthusing British tourists about this fabulous, lesser-known region, particularly at a time when tourist numbers to Greece were generally falling.

There was serious speculation now that Greece could be forced out of the eurozone, returning to the drachma because the government's austerity measures had not gone far enough to bring the debt under control. The Troika (the European Commission, the International Monetary Fund and the European Central Bank), which was overseeing the Greek bailout, were insisting that Greece had to speed up its fiscal reforms. And in the early summer of 2011, the government was set to approve yet another raft of measures to secure the next tranche of bail-out money. Opponents of the eurozone's strategy, however, were beginning to doubt that any amount of austerity measures would work and, worse still, they were hampering any chance of economic growth.

Many young Greeks suffering high unemployment were starting to pack up and leave. Thousands of Greeks who had been born or worked overseas – in Australia, America, Germany or the UK, as part of the Greek diaspora of last century – but now resettled in Greece, were also threatening to return to these adopted homelands.

So it was against this climate of unrest and general anxiety that Jim was to begin this challenging new job, and we were to take on another year in troubled Greece, with all the uncertainties that lay ahead. Caught between a crisis in Greece and a recession in Britain we had decided to stay where we were and take our chances in a country we were falling in love with.

We had a few weeks to go before we had to tell Desmond if we were renewing our lease or not, but were undecided whether we wanted to stay on in Spiti Mou. We had grown to like the location of the house, purely from a social point of view, with the steady stream of villagers who went past every day, but we hadn't got used to other aspects like garbage trucks rumbling by at five in the morning, and the bins themselves, still festering but at least without the addition of cow bones.

The house felt even more cramped than at the beginning. Without the benefit of a second bedroom we had had to create a study in one corner of the sitting-room upstairs under a window, which at least had a marvellous view of Mt Kalathio, but it took up valuable living space. We also wanted to find something with a lower rent. With Desmond still in Britain, we decided to use the time to check out other houses in the village, and I decided to involve some of the villagers in a bit of subterfuge. I told them of our plans to stay and that we wanted another house to rent in the village, for a year. I told them to keep it from the other expats.

They would rub their hands together and say: "Leave it with me."

Of course, I completely ignored perhaps the wisest *parimia*, Greek saying, of them all: *"To mistiko pou xeroun dio, to xerei olo to horio."* When two people know a secret, the whole village will know it.

I told them all we wanted a house for less than Desmond's rent and when I told them what it was they all said: *"Po, po, po,* you're paying far too much!"

After a week or so of hearing this refrain, and having people shake their heads and admonish me for paying so much for a *"spitaki"*, a little village house, I started to regret the subterfuge. One day in the Good Heart, I told Angeliki about our plans. She had the same response.

"You're paying far too much, Margarita. You can easily find something here for 300 euros a month, or less."

"I know, I know," I said to her, "but you're forgetting we need a place where the owner is happy to have a dog – inside. And we also need a house with furniture. We have none of our own."

Her eyes widened, then she roared with laugher. "Why do you need *opla*, weapons?" she said. "Are you planning a military takeover of the village?"

"What are you talking about?"

"That's what you said. You need *opla.*"

Another fiendish pair of words. I'd mixed up the word *opla* with *epipla*, the word for furniture.

She beeped me on the nose, like she always did when I got in a muddle. I laughed as well at my stupidity, but realised that I had been doubly stupid by forgetting to tell the other villagers as well that we needed furniture. I somehow assumed they'd know that we came here with nothing but a few suitcases of clothes and possessions packed into our old car, and that they would have remembered Desmond bringing things over to Spiti Mou on his wheelbarrow. Desmond's rental was high but in some ways it wasn't so outrageous when you considered that we had a proper lease, and more security. He took great joy in telling us that Greeks rented out houses that had no lease to earn black money.

Tax evasion in Greece had been widespread for decades and still was, despite the government trying to crack down on it as part of the austerity measures. It was particularly wide-spread in the retail and hospitality industries. Around Greece, many tavernas, bars and *kafeneia* still refused to give proper till receipts (to trusted clients at least), to cut their income tax bill and avoid paying VAT. The owners would write the bill on a scrap of paper, or scribble it on the paper tablecloth.

The rental property market was also awash with black money and dodgy receipts. In Kalamata it was commonplace for landlords to strike a deal with tenants to falsify records for the tax office. If a property was for rent at 500 euros a month, the landlord would offer to drop the price to say, 400, if the tenant signed a lease in which the rent was listed at just 200 and accepted receipts at this low figure, which would then be lodged with the tax department. Or deals were struck without a lease at all. As the crisis intensified, it seemed as if this practice was increasing in popularity, which meant that revenue from VAT and other taxes was going down rather than up.

The issue of tax evasion in Greece is a complex one that seems to go deep into the Greek psyche and is perhaps based on a widespread distrust and hatred of politicians and government officials, and rules of any kind. One Australian friend who had vast experience of Greek beliefs after marrying a local and living in the Peloponnese for a few decades, explained it this way: "Greeks have a huge sense of entitlement. They see it as their God-given right not to do anything they don't want to do. And particularly not handing money over to a government that they don't believe deserves it, which is most of the governments Greece has ever had."

At least Desmond was a stickler for doing things within the law. But that didn't stop the villagers from telling us we'd been paying too much, and they promised they could find us something cheaper, especially with everyone more eager than ever to cut a deal. Every time we walked through the village, someone would approach us, looking over their shoulder to make sure no-one else was about. Most of them had some house in mind that belonged to an uncle/cousin/friend. We looked at a few places but they were all either too old, damp, creaky, overlooked by other houses, no garden for the dog, too close to a chained dog, no furniture, diabolical furniture, ancient cooker, no cooker, leaking roof, no roof.

And so it went on, until one day one of the taverna owners told us she had a friend called Thekla with a modern house on the outskirts of the village with views over the gulf, and furniture, for only 350 euros a month – and the dog would be fine. Thekla took us to see the property and we took Wallace with us, as she was one of the few villagers who had never really seen him and we wanted to show her he was cute and well-behaved. In the time we had been in Greece, Wallace had calmed down a lot, especially since his health scare. A year ago, we wouldn't have considered taking him along to see a house because we couldn't predict what he'd get up to. The house was perfect and all was going well until she asked us if Wallace would be fine staying outside. I told her Wallace was never kept outside. She looked horrified. "I can't have that. Not inside. He'll make *zimies*, messes, surely?"

She didn't look convinced when I explained that in Britain dogs are house-trained and are as clean as most humans. It was an alien thought to her in a culture where dogs are chained to trees night and day, often standing in their own excrement. It was the most frustrating part of the Greek culture for us – the attitude to animals.

Along the coastline that runs from Kalamata down to the popular Santova beach, the area that expats called the Kalamata Riviera, there is an affluent beachside suburb where wealthy Greeks have built fabulous holiday villas, with high walls and security gates, which are generally used only in August. In many of these houses, big guard dogs are left to roam in the front garden for most of the year, and are fed by security guards who arrive in vans every day and hurl chunks of raw meat over the fence into the garden.

So we had to turn down Thekla's house and after a few weeks of searching, we still hadn't found anything else.

"I say we look further afield," said Jim. "There are other villages around here, or we could move further down to the sea. It would be nice in summer to walk to the beach, wouldn't it?"

"Leave the village? But we're just getting to know the Greeks here and they're so lovely. If we leave they'll forget us."

"We'd be leaving them anyway if we'd decided to go back to Scotland. What's the difference?" said Jim.

"But we're not leaving, and while we've got this opportunity to get to know these people better, we should take it, shouldn't we?"

"We can still come back and see everyone. It's a ten-minute drive up the hill. How can we handle another summer in Spiti Mou, with the heat, the bins, the hornets, the scorpions...?"

The word 'scorpions' nudged me along a bit, even though we hadn't discovered any more since the summer. I still felt remorseful about leaving the village, however.

"We just need someone to find us a nice place here," I said.

"Maybe there aren't nice places to rent. Greeks don't rent, do they?" said Jim.

We couldn't seem to agree and in the meantime we widened our search area.

25

Holy smoke

THE long lead-up to Easter in Greece is a case of feast, famine, famished. In the weeks before Lent, there is Meat Week, the last chance to eat meat, which culminates in *tsiknopempti*, quaintly translated as Barbecue Thursday, the day when everyone eats grilled meat and Greeks turn into Aussies, firing up garden barbecues and wearing outrageous aprons. The following week is Cheese Week, when women spend days in the kitchen constructing everything possible from cheese, which all sounds suspiciously like the brainchild of the Meat and Cheese Marketing Board of Greece. All of this culminates in *Kathari Deftera*, Clean Monday, the first day of Lent.

Lent in Greece becomes more abstemious as the days wear on, as meat, dairy foods, fish, eggs, and even olive oil is gradually phased out. By the end, you might be lucky to sit down to a plate of grass clippings with a squeeze of lemon juice on top and a few volcanic crusts of bread on the side.

Our Australian friend who had lived in the Peloponnese for many years told us that not everyone upheld all the restrictions of Lent any more. "Men don't. Greek men wriggle out of Lent by saying their wives do Lent for both of them." Other men probably say they are fasting and then retire to the comfort of a large wardrobe space to nibble on cold cuts of chicken, hiding the bones in their sock drawer.

A few weeks before Easter, Angeliki had asked if I would like to go with her to a special service being held in a small church near the fishing village of Kitries, with a marvellous position near the edge of a cliff overlooking the sea. The priest in attendance, however, was not Robert Downey Jr this time but a somewhat older village *papas*, with his hair tied back in a long, thin ponytail.

We arrived early. There were only a dozen or so people in church, sitting on the hard wooden chairs. We sat in the front row beside the *papadia*, the wife of the priest, called Polina, and another woman from our village, called Maria. Angeliki engaged them in some lively village gossip, as far as I could make out, though I wasn't paying much attention until Angeliki suddenly turned to me, nudging my arm.

"Tell them, Margarita, how much you pay for your house."

I was embarrassed and looked around to see if anyone in the church had lugged in or not. They had.

"No," I said petulantly. "I don't want to talk about the rent."

"Why not?" asked Angeliki, who was in good form that night, and slightly more mischievous than usual.

"It's personal, that's all."

Maria stared at me strangely, as if she'd never yet met a woman who didn't want to tell her life story in church. Polina gave me a look of sympathy and tried to quell Angeliki's enthusiasm for the subject, but it didn't work.

"TELL them, Margarita!" said Angeliki, her big brown eyes imploring me.

"I don't want to talk about money here – in church."

Polina nodded gravely in agreement.

"TELL THEM what you pay!" Angeliki insisted.

"N-O-O-O!" I said in a loud, shrill voice, like a buttoned-up librarian being groped unexpectedly in the back of the reference section.

"I will tell them then," she said defiantly, turning to the others and blabbing the amount. Sharp intake of breath on their part.

I hung my head in shame. The church was suddenly more crowded now. People waiting, fidgety, bored − listening. And now everyone knew what a mug the foreign woman was paying all that money for a village house. Oh dear!

"I know of a house on the edge of Megali Mantineia, not far from me. It's only 250 euros a month," said Maria.

"Will the owner take a dog?" I asked.

"I don't know."

"Does it have furniture?"

"I don't know. But you have furniture surely?"

"We drove here from Scotland. No furniture," I shrugged.

"The owner will put furniture in. I can ask him. Come tomorrow morning, we will go and see it."

"Yes, perhaps," I said, but only to end the conversation. I had visions of a Greek-style Desmond with a wheelbarrow, bringing us bits of furniture for the next two months, and I shuddered.

"I know where the house is. I'll take you," said Angeliki, nudging my arm again, and for one horrified moment I thought she was about to beep my nose as well.

When the chanting began, Polina slipped away, Maria and Angeliki were mercifully quiet and I was awash with relief at not having to talk any more about house rentals.

This was a long and devotional service with a hymn known as the *Hairetismi*, salutations chanted to the *Panayia*. One of the most famous and complex of Byzantine hymns with 24 verses, it is performed on four consecutive Fridays during Lent. During the whole service it is traditional for the congregation to stand. The priest was standing, his head inclined towards a flower-decked icon of the *Panayia*, propped on a wooden stand. Beside him, an elder of the church stood with a censer on its long silver chains. The incense, however, seemed to have a life of its own. It started off with fragrant puffs but quickly increased to billowing acrid clouds that shrouded the first few rows of seating, but most especially our side. We started coughing and choking. If this had been an aeroplane, oxygen masks would have dropped from the ceiling by now.

The rest of the congregation shuffled about as secondary waves of incense reached them, though less choking, yet neither the priest nor the elder seemed conscious of our distress, locked in a spiritual trance. Angeliki was soon gasping for air and clutching at her throat as it was also a warm night. I thought she was going to faint but she managed to scramble out of her chair, its wooden legs scraping loudly on the tiled floor, and every eye was on her as she staggered up the aisle to the back of the church, where there was another scraping of chair legs and five minutes of coughing.

I tried to hold out a while, but I couldn't stand it any longer either. I felt like I was smoking some kind of ecclesiastical whacky-baccy and my head was spinning. I escaped to the back of the church as well, with Maria not far behind. We found Angeliki sitting by the open door, breathing deeply from the fresh sea air.

"What was the idea of choking us with incense?" she said loudly, fanning herself with the service programme.

"God's wrath," I said.

"What?"

"Punishment for talking about money in church, don't you see?"

She gave me an arch look.

"You think so, do you?"

"Yes. And *elpizo tha zisoume*. I hope we'll live," I said, using her favourite expression and enjoying this moment of divine retribution.

In the car, on the way back to the village, she apologised for having embarrassed me in church. I tried to explain that in Britain we don't talk about personal things like wages, rent, mortgages, unless it's with people we know very well. I could tell the idea was totally alien to her. Greeks have different notions about privacy.

They seem happy for other people to know personal facts like age, wages, health problems, but are more rigid about the personal impression they make on others: wearing the best clothes to special services, carrying the biggest, most decorated candle at Easter. *Ti tha pei o kosmos*, what will people say, has much more weight in Greece than it now does in Britain.

"We don't bother hiding the facts here. The eyes of the villagers look inside your soul," she said.

"Is that another one of your *parimies*?"

"No, it's just the way it is, Margarita."

The next day I was trying to construct a feasible excuse for not going to see the house Maria had suggested. As I was mulling it over, the phone rang. It was our Kalamatan real estate agent, Rochelle. She said she had a house for rent that we might like, though it wasn't in the village. It was down near the sea, in Paleohora, which was where we had gone for the Epiphany celebration in January.

Jim was keen to see it. "A house in Paleohora would be great – right near the sea for swimming all summer."

"Rochelle said the Greek owners live in Kalamata and have been using this family house at the weekends, but now they want to rent it out long-term. They don't mind the dog as they have one of their own…"

Jim cut in: "That's perfect. A Greek couple who like dogs…"

"Not so fast. They have a big dog and it goes with the property. It's kept in the corner on a chain as they don't have anywhere else to put it. It's a kind of guard dog."

Jim's face fell. "Hmm, I suppose Wallace will freak out with a big dog on a chain."

We were used to this routine now, hearing about great houses and then finding snags with them. Every rental property in Greece seemed to have a snag.

"Let's go and see the place anyway, it won't hurt will it?" said Jim.

26

House of olives and Zina the minx

WE decided to leave Wallace at home as we didn't have high hopes for the house at Paleohora, as the main snag, apart from the owners' dog, was the fact the couple wanted a lot more money than we were paying Desmond. Houses on this strip of coastline were more expensive than village houses.

The house was built on a low hill overlooking the sea and the narrow, dusty road that wound up to it was called *Odos Elaionon*, Road of the Olive Orchards. I admit to being seduced by its name and by the thick orchards on the hillside that rambled all the way up to the lower edge of Megali Mantineia. It was quiet and dreamy here in the afternoon sun. When we arrived at the front gates, the couple were waiting for us. They were younger than we expected, in their 40s, and Andreas the husband spoke quite good English, apart from having some strange grammar. We decided to look at the house first before we checked out the dog, though we could hear it barking from a tiny stone house nearby, set in the corner of the property.

The main house belonged to the wife Marina's family and was more typically Greek, like a bungalow set high on massive concrete stilts under which was a mess of junk and a pile of olive wood for the fire. It had an open-plan living/dining room with a lovely fireplace and was comfortable though slightly dated. The main balcony off the living room was huge and overlooked the gulf and Kalamata and it wasn't hard to imagine how nights would be spent here, sipping a glass of chilled wine, watching the sun set over the Messinian Peninsula opposite.

Desmond's house had balconies, but the larger one had no view. The best one, facing Kalamata and the mountains, was too small to set more than two chairs on. Many nights in the summer we had squeezed on to this balcony to gaze at the view and out over the edge of the village towards Foteini's old house and, further up the hill, Eftihia's terrace, where she and her mother Pelagia would sit side by side well into the night, talking and laughing, which was a strangely reassuring sound to us.

After the house viewing, we looked around the property which had olive trees and some fruit trees, and a collection of animals, including five cats. We walked down a short path to the other dwelling they called the *spitaki*, small house. It was a charming old place in need of work. This had been the original house on the site.

The couple's dog, Zina, was a big, brown cross-bred female that looked more like a wolf, with pale brown, fierce-looking eyes. As we approached, she barked loudly and strained against her chain, and I didn't doubt she would scare intruders. She was having the same effect on me. This would never work, I said to myself. Wallace would have a panic attack here. Andreas managed to calm Zina down, however.

"Is she always on the chain?" I asked him.

"Only when we are not here. She might get out."

I couldn't see how that was possible, as the property had a high wire fence all the way around it and two locking gates. It was very secure. I explained to him that Wallace was small, lively and nervous and we didn't know if the two dogs would get on.

"That could be a problem. But Zina is in our family for ten years. First she live with us in Kalamata, but she too big now

262

and there is nowhere else for her to go. But she is a good dog, not so wild as you might think."

It all seemed like an odd arrangement, even stranger when they told us they would come every other night after work to feed the dog and the cats. Marina was keen to learn English and had a rough stab at it when she said: "We have sex kitchens here."

"Sex kitchens?" Jim and I arched our brows at each other. I had visions of strange goings-on with chefs in aprons.

"There," said Marina, pointing to a stone outhouse nearby. That seemed even kinkier.

A nervy chicken suddenly flew out the outhouse door in a cloud of feathers.

"Ah, you mean you have six chickens?"

She nodded. Jim and I relaxed, briefly. The couple told us the chickens normally roamed the property during the day. Wallace, who went mad over flies, would go scatty with chickens, I imagined, but I kept that to myself.

The couple also told us they would be at the property on weekends, as they were slowly renovating the small house. And their two children, now at university, would spend time here in the summer, and occasionally the surviving parents of the couple – the two mothers from Kalamata – might make an appearance. A crowd, by the sounds of it.

Marina must have sensed our disquiet. "Don't worry. We are all very private people. You will hardly ever see us."

Andreas seemed keen to emphasise the more positive things about the house, mainly that it was very quiet, not overlooked by any other properties.

"Outside July and August, when people come for holidays, there is no-one. In the winter you have the hillside for you," he said, opening his arms out wide and smiling.

"Are there any foreigners living around here?" Jim asked.

"Foreigners? *Xenoi*? I think, no. It has only Greeks in Paleohora."

It wasn't just the grammar that made us smile. No *xenoi*. Jim and I looked at each other and our eyes were doing high-fives.

"The last bit was good news at least," said Jim as we drove back to the village.

"The house at Paleohora is lovely, but the dog's a big problem, isn't it? Despite what Andreas said, Zina still looks a bit wild to me. She looks like she could eat Wallace for breakfast and floss with him afterwards."

Jim laughed and nearly drove into a big pothole in the road. "It's an odd set-up though, having your landlords beside you at the weekend. I fear we might get in each other's way."

"I like the couple though and it could be lots of fun," I said, trying hard to expand my horizons.

"We can't afford the rent they're asking. If Rochelle can't knock it down a bit we won't be able to take the house."

We called the agent the next day and told her the rent was the main problem.

"I'll talk to them. I know they're very keen to rent out the house."

@@@@@@@

We were in the kitchen a couple of days later, making dinner, when we heard the familiar screeching sound of Cyclops being manhandled. It could only have been Foteini. She walked inside, brushing the front of her black cardigan as if it were suddenly contaminated.

Foteini looked keenly around the room and her gaze stopped at Jim, standing by the cooker wearing an apron featuring a large carrot with a cartoon face. Her eyes were full of disbelief. No wonder the goats run away from the *xenoi*, she must have been thinking. She was wearing a smart outfit under the cardigan and fashionable ankle boots. Without her usual headscarf and scruffy layers, she was transformed again. Even her voice seemed quieter.

"Here," she said, handing me a plastic box. "It's some of my mizithra cheese that I promised you."

She took the lid off so we could admire the two chunks of white cheese with their sticky sheen, and a pungent goaty smell spiked the air.

"Try some, it's good," she said, beaming with pride.

"Thank you, Foteini. We'll try some after dinner if that's all right," I said, quickly putting the box away in the fridge. "Sit for a while," I added, pulling out a chair at the dining table.

"Only for a minute. I am having a meal in the village with a relative from Kalamata."

I didn't ask what the occasion was, though I imagined it was something important since Foteini rarely ate out in the village unless it was for a *mnimosino*, memorial service. I asked her who the relative was and she started to describe the complicated connection in the way Greeks do: a great uncle of the brother of a second cousin thrice removed... until in the end, the relationship was stretched out like a violin string.

She was brushing hairs from her black skirt with a sullen motion. "You never said you were looking for another house."

"Ah ... I planned to, soon. Do you know of something?"

She shook her head. "Are you staying in the village?"

"I don't know, Foteini. There doesn't seem to be anything suitable in the village."

"Why can't you stay on here?" she said, her eyes ranging around the room and up to the lovely wooden pitched ceiling, one of the nicer features of Desmond's house, the roof that Foteini said wouldn't leak, and it hadn't. It seemed like a re-run of that first day on the road when she asked why we wouldn't want to rent this house. When I told her it was too small for us, her eyes widened in disbelief.

"This isn't SMALL! And it's *poli oraio*, very lovely. You don't need another one," she said, and again I felt shamed by her simple logic. Desmond's house was huge, a palace, compared to her village home, or at least what we'd seen of it from the outside.

I knew that everything I said would sound feeble now. "It's very hot in summer, and noisy...and it's quite expensive for what we're getting here. We looked at a house the other day in Paleohora and it was three times bigger than this."

"You're not going to Paleohora?" she said, as if I'd said Poland. " I'll never see you if you go there, Margarita."

"It's only down the road."

"You won't bother to call by if you're living by the sea. You'll forget me," she said like a child with separation anxiety. "I like to look across from my house at night and see lights on here. Now I'll look and see nothing but darkness."

She sat, her big fingers worrying her knees through the soft material of her skirt. I was touched by her anxiety, and I felt bad. It was what I feared all along, that the villagers would think we were letting them down, spending so much time getting to know them all, taking part in their lives, their celebrations, their services, and then leaving.

"Will you be here for Easter at least?"

"Yes, of course. We won't leave – if we leave – until May."

After she left I almost began to wish the agent wouldn't be able to hammer down the price and we'd be forced to stay in Desmond's house. But things were never meant to be that straightforward. A week after we saw the Paleohora house the agent phoned us to say she had persuaded the couple to drop the price to slightly lower than we were paying in the village.

"With two kids at university and what with all the anxiety about the economy and wages, they won't accept any less," said Rochelle.

Jim was philosophical about the small drop in rent.

"At least it will be nice renting a house from a Greek family for a change, who want to help their kids."

"Yes, that part's very good," I said.

"What bit isn't? Wouldn't you love to live in that house with that wonderful sea view? Imagine it."

"I don't know."

"Ach! You're not thinking about Foteini now and what she said the other night? Look, the villagers will get by without us. Anyway, I sometimes think the poor Greeks must get fed up sometimes with the *xenoi* in the village, there's enough of us, and all our strange cultural ideas."

I didn't think the Greeks *were* tired of the expats or their foreign customs, but I had to smile at some of the peculiar things the village expats had said about Greek life and culture. One Londoner called Roger told us he never ate out in the tavernas because Greek food gave him indigestion. "It's all that olive oil," he said, which I thought was hilarious at the time, and ironic, in an area that produces some of the finest olive oil in the world. A northerner called Charlie was an affable but shy man, who spent most of his time in his vegetable patch growing things like leaks and Brussels sprouts. He told us once he was determined to produce Greece's first sprout to go with his Christmas roast.

One easy-going couple from Kent with a holiday house outside the village divided their time between the Mani and the UK, coming and going up to six times a year. Although they said they loved the Greek lifestyle, they suddenly put their house up for sale. We asked them why, sure that they'd confess to being worried about their investment in these economic times, but the wife surprised us by saying: "We've been here long enough. We need to reconnect with mother England."

"That's funny," said Jim later. "I thought they were already pretty connected with it. It's mother Greece they need to bond with."

The more Jim and I talked about where we should live next, the more puzzled he was about my attachment to Megali Mantineia.

"We only came here for a year remember? We wanted to live somewhere remote. We've done that. Now we happen to be staying longer, and wouldn't it be nice to experience a different location? And the sea...as well."

I didn't answer. He stood looking at me, rubbing his chin in exasperation.

"I'm taking Wallace for a walk," he said, fetching Wallace's lead. He gave me a dark look as he led the dog towards the front door. "I think you're making a big mistake not to consider this move."

Wallace dragged him out the door, like a pent-up greyhound, well over his health scare.

@@@@@@@

My problem with where to live was how quickly the year had gone. When we first arrived in the village the year stretched out gloriously long in front of us, full of unknown encounters and adventures. Now it was nearly at an end. The quickest year of my life.

I hadn't expected to like village life as much as I did, given the historic reputation of Maniots for being uncompromising and suspicious of incomers, though I have since learnt that nothing much fazes them these days. It began to feel as if Jim and I, despite spending so much of our waking time together, and knowing each other so well, had been looking for different things in our adventure. I just hadn't noticed it before.

Always the more sensible one, Jim was happy to take things as they came along and not expect too much, whereas my aims now seemed complicated, or even muddled. I was the one with the long attachment to Greece that had started through my friendship with Anna, my outgoing Aussie/Greek school friend, in Australia. Now that I had a chance to live in Greece, I wanted to learn more about it and delve deeper into the culture.

But how deep could you go in just a year or two? I thought about the expat who had warned us right at the beginning that no matter how long you stayed in a village like Megali Mantineia you only ever scratched the surface. After a year in the village, I realised the comment was true for him because he hadn't aimed any higher. Yet I knew that it would probably take many years of living here, and much better Greek than I had, to connect on the level I wanted, or even discover what it was about the place that had gripped me for so long. What I didn't want from our adventure was for it to create a rift between Jim and me when we had already been through so much together.

Even that wasn't the whole story though. If I were to be really honest, one of my main anxieties about moving to Paleohora was the chained dog, Zina. Would it be brutal to subject Wallace to that scary scenario? And would we all go nuts over it? To sort out this particular problem we decided to go back to the house for another viewing and take Wallace with us this time, to see how the two dogs got on.

After looking around the house again with Andreas and Marina, we took Wallace on his lead down to the *spitaki*, where Zina was chained, ready to do the introductions. Even before we got to the dog, Wallace started whimpering and growling softly, but once the dogs were facing each other, they both went ballistic. Zina pulled hard against the thick chain that was fastened to a concrete pillar, and barked viciously. And Wallace? Well, he just ran the gamut of Jack Russell lunacy. He barked, screamed, leapt in the air a dozen times like he was dancing on a hot-plate, and then finally skulked behind our legs, quivering with fear.

Jim looked pale. The Road of the Olive Orchards had turned into the Road to Hell. He was caressing his chin with nervy fingers. We told the couple we would make a decision soon and retreated back to the village again to discuss the dog problem. We still had a week or so before Desmond returned to Greece.

"What if we took the place and the dogs never calmed down? We'd have to keep Wallace in all the time," I said.

"I suppose we could take Wallace back just once more, and see if there was any way they might get used to each other," said Jim.

"Are you serious? Do you like the place that much?"

Jim merely raised his eyebrows and tutted, the 'no comment' sign. That's all we needed now – Jim was turning into a Greek.

27

Oracles and Foteini's catastrophe

"VILLAGERS can see right into your soul," Angeliki had told me weeks earlier, and she was absolutely right. Just how they do it is mostly mysterious. Sometimes, however, it's rather blatant.

One morning I went to the village shop, where a few tables and chairs were always set outside under an olive tree, making it a popular gossip haunt for villagers. The place was breezily elevated, overlooking the village centre with the old church and its lofty bell-tower, cracked all the way down the front from the 1986 earthquake. Next to the church was the Good Heart and a cluster of stone houses, some renovated, some hanging on for dear life. From the shop, there was also a wonderful view over the olive orchards down to the Messinian gulf and the peninsula beyond, with its low rippling hills suggesting a gigantic boa constrictor digesting different-sized boulders.

I sat down to drink a coffee, hoping to be entertained by the usual spectacle of villagers doing mad things on vehicles and was rewarded by a sight I'd never seen before – a man on a motorbike roaring up the road towing a small trailer in which another man sat awkwardly on his haunches, holding aloft a long metal ladder.

At the table next to me was Adonis, president of the village *syllogos*, council. He was a confident man with striking Levantine features – a swarthy complexion and dark eyes like the peaty lagoons of Scotland that never lighten, even when the sun occasionally skitters over them. A few other men were milling about him, smoking, drinking coffee, cracking jokes.

He seemed to think my attention had been caught by the view and not the man with the ladder.

"You think our village has the best views of the gulf?"

"The shop certainly does," I said, looking out towards the long slip of calm blue water in the distance, on which small caiques trailed back and forth.

"I think you love this village, yes?" he said, drawing deeply on his cigarette and puffing out a thick cloud of smoke, almost obscuring the view we were admiring.

"Yes, I do."

"But you are leaving soon, I think, for Paleohora?"

I had no time to cover up my surprise.

He laughed raucously, then added. "It will be a good move. The house is good. Much bigger than Desmond's. A big garden, plenty of space for the dog." He even knew what house it was.

"We've looked at a house, that's all. We haven't said we'll take it," I said, trying to figure out how he knew all this.

"You should," he said.

"How do you know about the Paleohora house? Did Foteini tell you?"

"She didn't have to. The president of the village knows everything," he said, holding his arms apart in an expansive gesture and laughing loudly. It was the low rumbling sound of a keen smoker. His cronies joined in. Yet there seemed to be no offence intended.

He let me ponder all that a while, then added: "I know the family who own the house. I've done some work for them in their olive fields."

"I see."

"Nothing is a secret in a Greek village – nothing."

"Yes, apparently. Next you're going to say you can read my mind."

He laughed then puffed again on his cigarette. "Yes, I can, and you think I'm being cheeky."

I laughed, nervously.

"Is the rent cheaper?" he asked.

"Yes, a lot," I said, sipping at my lemonade again with certain gusto.

"Good," he said with a wink. I expect he knew exactly what the rent was, but at least he didn't embarrass me by mentioning it.

Before I left I decided that perhaps the village president could be useful after all. I asked him: "What about the big dog, Zina, chained in the property? Is she okay, I mean, not aggressive?"

He puffed out a great cloud of smoke and then looked into the distance a moment, with a dreamy expression. I felt like I was consulting a male version of the Pythia at the Oracle of Delphi, sitting on her rock amid mystical vapours, waiting for an answer from the gods.

"Zina won't be a problem for your little dog, if that's what you're thinking," he said.

I don't think he quite answered the question, but it was slightly reassuring all the same.

The phone rang early one evening. The voice was frantic.

"Margarita, I'm heartbroken. Three of my young goats have been killed. Someone broke into the *ktima* last night, slaughtered them in the *mandri*, and took them. Who does such evil things?"

I was shocked when I heard Foteini's story. It seemed out of keeping with this quiet rural region.

"Did you call the police?"

"Yes. They came out to the *ktima*, looked about, but they won't catch these thieves. There are too many people like them...cunning. They came late and cut through the chain on the front gate. I found a knife in the *mandri* and saw all the blood on the ground, where they did it...." Her voice went high and squeaky.

"Do you want to come over?"

"No thank you. I will sit with Eftihia a while, then go to bed. Come tomorrow for coffee. Not the *ktima*. I don't want to stay there all day. Not right now. Come to my house. At 11."

I felt relieved not to have to go to the *ktima*. I didn't want to see where the goats had just been killed.

In the morning, we walked up the donkey track that ended in a cluster of stone houses, most with outhouses for goats and chickens. We had never been to Foteini's house before. We only ever saw it from the small side balcony, an old stone house with dilapidated roof tiles. We knocked at the weather-beaten door and heard her rattling keys on the other side. As she pulled the door open, the buckled wood scraped across uneven flagstones.

"Come in *paidia*," she said. Her eyes were red and puffy.

We stepped straight into her small kitchen and it was much as I had imagined it would be. Old and neglected. The walls were plastered and in need of a coat of paint. An old-fashioned wooden kitchen dresser stood to one side, crammed with crockery and glasses and a few rattan chairs with bendy legs were arranged along one wall. It had a small *petrogazi* cooker and a big open fireplace, the smoke from which we had seen throughout winter, curling into the cold night air. Some of the window panes were missing and patched with thick sheets of plastic.

She made some coffee and put it down on a low table that she fetched from the inner part of the house that glowered through a doorway, a dark, sombre space but with the curious addition of a tall fridge on one wall. She sat opposite us on a tiny wooden stool seemingly fashioned for one of the Seven Dwarfs, her big hands wrapped around a white coffee cup.

"Ach!" she said with a sigh. "This theft has really put me on edge. The chain was cut clean through and I had to get another thicker one. Thieves can still get in. The fences are old. Now I am afraid they'll come back for the rest of my goats."

She went quiet and then started crying, but almost soundlessly, mopping the tears away with the back of one big hand and then the other, shifting the coffee cup from hand to hand. It was a distressing sight in someone like Foteini, who seemed too tough for tears, yet losing her goats was no small misfortune as she relied on them for some of her income. More than that, she had a profound attachment to these charming creatures, as all rural Greeks do. Foteini had often told us: "The goats are like *anthropoi* (people) to me."

"Do you know who did this terrible thing?" I asked her.

"Many different people go up and down that road, selling things, buying things. It was probably two or three people. That's how they operate. The other day a couple of men came to the *ktima* looking to buy scrap metal. They were gypsies, and I showed them the old car in the next field. One was cheeky, offering me next to nothing. I told them to leave. But they probably got a good look around while they were there. They would have seen all my goats in the fields."

We had seen the old car, left to rot away in the field like so many cars in Greece that have broken down, the owners unable to fork out enough money to get them fixed or to tow them away. Her car had belonged to her husband and now weeds grew through the front smashed windscreen, and the top of the car had become a place for her otherwise shy goats to do some tabletop dancing, when the mood took them.

"Did you tell the police about these men?"

"Pah!" she said, implying it was a waste of time as there were plenty of crimes like this with people desperate for money, selling on goats for meat, especially before the great Sunday feast at Easter.

She got up and went into the other room, bringing back a small picture frame. It was slightly battered round the edges and inside was the photo I'd once taken of Foteini and her favourite kid goat, Samaro.

"They got that one," she said, and her eyes started to mist up again. Jim and I looked helplessly at each other.

She gripped her lower lip with her top teeth, and stared at the photo for a long time until she'd calmed down.

"I've always had goats you see…that's the trouble. Have you seen the two big caves on the mountainside above the road to Altomira? Have I pointed them out?"

She hadn't, but they were clearly visible from the *ktima*, two spectacular ochre-coloured gashes on a steep cliff-face.

"When I was a teenager, I used to take my father's goats from Altomira along the mountain tracks to the caves on hot summer days. It was cool there, and quiet. I loved it. I would sit all day with the goats and look down towards the sea for hours, and the *ktima* – my grandfather's then. I'd just dream…." She trailed off.

"About what?"

She lifted her eyebrows and shut her eyes. No comment.

Then she said: "Tell you what. After Easter we'll go up to Altomira, in your car. Take some cool drinks, some bread and I'll show you around my village. Okay?"

Ah, that old promise again.

"*O'ti theleis.*" Whatever you want. That had become my stock phrase now, not only with Foteini, but with most Greeks, who it seemed took more joy in talking about future plans than actually carrying them out, not because they were unreliable but because they had a different concept about time and had trouble thinking beyond the present moment.

I once asked a village woman if she was going to a certain *yiorti*, celebration, in the village later in the week, and she merely shrugged. "How do I know if I can go on that day? How do I know what will happen between now and then, if I won't fall off a ladder in the olive groves and die of a heart attack, like my cousin did this time last year?" she offered, cheerily. "You see," she added. "How can anyone make a plan?"

Foteini stood up to take the photo back. "Come and see the rest of the house," she said, but with little enthusiasm, and we quickly discovered why. The main part of the house was more dilapidated still. She took us into the bedroom, where a dull, cracked window looked out on the olive groves and the gulf beyond like a rheumy eye. There was a small bed against one wall, an icon of the *Panayia* above it. Below the pitched roof, balancing on two wooden beams, was a piece of hardboard to catch water from a leak.

Scuffed lino covered the floor, with a threadbare rug on top of indeterminate design. There was such a dank, musty reek about the place it took our breath away, and in winter I thought it must be perishingly cold here. I thought that no-one in Britain would believe that in modern-day Greece, even with

277

a crisis, a pensioner could survive like this, like a hermit in a cave, and there were thousands of rural Greeks living in these conditions all over the country. Not for the first time in Foteini's company did I feel ashamed of my own carefree existence, and bowled over by her stoicism.

If there was a spark of redemption in this meagre dwelling it was the huge treasure trove of framed photographs on the walls: mountain scenes from Altomira; black and white photographs of ancestors, men with shotguns riding mules; doughty matrons in black with the family trait of pale, alluring eyes; the handsome portrait of the brother who had been murdered.

Against one wall was a narrow table displaying more framed photos. Foteini put the picture of Samaro there and as she did, I noticed something else I'd given her. It was a picture of Foteini and me taken by Jim in the *ktima,* sitting under a mulberry tree in the summer, wearing straw hats and laughing. I was touched to see it had pride of place in the middle of the table, as if I had now been annexed to her family history.

But this photographic display didn't show the whole story.

"Sit in the kitchen, *paidia,* finish your coffee. I have one more picture to show you."

She came back moments later with a dog-eared photo and handed it to me. It was a colour shot of a young, attractive woman, leaning against a wall, her head thrown back slightly, laughing. She was modern-looking, wearing a blue denim skirt and T-shirt, the brown hair cropped short. I stared, uncomprehending.

"What do you think?" she said, impatiently.

It didn't look like anyone we knew.

"I don't know."

"It's *me,*" she said.

I was shocked. I nudged Jim with my elbow.

"It's Foteini in the picture, look." He drew close and gasped.

"I was just 20 then," she said, smiling for the first time that day.

Jim muttered under his breath. "She looks .... quite trendy."

It was true. We might as well have been looking at a young woman from another part of the world, a young Londoner even, in the sixties or seventies, not a shepherdess from a remote mountain village, or even the black-clad, church-going Foteini. But then she'd already told us about the twists and turns of her life. Had one or two of those corkscrew turnings been quite different, what other, easier life might have materialised for the carefree girl in the denim skirt? I almost couldn't bear to think about it, especially when I'd just seen the rest of her house. I guessed that the things Foteini might have dreamed about on summer days up in the caves she mentioned were very different from the life she eventually found in Megali Mantineia. Maybe that's why she only ever *talked* about going back up to Altomira.

When we said our goodbyes, she touched her heart, thanked us for coming, then went back into the house, still clutching her photograph.

@@@@@@@

Foteini's goat slaughter was one of the worst things that had befallen the village in a while and news of it quickly spread, with everyone offering an opinion on who did it, and how they got away with it. It became clear to me that although Foteini had many friends in the village who admired her stamina and cherished her warmth, there were a few who thought that, for a pensioner, she was foolhardy.

"How can a woman of that age go swinging about in olive trees like Tarzan? She'll kill herself one day," said one villager.

Many people blamed her for being too trusting, befriending the hawkers and gypsies who regularly passed her *ktima*. Yet kind and well-meaning friends like Eftihia agreed it was probably time for Foteini to hang up her hacksaw, let the farm go and live off her modest farmer's pension.

"How will she manage on such a small income?" I asked Eftihia.

"How will anyone manage in Greece now?" she said. And there was truth in that.

When we helped Foteini with the olive harvest in the autumn I had the same thoughts myself. How long could she continue with this punishing, dangerous work? One day, after the harvest, she complained about an aching back. I felt bold enough to ask her: "Have you ever thought of selling most of the animals and just keeping a few, especially Hercules?" Villagers often brought their nanny goats to the *ktima* to mate with him. Foteini didn't charge for his 'services' but she was offered food or animal fodder in return.

"I'll never give him away," she said. "But what would I do every day without all my goats, tell me that? Sit in that old house all day knitting pullovers?"

I laughed at the quaint image of Foteini with her big muscly paws, worrying balls of wool. She laughed heartily as well at the idea of a forced retirement. Sadly, I hadn't seen her laugh like that lately. These days it was hard enough just to make her smile. I couldn't help but remember the first time we met Foteini on the village road, a vivacious spirit in a big hat, waving her stick, urging on the little donkey that carried half her house on its back. Now she looked like she was carrying half the world's problems on her own shoulders.

28

What would Zorba have done?

A FEW days before Desmond was due back in the village and we would be required to give him a month's notice to quit Spiti Mou, I still hadn't made up my mind.

Jim was still full of enthusiasm for the house in Paleohora, and with his travel job due to start he was keen to have an extra room for a study where he could start producing the travel packs he was contracted to finish by early May. But he had no idea how to resolve the dog problem, short of flying canine expert Cesar Millan over from America for a therapy session.

"We must decide today," he said, looking exasperated.

He got Wallace's lead out, ready for the evening walk. "By the time I get back, I need to know what you've decided."

I stood and watched them from the front kitchen window, walking up the road where it starts to ascend to the top part of the village. It takes a lot to make Jim angry. He's the most even-tempered guy I've ever met. But this time, he'd lost patience. I stood a while at the window, watching the late-afternoon flow of life up and down the road. Konstantina carrying some of her farming implements home; Ilias from the Good Heart *kafeneio* scrumping some late-season sweet oranges; Leonidas, looking handsome on his small tractor, sitting tall as he always did, a pile of olive branches in his small trailer.

That reminded me of a few days earlier, when it was raining hard. I saw Leonidas again on his tractor, straight-backed, steadying the wheel with one hand and holding aloft in the other a large, striped umbrella, like Mr Polly Comes to Greece.

Again, I recognised the best feature of Desmond's house: its position.

Moments later I saw Jim and Wallace reach the top of the incline where the road swings round past the shop, Foteini's house, the small church of Agia Triada (Holy Trinity), the cemetery and the edge of the village. Wallace was pulling in his usual fashion, with Jim hurrying along behind him.

Wallace had always done this when we took him for a walk, even when he was just a few months old. It was as if he was in a hurry to devour every moment of the day, as if life were nothing more than a hot roast dinner – chicken, of course. In our Scottish village, people used to comment loudly when they saw Wallace dragging either of us along the main street, debating whether we were the ones being taken for an airing. His energy was immense. But it was the Paleohora house I was thinking about when I later saw Wallace pulling Jim back down the road.

While I was agonising over what to do, a certain passage came to mind from *Zorba the Greek*, by Nikos Kazantzakis, which I had re-read while in the Mani, as the region had inspired so much of this literary classic. The book is a wonderful study of what the Greeks would call a *mangas*, a tough, spirited, uncompromising guy, the kind that often features in the popular *rebetika* (Greek blues) songs of the past century with their themes of poverty, love and sorrow. I had once asked a taverna owner how Greeks would survive the economic crisis and harsh austerity measures. He said: "Every Greek is a *mangas* now. We can survive anything."

Yet Zorba is so much more than that, he's a colossus who rushes headlong at life: "A great brute soul, not yet severed from mother earth."

The passage I had in mind was short and simple, near the start of the book, when the maverick Zorba is trying to persuade the priggish narrator to hire him on a business venture in Crete. "You keep a pair of scales, too, do you? You weigh everything to the nearest gram, don't you? Come on, my friend, make a decision. To hell with your weighing scales!"

No-one could accuse me of having hugged my weighing scales too tightly. I'd already taken a few too many risks in my life, moving about the globe. Perhaps that was the problem. That afternoon, looking out at this small Greek village in which I still felt more or less a stranger, it seemed to me that I was not just one of those women who had forgotten to have babies, I had forgotten also to put down some roots, any roots.

My mind wandered back to a conversation I'd had with my mother in Scotland not long before she died. We'd been talking about the move back to Scotland from Australia and she finally confessed, with nothing more to lose I suppose, that she'd been disappointed we ended up there, for which I felt consumed by guilt, and probably still do.

"I always thought you'd put down roots in Australia and we'd all end our days there. But maybe that's because I loved the place. And you didn't. I can see now that you've been restless most of your life, haven't you?"

That was true. But I had been restless since my first move ever, out of the birth canal. I'd been restless since I'd left Scotland as a kid, when we emigrated. I suppose I was restless still, even though Greece had already taken a firm grip of my heart. Some wise soul once said: "When you've left one country for good, you've left them all." And there was sense in that.

My mother didn't want to let the issue go, however. "Are you finally settled here then? Has Scotland turned out to be better than Australia after all?" she asked, not without a note of challenge in her voice.

I thought it over a moment. "No, it isn't better. No one place is ever better. It's just different, isn't it?"

"Was it worth all this upheaval then, pet, moving back, just for a different place?"

The words chilled me then, and they still do now. Was that what every move in my life was about, a different place, not some sinking of roots into more compatible earth, some sense of completion at last? I didn't have the answer. And perhaps there wasn't one. Throw away the scales again, take the plunge. It's the plunge that matters, not the destination, Zorba would have said.

When Jim and Wallace walked in the front door I was still standing at the window, looking down on to the road. Jim gave me a petulant look while he unclipped Wallace's lead.

"You look thoughtful," he said.

"Hmmm," I said, drawing my thoughts back to the present conundrum. At least I wasn't faced with the decision of where I should spend the rest of my life. I only needed to focus on a house for now.

"I was watching the two of you out walking just now and I'm thinking ....We love this silly dog, and his health scare has just given us a jolt, right?"

Jim nodded.

"But we can't let Wallace decide in which direction we're going, and what house to live in. He's a dog, not a house whisperer..."

"I didn't think we were letting Wallace....." Jim cut in, looking confused.

"Shhh....Here's the thing: You like the Paleohora house. I like this village. But the house is growing on me. It might take a while to get the two dogs sorted. We might lose a few fingers along the way. Wallace might develop more nervy mannerisms. He might even try to dig his way out, but we've proved over the years we really CAN control his compulsive, obsessive and disorderly behaviour ... em, more or less."

Jim's eyebrows shot up in surprise. "Well...I didn't think this was all about Wallace, really."

"It's not. And yet it is...if you get my drift."

"Not really. But if that's how you feel, and you're not just saying it to please me. Then, fantastic, let's go for it."

He came over to where I was still standing by the window and kissed me. Suddenly everything else seemed like geography and nothing more.

When Desmond came back from overseas, he had no idea I had engaged some of the villagers in the house hunt and I saw first-hand how well Greeks can keep a secret if they really want to. Desmond was strangely cool when we told him we were taking a house at Paleohora, or perhaps he was tired of yappy Wallace, complaints about furniture, hornets, scorpions, bones in bins, or too proud to show that our leaving bothered him. And he had to have the last word on the matter.

"Is the Paleohora house owned by Greeks?"

"Yes."

"You won't have a lease then."

"Yes, we do."

"Ha! That'll be a first...but I wish you well, my friends."

And off he went, pushing his wheelbarrow up the road, filled with lemons.

29

From bier to eternity

"HOW do you think Wallace will react when the procession goes past the house tonight?" Jim asked nervously, referring to the procession through the village of the Epitafios on Good Friday. "Do you think he'll howl like a banshee?"

"Probably. But it will only take a few moments to pass, won't it. Everyone in the village has heard Wallace spit the dummy before. But Robert Downey won't be impressed, I'm sure."

"Hmmm. Eddie Edit tells me we should lock him in the bedroom," said Jim.

"I don't think the priest will like being locked in our bedroom."

"Oh, very funny. I mean that if we lock Wallace in the bedroom, people won't hear him bark so much. It's further away."

"You know what? I'm beginning to regret inventing Eddie Edit. He's taking over your life."

"You won't say that when everything goes pear-shaped tonight."

"It won't," I said, not believing that for one minute, remembering a time in our Scottish village when a summer fete was held in the park across the road and a Scottish pipe band went right past our house. Wallace went bonkers, howling and leaping around on chair backs and tables, just to get a better look through the windows at this evil-sounding (to his ears) tartan pack swaggering down his road, and I swear his performance was more diverting than anything the villagers saw that day.

The procession of the Epitafios is one of the most solemn and impressive rituals of the Greek Orthodox religion to mark the crucifixion of Christ and his death on Calvary and takes place in most villages and cities in Greece. A wooden bier (epitaph), its canopy richly decorated with posies of spring flowers, represents the tomb of Christ. An icon of Christ, representing his body, is laid inside.

It is carried from the church just before sunset and taken around the village, or the city streets, with a crowd walking behind, singing and holding lanterns. Firecrackers are also thrown, for reasons that seem perverse, which turns the event briefly into Chinese New Year, complete with cats going ballistic, and dogs barking in concert, hence the worry over Wallace.

This procession is part of the spine-tingling finale in the week called the *Megali Evdomada*, the Great Week, in which the whole story of the crucifixion and resurrection of Christ is played out every day in dramatic and moving services. This is the week when people will also offer the quaint greeting/ farewell, *kali anastasi* (have a great resurrection), and who hasn't wanted a timely resurrection now and then, especially when the latest anti-ageing cream hasn't quite delivered?

The Saturday night service, however, brings Easter to a dramatic but joyful close, as it portrays the resurrection itself, first with the church being plunged into darkness at midnight and then illuminated by a single priestly candle carried from the sanctuary of the church, towards which the congregation will rush to light their own candles, saying the words *Christos anesti* (Christ is risen). The Lenten fast is then broken with the traditional *mayeritsa* soup after midnight, and the feasting returns in earnest on Sunday, when families gather for a long, leisurely meal of roast lamb or goat.

The service before the procession on that particular Friday was long, starting at 5.30pm, and only the devout few, and curious *xenoi* (the two of us), turned up at the beginning, the men to the right as usual, the women to the left. It is a sombre service, the flower-decked bier set before the iconostasis, reminding the congregation of the death that precedes resurrection. The darkness before the light. The sweet old woman who had made me join the bread queue on our first church visit was installed in one of the high chairs again and smiled gap-toothed towards us.

Angeliki was next to me. She whispered, "I hear you've got a place in Paleohora?"

"Yes. Don't ask me about the rent though."

She laughed softly. It was lost in the chanting. Around seven o'clock, there was an intermission of sorts, when the villagers gathered outside in the forecourt for a breather before the next part of the service began. Children stood in nervy huddles, impatient for the procession to start. Some of the farming men sneaked away for a drink in the Good Heart that also opened onto the forecourt. Everyone had *kefi*, high spirits.

The papas sat down on the stone wall that ran the length of the *kafeneio*, taking an informal break from the solemnity of the occasion, loosening the collar on his purple and gold robe and shooting the breeze with some of the village boys. I had learnt long ago that his real name was Papa Nektarios, from Kalamata, but in my mind he would always be Robert Downey Jr, even though close up, he didn't really look like the actor at all. What was I thinking? But he was handsome nevertheless and his Italian leather shoes had star quality, as always.

We stood in the forecourt, enjoying the last fiery rays of the setting sun that had lit up the side of the village with a tangerine glow. Within twenty minutes, most of the people we knew in the village had gathered outside the church: Sweet Konstantina who brought us oil at Christmas, Adonis, the president of the village *syllogos*, Chrisanthi and her family from the taverna, Angeliki and Ilias, the latter asking us what we'd done with crazy Vassie for the night, making a claw of his hand and twisting it back and forth beside his head. Eftihia and Pelagia stopped to offer best wishes for our move, bear-hugging us in their big, warm arms. It felt like the safest place in the world to be. We promised to visit them regularly.

The one person we hadn't seen yet was Foteini. It wasn't like her to miss an important church service. When I saw Leonidas in the crowd I waved him over.

"Have you seen Foteini?" I asked him.

"No, I haven't," he said, rubbing his cheek thoughtfully and looking carefully around the assembled villagers. "Don't worry, I'll find out for you. She's probably had something urgent to do at the *ktima*. "

"Nothing bad, I hope."

He shook his head. "I hope not...By the way, I hear you're staying another year in Greece after all and moving to Paleohora?"

"It's a nicer house but we're sorry to be leaving the village."

He merely nodded, and I thought of how he had almost predicted in the winter that if we stayed we'd move to another village. What did he know that we didn't? Was he perhaps a secret expert on the pitfalls of Greek rental property?

"One day perhaps you'll buy your own house in the village," he said, with a shrewd smile.

"Who knows?" I said, wondering, not for the first time, if this was a place I could finally put down a few roots at last.

"Remember to come back and see us all, now and then."

Was he kidding? Leonidas, with his wise blue eyes glimmering in the setting sun like antique mirrors; Leonidas, with his gracious attitude, not to mention his kick-ass negotiating, was one of its main attractions.

Around eight o'clock, the wooden bier was carried from the church by four village men, with Father Nektarios walking in front, clutching a Bible to his chest and Leonidas holding aloft a wooden cross. The planned route for the procession was firstly up to the graveyard at the top end of the village, where the group would stop and offer prayers for the dead, then it was to turn and come back down the hill, past Spiti Mou and up to the other end of the village to a tiny church called Agia Eleni. After a few minutes' break, it was to turn and go back to the church via the narrow, original road through the village.

The procession, once it started, kept up a cracking pace, the four men carrying the bier struggling slightly with the inclines. Everyone was euphoric, probably relieved to be on the home stretch with weeks of fasting nearly at an end. The children from the village darted up the sides of the procession, some carrying paper lanterns, others lighting small firecrackers, with old women in black trying to struggle clear. I only hoped the crackers would run out before we got to our house. As we toiled along in the wake of the procession, edging closer to Spiti Mou, Jim tapped me on the arm.

"I'm busting for the toilet. I'll run ahead and go back to the house and I'll catch up with you in a minute." It must have been the long church service, I thought. And off he scurried.

When the procession reached the house there was no sign of Jim, no sound from Wallace. Cyclops was sitting on the wall by the front gate, like a one-eyed oracle of doom. The procession rippled on up the road, the bier in lead position, its blooms bright in the setting sun. Suddenly my stomach did a queasy back-flip. I heard one of the children behind me shouting: "Look, there's Vassie!"

Before I had a chance to turn around, a white furry shape streaked past, running up the side of the procession, where moments before one young lad had set off a large firecracker, the sulphurous smoke still fizzing in the evening air. It only made Wallace move faster. No sign of Jim yet. But I could sense what had happened there. Doors left open, Eddie Edit napping.

In the distance I could see the priest's robes flapping around his legs from his relentless pace, then I heard a round of screamy barking from somewhere near the front of the procession. Still no Jim. I squeezed my hands together in anxiety.

'Oh God, please don't let Wallace disgrace us now, or devour small members of the congregation,' I said to myself, 'And if you answer my prayer, I promise to buy the biggest votive candle in Kalamata and stagger up the church aisle with it the following Sunday'.

I started running up the side of the group on the rocky edges of the road, setting off small puffs of dust behind me. A few kids started running as well and I could hear old people moaning as we sprinted past about Easter Friday turning into an Olympic marathon. We were now overtaking the procession on the right-hand side, with people jumping out of the way of us. Some of the younger kids were now hysterical, shouting: "Catch Vassie! Catch Vassie!"

The procession arrived at Agia Eleni, at the other end of the village on the junction of the new and old roads. A blessing was offered by the papas, then the procession circled and stopped for a moment so the men carrying the heavy bier could catch their breath. Papa Nektarios stood resolutely at the head of the procession, seemingly aware of the furry white thing shooting in and out of the procession like a rugby ball in a scrum, yet managing to remain celestially calm.

I kept to the opposite side of the junction, my forehead beading with sweat as I tried to figure out what the dog's next move would be and if he was going to trot down the old road with the group and into the church as well. Finally Wallace appeared, shooting out the side of the procession group.

"Wallace, come HERE!" I shouted. Nothing happened. I repeated the command, louder this time.

One of the taverna owners in the village, a spry, good-natured man, was standing near me. He tapped me on the arm.

"Don't worry. Vassie is fine. He's one of us now."

I gave the man a horrified look. Megali Mantineia didn't deserve this today, of all days, to be adopting The Crazy One. I looked at Wallace. He was in his element now, his tongue lolling out of his mouth, his fur fluffed up on the top of his head from all his efforts. He looked like a demented Aussie cockatoo.

"Thank you," I said to the man. "That's lovely, but I must get the dog back."

That's when Jim finally arrived, slightly out of breath.

"Bugger it! Wallace slipped past my legs when I opened the front door and I couldn't catch him. Don't worry, I'll go get him," he said, ready to mount an assault on the procession.

I pulled Jim back by the arm. "Don't bother. You won't catch him. And he won't come when you call. You know what he's like."

"Well then, you know what we have to do now, don't you?" he said.

"Okay, I know what you're thinking. It's disgusting really but it must be done."

And so we both took a deep breath and shouted: "Chicken! C-H-I-C-K-E-N!"

Most of the Greeks knew what 'chicken' meant, as the village was steeped in the taverna business, and they must have been confused hearing the word in the middle of a religious event. The kids were massed at the front of the procession, beaming with amusement. Easter Fridays were never this diverting, their faces seemed to say. They started giggling. Irini, standing to one side of the group, was clapping her hands with glee.

We shouted again: "CHICKEN! CHICKEN!"

Wallace's ears popped up like hot bread slices from a toaster. He skittered across the junction towards us, ready to plunder pockets for chicken morsels. Jim scooped him up, saying loudly, "*Poli kakos skilos*, very bad dog", while wagging a finger at him and looking towards the group opposite. Heads nodded.

The procession revved up again and trotted past us, down the old road towards the church for the conclusion of the service, which we would now miss. But we could finally relax. Mayhem over.

As we walked back to the house, I told Jim what the taverna guy had said, about Vassie being 'one of us'.

Jim laughed heartily. "Mani's best friend, eh?"

"I like that. It has a ring about it," I said, smiling at the sight of Wallace tucked contentedly under Jim's arm.

"Honestly," said Jim, rubbing his hand over his forehead. "I never thought we'd come to Greece and be standing shame-faced in front of a Greek priest and his congregation, in an Easter procession, with Wallace running amok, kids going hysterical and us yelling 'Chicken!' Did you?"

"Never, but I'm well pleased. You just can't put a price on crazy!"

30

Yeia sas and farewell

AFTER we got home, we broke our Lent-lite fast of two weeks (including no alcohol) by having a stiff drink. As we were getting ready to go out for a meal in the village, we heard the sound of Cyclops being airlifted from the front door. I began to think that Cyclops was better than a door bell, and that we'd probably have to end up taking him with us to Paleohora. I'd grown used to his tatty face and his lonely orb.

I opened the door to Foteini. She stepped inside.

"Ah, there you are," I said. "Why didn't you go to church? I was worried about you."

"The goats needed me. I got to the church late, just as the procession was coming back. I only had time to light a few candles, a quick prayer to the *Panayia*," she said, lowering her voice to a stage whisper, as if afraid someone would take note of her lapse in devotion.

"When I got home from church I noticed your light was on. I thought, 'I'll just slip over for a minute'," she added.

She was still in her best black clothes, her hair brushed back and fixed under the tortoiseshell hair band. She looked better than I'd seen her for weeks. The blue eyes were sparkling, her skin scrubbed and gleaming. Ingrid Bergman, retired and living in rural splendour in the Mani. Except that Foteini wasn't about to throw in the towel. Against all advice given, she was resolved to continue with her beloved goat farm and make the perimeter fence more secure. I asked her if she'd heard any more about the goat theft, and she waved her big hand around.

"Nothing. The police won't do anything. Might as well boil a stone," she said, using an old expression for doing something useless. "But listen. Some of the nanny goats are pregnant again. I'll have plenty more baby goats soon. Maybe another Samaro."

"*Ftou, ftou, ftou.*" I performed three pretend spits on the ground, just as she'd shown me once, to ward off evil spells. She followed with three of her own. "*Ftou, ftou, ftou.*"

"So, old Hercules has turned out to be a bit of a stud, eh?

She laughed loudly. It was the first time I'd heard her laugh in weeks. And that's when I noticed she'd finally had something done with her missing teeth. The gap had closed. I felt strangely relieved in my own quirky, tooth-obsessed kind of way.

"When are you leaving for Paleohora?" she asked.

"Not for a few weeks yet."

"You won't forget to come and see me when you leave? You won't forget me?"

"How could we ever forget you, Foteini?" I replied. "We'll visit you regularly, don't worry."

"I won't forget the two of you, ever. Here," she said, opening the black shopping bag she was carrying in one hand. Out came a round tin with a classic London scene painted on the lid — the Houses of Parliament, a red double-decker bus. It looked incongruous in her big farming hands.

"Binid brought this back from *Londino* (London)," she said, proudly.

Jim's eyebrows shot up when he heard the word 'Binid'.

"Another present to Foteini from Bernard," I said to Jim quietly. "And now it's ours. It looks like a tin of chocolates, and fairly new." I licked my lips.

"Hard centres probably," he said with a pout.

"Open it, *koritsara mou*, my girl," said Foteini, thrusting it into my hands.

I struggled with the tight lid, anticipating rows of gleaming chocolates bedded down in their frothy paper casings. The lid finally came off and even before I peered inside, a familiar, ghastly aroma whacked me in the face. Goat cheese. Hidden in a chocolate tin. No wonder they say: Beware of Greeks bearing gifts. I finally got the point of that.

Jim coughed and took a step backwards. Inside the tin, wrapped in see-through plastic, was a large slab of mizithra so luminescent, it almost throbbed. My eyes started to water with the smell, and the frustration of it all.

"It's a big piece, Foteini. You shouldn't have."

She shrugged majestically, holding her arms out at the same, as Greeks do.

"Margarita, you think I can't spare a big piece of cheese for my two dear friends. And I thought you'd like the tin. Binid's city. He told me," she said, tapping her fingers on the lid.

"Yes, Foteini, I like everything. *Efharisto para poli*, thank you very much," I said, snapping the lid back on the tin. I put it on the kitchen table, my eyes still watering.

"Ach!" she said. "Don't get all weepy now, *koritsara mou*, it's only a small present."

Then she gave me a hug, almost squeezing the life out of me. I caught a heady aroma of lavender, goats and incense.

It wasn't a small present she'd given us though. For a woman who had little, the tin of cheese was a generous, heartfelt offering. Whether I liked it or not, I owed it to her to develop a taste for mizithra in the coming weeks.

"I'll see you tomorrow then in church," she said, referring to the midnight service, for *Megalo Savato*, Great Saturday, the most important day in the Greek calendar.

"Some of the villagers are going to Chrisanthi's taverna afterwards for some *mayeritsa* soup," I said. "Would you like to come with us?"

She didn't say anything at first but her eyes were lit up with wonder at this novel idea, being invited out for a meal with *xenoi*. She was no less surprised than if I'd suggested we charter a Lear jet for the weekend and fly to Bermuda. But I doubt she'd have left her goats that long.

"*Endaxi, ta leme*. Okay, I'll see you tomorrow then," she said, stepping lightly out the front door as if she'd just shrugged off a lifetime of worries. Then she turned, offering the most beguiling Greek farewell of all, to our ears at least.

"*Kali anastasi*." Have a great resurrection.

Epilogue

AT the end of May 2011, the RAF's aerobatic team, the Red Arrows, flew over Kalamata, just as Harry had envisaged, as part of the 70th anniversary of the Battle of Kalamata. We joined hundreds of other people to watch the jets in formation roar up the Messinian Gulf and fan out over the city, trailing the famous red, white and blue plumes of vapour. Sadly, Harry didn't live long enough to see this tour de force, but if he had, it would have been one dream of life in the sun coming true – big style.

Within weeks of moving to our new rented house in Paleohora and starting another year's adventure in the Mani, Greece was entering another phase of its economic crisis, and one of the most chaotic eras in its history. In the spring of 2011, with the Greek budget deficit worse than expected, the group overseeing Greece's financial future, the Troika (European Commission, International Monetary Fund and the European Central Bank) criticised the Greek government for not taking its fiscal reforms and austerity measures far enough.

In June, the government passed a tough new austerity bill, a pre-condition of further economic aid, and this sparked a two-day general strike and violent clashes between protesters and police in Syntagma Square in Athens. The demonstrations took place in a mood of mounting hostility towards the government and the heavy-handedness of the Troika. New austerity measures would see Greeks hammered by severe wage and pension cuts. The greatest threat was to the public sector, with a government pledge to cut 30,000 jobs.

By autumn, spectacular events unfolded as Prime Minister George Papandreou, the leader of Pasok, resigned and a government of national unity was scrambled together from the main parties, with an interim Prime Minister appointed, former banker Lucas Papademos.

The following year brought some of the darkest days of the crisis, as the interim government began debating the punishing terms for a 130 billion euro rescue package, needed to save Greece from imminent bankruptcy. Papademos insisted the harsh new measures were crucial. He said: "A disorderly default would plunge our country into a catastrophic adventure. It would create conditions of uncontrolled economic chaos and social explosion."

Despite the rescue package being approved, the financial crisis had become a humanitarian one, with general unemployment at 21 per cent, and rising, and a cut of 22 per cent to the minimum wage.

Few people in Greece were left untouched by the crisis. In Megali Mantineia, where we spent our first year, most villagers felt the effects of austerity in one way or another, especially with the new and unpopular property tax, known as the 'haratsi', levied on all property, however small, or however poor the owner. Hardest hit were farmers with modest incomes, like Foteini, who struggled to survive as it was. Many villagers saw their incomes plummet, their pensions drop. Taverna owners reported business was down as beleaguered Greeks began to sacrifice the much-loved ritual of eating out in big family groups. Yet, despite the crisis, traditional life continued, and the spirit and stoicism of the villagers survived, proving that Greece has heroes, if not euros.

In our second year, in the village of Paleohora, we were just as smitten with the country as we ever were, even if it was sliding towards Hades in a handcart. But how would we survive life on a sprawling olive orchard with one crazy Jack Russell, Zina the hungry wolf-dog, a rabble of cats and chickens, one extended Greek family beginning to feel the pinch of austerity, and a gun-toting farmer next door? With a great deal of laughter, more outrageous escapades with Wallace, and a dash of luck from the gods.

THE END

The Peloponnese series

If you enjoyed this travel memoir about living in southern Greece during the economic crisis, I hope you will like the following two books in the series, which continues our adventures in this region.

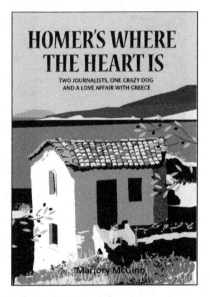

Book 2: Homer's Where The Heart Is

Book 2 continues where *Things Can Only Get Feta* left off. Marjory, Jim and Wallace move to a nearby village and a house in an olive grove with Greek landlords, as the crisis intensifies. As well as a new cast of characters, the book reconnects with some of the Greeks from the original village of Megali Mantineia.

Chosen as one of the best non-fiction expat books of 2015 by The Displaced Nation website.

Available in paperback and Kindle on Amazon.

Book 3: A Scorpion In The Lemon Tree

Book 3 charts the couple's second long adventure in Greece when, although they set out to live once more in the Mani, they never quite make it. Instead they end up in a peninsula they didn't choose and a house they never thought they'd live in. How did this happen? Easy, it's Greece, and nothing ever goes to plan.

This new odyssey takes them on another perilous and funny journey, with a cast of new characters and a few old friends from the Mani as well, including the inimitable Foteini.

Available in paperback and Kindle on Amazon.

For more information about Marjory's writing and the couple's adventures visit www.bigfatgreekodyssey.com.

Praise for Things Can Only Get Feta

"Honestly, you won't be able to put this book down."– **Maria Karamitsos**, reviewing in *The Greek Star* newspaper, Chicago.

"A book to relax into, a wonderful record of Greece's uniqueness, written with wonderment, admiration and wit, all in equal measure." – **Anne Zouroudi**, award-winning author of the Greek detective series of novels.

"I respectfully suggest to all wannabe authors of an 'expat life' type of book that you read this book before putting pen to paper. It's an object lesson in how it should be done. Congratulations, Marjory!" – **Peter Kerr**, best-selling author of *Snowball Oranges*.

"Marjory is a very talented storyteller, and many descriptions of events and turns of phrase she used in this book actually made me laugh out loud while reading silently to myself, a feat that until now was only achieved by Douglas Adams and P.G. Wodehouse." – **Gry**, Good Reads reviewer.

"A tale full of adventure and wit, delving into the heart of the communities in this area (Mani)... This book might become a future reference source about life in 'unspoilt' Greece." – **Stella Pierides**, author of *The Heart And Its Reasons*.

Praise for Homer's Where The Heart Is

"Beautifully written, at times funny and always insightful, it entertains and at the same time gives us a unique perspective on an indomitable country coping with crisis. What more could you ask for?" – **Richard Clark**, author of the *Greek Notebook* series.

"Through her stories, sentiments and humour, we see and feel her love for Greece. Put this at the top of your summer reading list." – **Maria A. Karamitsos**, founder and editor of WindyCity Greek, in Chicago.

"Marjory takes us on an odyssey with mind, heart and great skill. I loved reading this book." – **Pamela Jane Rogers**, author of *Greekscapes*.

"Another wonderful book by Marjory McGinn. The ending tugged at my heart." – **Linda Fagioli-Katsiotas**, author of Greek memoir, *The Nifi*.

"Marjory writes at a level that sits with the best of the travelogue genre. Her depth of characterisation and turns of phrase are outstanding." – **Amazon reviewer**.

"Beautifully written. Her historic insight gives this book a gravitas far beyond its genre, without taking anything away from a charming read." – **Anthony Hooper**, author of *The Glass Lie*.

"A fascinating and heartwarming memoir. I absolutely loved this book and had a huge lump in my throat at the end of it." – **Valerie Poore**, author of *Watery Ways*.

Praise for A Scorpion In The Lemon Tree

"This book is rare within the travel genre. It cleverly combines a travel narrative with enlightened observations about Greece." – **Peter Kerr,** best-selling author of *Snowball Oranges*.

"If you enjoyed Marjory McGinn's first two memoirs, you will love *A Scorpion in the Lemon Tree*. This book is her best yet, and that is saying something. McGinn's deeply-held affection for Greece always shines through. She has a lightness of touch that even makes reading about the dark shadows cast by the current crisis a joy. Her empathy with Greece and refusal to lapse into sentimentality makes this a witty and poignant book." – **Richard Clark,** author of the *Greek Notebook* series.

"I could read this series forever." – **Amazon reviewer.**

"I loved this book. If you can't get to Greece, pick up a copy of 'Scorpion' and enjoy the ride." – **Maria Karamitsos,** founder, the Chicago internet magazine *Windy-City Greek.*

"I absolutely love all three books in this series ... written with warmth and with humour." – **Dawn,** *Goodreads* reviewer.

"Fun and enlightening." – **Expat Bookshop** website.

"An utter joy." – **Amazon reviewer.**

Marjory McGinn's new novel

A Saint For The Summer
A compelling story of heroism, faith and love

This novel, set in the wild and beautiful Mani region of southern Greece, is a contemporary story, with a cast of memorable characters. It is set during the economic crisis and combines family drama and a gripping narrative thread going back to a Second World War mystery, during the little-known Battle of Kalamata, which has been described as 'Greece's Dunkirk'.

It's also a love story between the protagonist, journalist Bronte McKnight, and the charming, enigmatic doctor, Leonidas Papachristou, with a heart-warming conclusion.

Available in paperback and Kindle on Amazon.

Made in the USA
Columbia, SC
13 December 2020

27578424R00173